COMMON
PHRASES

Also by Max Cryer:

Hear Our Voices, We Entreat (Exisle 2004)

The Godzone Dictionary (Exisle 2006)

Love Me Tender (Exisle 2008)

COMMON PHRASES

...AND THE AMAZING STORIES BEHIND THEM

MAX CRYER

Skyhorse Publishing

ALAEditions

American Library Association
Chicago, 2010

Skyhorse Publishing books may be purchased in bulk at special discounts for
sales promotion, corporate gifts, fund-raising, or educational purposes.
Special editions can also be created to specifications. For details, contact the
Special Sales Department, Skyhorse Publishing, 555 Eighth Avenue, Suite
903, New York, NY 10018 or info@skyhorsepublishing.com.

www.skyhorsepublishing.com

10 9 8 7 6 5 4 3 2 1

Library of Congress Cataloging-in-Publication Data

Cryer, Max.
  Common phrases : and the amazing stories behind them / Max Cryer.
    p. cm.
  ISBN 978-1-61608-143-0 (alk. paper)
  1. English language--Terms and phrases--Dictionaries. 2. English
language--Idioms--Dictionaries. 3. English language--Etymology--
Dictionaries. I. Title.
  PE1689.C79 2010
  423'.1--dc22

                                        2010023863

ALA edition ISBN: 978-0-8389-1097-9

Printed in the United States of America

ACKNOWLEDGMENTS

The author thanks Joe Gilfillan, Graeme and Valerie Fisher, Robbie Ancell, Nigel Horrocks, Bryan Staff, Stephen Jennings, David Stevens, Geoffrey Pooch, Paul Barrett, Richard and Pamela Wolfe, and Ian Watt.

INTRODUCTION

After seeing a performance of *Hamlet*, a little old lady supposedly remarked, "So many quotes!" But she could well have said the same thing at any other point in her day. We are surrounded by quotes in everyday speech, not necessarily from Shakespeare.

Other bright minds have come up with expressions we now take for granted as part of the English language, and which we use freely in vernacular speech. But unlike Hamlet, the originators of many of our most useful second-hand remarks go uncredited.

Who said it first?

This collection sets out to credit—as far as it's possible to do so—the people who actually created many familiar terms in common use. For example, poor Ernest Dowson is all but forgotten, but author Margaret Mitchell read his 1891 poem "Non Sum Qualis" and brought one phrase from that poem to the attention of millions. The phrase that caught her eye was "…gone with the wind." (In 1867, Dowson also wrote another familiar phrase: "…the days of wine and roses.")

And who remembers Mrs. Daeda Wilcox? In 1887 she told her realtor husband about an attractive name she heard mentioned on a train as she was returning to her home in Los Angeles. Mr. Wilcox liked it and immediately registered the land he owned nearby as—Hollywood.

Sometimes it has to be acknowledged that an expression became known because someone other than the originator introduced an existing term to a wider public, either in print or by exclamation.

Only a limited number of people would know of Sir Edward Spencer Ford, but in 1992 he wrote a letter to the Queen making a kindly comment on the difficult year she'd had. He included a variation on a phrase taken from the title of a 1667 poem by John Dryden.

In a speech soon afterward, the Queen said:

> *1992 is not a year I shall look back on with undiluted pleasure. In the words of one of my more sympathetic correspondents, it has turned out to be an annus horribilis.*

The term "annus horribilis" hit the headlines immediately, clearly because of the impact of Elizabeth Windsor saying it, rather than Dryden or Sir Edward Spencer Ford.

This collection does not claim to include every expression in common usage that arose from a specified person—there are too many to cover in one book. Two major (and rich) sources of English expressions—the Bible and the works of Shakespeare—have generally been excluded, partly because they have been covered many times before. One exception can be found under "Red Sky", and Bernard Levin's brilliant condensation of just some of Shakespeare's expressions is reproduced by permission on pages 315–16.

Some of our favorite and frequently used expressions date back to ancient civilizations and an impressive number come from nineteenth-century literary luminaries. Dickens, Thackeray, and Scott have all left small but active landmarks on our speech—but then so has party-girl Mandy Rice-Davies, who simply said, "Well he would, wouldn't he?"

Sometimes there are gentle surprises: "brunch" was invented in

England in 1896; Graham Greene first linked "fame" with "aphrodisiac"; "iron curtain" had been in use for forty years before Winston Churchill said it; we have P.G. Wodehouse to thank for "straight from the horse's mouth"; and H. Rider Haggard for "she who must be obeyed."

There is no evidence at all that Queen Victoria ever said, "We are not amused," or that Marie Antoinette said, "Let them eat cake." But Andy Warhol *did* say that everyone would be "famous for fifteen minutes."

Where did he say it, and when? Read on . . .

A-1

In London in 1716, **Edward Lloyd** began publishing a weekly *Lloyd's List* of shipping information. Ships were given two symbols: a letter of the alphabet used to classify ships' hulls, attached to one of the initials G, M, or B, signifying the ship's equipment as "Good," "Middling" or "Bad."

In 1776 the quality of equipment symbols G, M, B were replaced by the numbers 1, 2, 3, 4, 5, still in combination with A, E, I, O, U. Thus A-1 became a designation of the greatest excellence.

Absence makes the heart grow fonder

Born around 50–45 BC, the Latin poet Sextus Aurelius Propertius in one of his *Elegies* pronounced, "Passion is always warmer towards absent lovers" (Semper in absentes felicior aestus amantes).

The phrase first appeared in English 1,500 years later as the title of a poem by an anonymous writer. This poem and others on the theme of absence were included in the collection called *Poetical Rhapsody* (1602), put together by Elizabethan poet (and spy) Francis Davison.

But the expression only began to assume the status of a proverb after 1844, following the publication of Englishman **Thomas Haynes Bayly**'s poem "Isle of Beauty." The stanza which drew attention:

What would not I give to wander
Where my old companions dwell?
Absence makes the heart grow fonder:
Isle of Beauty, fare thee well!

Bayly never knew how widely used the phrase would become—his poem appeared over a decade after he had died.

See also **Out of sight, out of mind**

Accidentally on purpose

Combining as it does two normally contradictory terms, "accidentally on purpose" is a fine example of an oxymoron. Its first known appearance was in the memoirs of prolific Irish writer and poet **Sydney, Lady Morgan,** published in 1862. Her use of quotation marks suggests the phrase may have already been known to her:

> *Dermody neglected the order –*
> *perhaps "accidentally on purpose."*

(The) affluent society

As far back as AD 115, the Roman historian Cornelius Tacitus acknowledged that

> *Many who seem to be struggling with adversity are happy;*
> *many, amid great affluence, are utterly miserable.*

So the awareness wasn't new. After World War II, Canadian-born economist **John Kenneth Galbraith** contemplated the growing prosperity and materialism of America—the increasing ownership of cars, televisions, home appliances, etc., but observed that these consumer "needs" could be considered trivial against the importance of larger and less well financed public systems.

He coined a term intended to be ironic—"the affluent society," which in 1958 became the title of his widely discussed book. In later usage, the term lost its ironic overtones and simply came to mean general prosperity.

Agree to disagree

John Wesley, the English theologian who developed Methodism, had doctrinal differences with the evangelist George Whitefield, yet respected the other man's strength of belief and firmness of opinion. When Whitefield died in 1770, Wesley said in his sermon:

> *There are many doctrines of a less essential nature . . .*
> *In these we may think and let think; we may "agree to*
> *disagree." But, meantime, let us hold fast the essentials . . .*

Wesley's use of quote marks suggests the phrase was a term already in use, but his sermon marks its first known appearance in print.

John Wesley and his brother Charles were also at odds over religious matters. Charles Wesley gave us an alternative version, replacing "disagree" with "differ." In 1787 Charles wrote to John: "Stand to your own proposal, 'let us agree to differ.'"

All dressed up and nowhere to go

A lament of the socially isolated, the term originated as "no place to go," from two separate songs in 1913. The Indiana University holds "All Dressed Up and No Place to Go" by Joseph Daley and Thomas Allen, though it is not heard of much elsewhere. But the other song from the same year, "All Dressed Up and No Place to Go," music by Silvio Hein, words by **Benjamin Hapgood Burt,** was a huge success in the Broadway show *Beauty Shop* (1914), as sung by Raymond Hitchcock.

When you're all dressed up and no place to go,
Life seems weary, dreary and slow. My heart has ached and
bled for the tears I've shed, When I'd no place to go unless I
went back to bed.

All of a doodah

American songwriter **Stephen Foster**'s song officially called "Gwine To Run All Night" was published in 1850, telling of a haphazard race meeting near a workingmen's tent city. The opening line introduced a famous catchphrase with no particular meaning: "Camptown ladies sing dis song, doo dah, doo dah."

A century later **P.G. Wodehouse** launched an adaptation of the phrase into the language, having created a meaning for it signifying that someone (or it could be something) was being distinctly aberrant in behavior. In *Pigs Have Wings* (1952) we are told that Galahad Threepwood observed that Lord Clarence Emsworth had the look of a dying duck and was clearly in distress:

Poor old Clarence was patently all of a doodah.

All over bar the shouting

Although the meaning is clear—that the conclusion of a matter appears evident—the actual genesis of the expression is clouded. It could have arisen in the context of nineteenth-century sports or politics.

It appeared in print for the first time in 1842. **Charles James Apperley**, born in Plas-Grenow, Wales, began writing for *The Sporting Magazine* in 1821, often using the pen-name Nimrod. His 1842 book *The Life of a Sportsman*, while depicting a horse-racing situation, carried the first printing of what became a vernacular term:

"I'll bet an even hundred on the young one," roars O'Hara.
"Done with you," says Lord Marley.

> *"I'll bet 6 to 4 on the young one," roars Nightingale, with a small telescope to his eye; no one answered. "It's all over but shouting," exclaims Lilly; "Antonio's as dead as a hammer."*

This was the forerunner of the variants "all over bar the shouting" and "all over except the shouting."

All's fair in love and war

The centuries have smoothed out the syntax a little, but the meaning is clear in **John Lyly**'s *Euphues, the Anatomy of Wit* (1579). Written in the elaborate and artificial style (euphuism) that was eventually named after it, there is the line:

> *Anye impietie may lawfully be committed in loue, which is lawlesse.*

All's right with the world

In 1841 the people of Asolo in Northern Italy were rather offended by a series of poems depicting a poor orphan girl wandering through the less savory areas of their town and describing in a matter-of-fact manner the squalid sights she encountered.

Poet **Robert Browning** created this girl in his poem "Pippa Passes." The scandalous goings-on Pippa recounts (including those of Ottima the adulteress) are long forgotten, but the line in which Pippa's optimism transcends her hard life has remained in collective memory:

> *God's in his Heaven—All's right with the world.*

This line is sometimes misquoted as "All's *well* with the world."

All the things I really like to do are either illegal, immoral, or fattening

American writer and drama critic **Alexander Woolcott** told *Readers Digest* in 1933:

> *All the things I really like to do are either immoral, illegal, or fattening.*

In use, the order of the first two adjectives is sometimes reversed. Comedy movie actor **W.C. Fields** repeated a version of the line the following year, as the sheriff Honest John Hoxley in *Six of a Kind*.

(The) almighty dollar

British writer **Ben Jonson** recognized that the regard for wealth often engendered a quasi-religious respect when he wrote to the Countess of Rutland in 1616:

> *Whilst that for which all virtue now is sold,*
> *And almost every vice, almightie gold.*

Two centuries later the American writer **Washington Irving** travelled through the riverbank settlements of Louisiana and, noting their "contented poverty," wrote that:

> *The almighty dollar, that great object of universal devotion throughout our land, seems to have no genuine devotees in these peculiar villages.*

When Irving's remarks were published in 1836, a new catch-phrase entered the language.

Annus horribilis

When **Queen Elizabeth II** used the expression during a speech at the Guildhall, referring to the year 1992, its aptness and novelty caught immediate attention. Her use of the expression was widely quoted and the term was often attributed to the Queen herself. But the conduit which brought it to her, and the English-speaking world at large, was sidelined by commentators who overlooked one part of the Queen's speech. She said:

> *1992 is not a year I shall look back on with undiluted pleasure. In the words of one of my more sympathetic correspondents, it has turned out to be an "annus horribilis."*

The expression was a modern reversal of the term known in the 1600s and used by John Dryden as the title of his 1667 poem "Annus Mirabilis, the Year of Wonders, 1666."

Prior to the Queen's speech, the "Mirabilis" version had been seen occasionally as an expression in newspapers and as the title of a Philip Larkin poem in 1967. But the Queen's "sympathetic correspondent," **Sir Edward Spencer Ford**, who had been secretary to her father King George, reversed the term in a letter to the Queen, which she quoted in her Guildhall speech.

When Sir Edward Spencer Ford died, the *Guardian* described him as the person who gave "the Queen's worst year in office its Latin tag."

Any port in a storm

The idiom suggests taking any chance that offers itself, especially when connected to storms at sea, but the expression's first outing in print involved "ports" of a rather more ribald kind. The words come from **John Cleland**'s *Fanny Hill—Memoirs of a Woman of Pleasure* (1749). One of Fanny's love partners is a sailor who, in the throes of passion, confuses Fanny about what might be called his sense of misdirection and which "door" he is approaching. Fanny reports that the sailor uses nautical imagery in replying:

"Pooh," says he, "my dear, any port in a storm."

A-OK

The possible origins of OK have resulted in the world dividing into numerous factions, each of which believes their derivation to be the correct one.

A-OK has a slightly narrower reference base. In 1961, when American astronaut Alan Shepard was in suborbital space flight, he made at one point a particularly jubilant call of OK.

Back at the NASA base, Colonel John Powers misheard the call as A-OK. This had a certain logic to it—an amplification of satisfaction surpassing good old OK to mean "very OK" or "beyond OK," and Powers put the term about the base and the media before he had the opportunity to discuss it with Shepard in person.

Some confusion later arose about whether Shepard did actually say A-OK, or whether Powers misheard him.

Either way, those two are the term's only begetters, with the added "A" universally recognized as an "intensifier." A-OK now means *All* OK.

Apple-pie order

Although claimed by Americans ("as American as apple pie"), pies made with apples in England date back as far as Chaucer and beyond, well before a single apple tree grew in North America. But linguists assign the association of apple pies with neatness and order to the French language originally, and it may well have remained in French.

However, in 1780 the English version of the expression was launched by Admiral **Sir William Pasley**, whose published *Sea Journals of HMS* Sibyl contained his weekly plan:

Tuesdays and Fridays—exercise great guns and small arms;
Wednesdays and Saturdays—fire volleys and fumigate;
Mondays—air spare sails;
Thursdays—muster the men;
And their Persons Clean and in apple-pie order on Sundays.

Arm candy

An attractive woman, escorted by a man with whom she need not have any relationship, creates such a lasting impression that it arouses envy toward the man among those who see them together.

The origin of this term is attributed to journalist **Marcia Froelke Coburn** in the *Chicago Tribune* (August 21, 1992) when commenting on Marilyn Monroe's brief appearance (as George Sanders' party partner) in the 1950 film *All About Eve*. Later the term achieved gender-equity and may refer to a good-looking man partnering a woman.

See also **Ear candy**. Both terms are related to "eye candy," which surfaced in the mid–1980s and went into overdrive when *Baywatch* started on television in 1989. Eminent British etymologist John Ayto observes that "eye, ear, and arm candy" may have developed from the 1930s slang term for cocaine: "nose candy."

As fresh as paint

In the 1850 novel *Frank Fairleigh*, British writer **Francis Edward Smedley** introduced the line:

> *You are looking as fresh as paint; getting round again,*
> *wind and limb, eh?*

As good as gold

In **Charles Dickens'** *A Christmas Carol* (1843), Mrs. Cratchitt asks:

> *"And how did little Tim behave?"*
> *"As good as gold," answered Bob.*

Ask me no questions and I'll tell you no lies

In the course of the complex plot of *She Stoops to Conquer* (1773), by Irish playwright **Oliver Goldsmith**, the character of Tony Lumpkin retrieves a casket of jewels and is asked how he achieved this. He answers:

> *Ask me no questions and I'll tell you no fibs.*

Over the years, fibs became lies.

As long as they spell my name right

There are many and varied versions of this original line. It may be the ancestor of there being "no such thing as bad publicity"—as long as the name is recognizable. Even more numerous than variations on the original line are the names of those who are supposed to have said it first: Mae West, Oscar Wilde, P.T. Barnum, Will Rogers, W.C. Fields, Mark Twain, American politician Tim Sullivan, Dame Nellie Melba, or Edith Head.

The variations have flowed from the original remark by American author, dancer, and singer **George M. Cohan**. He was an undisputed star of musical theater, but in 1912 word got around New York that Cohan was planning to appear in a straight play, which aroused curiosity.

His biographer John McCabe, in *The Man Who Owned Broadway*, reports that when a journalist queried Cohan, he replied:

> *I don't care what you say about me, as long as you say* something *about me, and spell my name right.*

Two years earlier, speaking to a gala dinner for 1,500 theater people, Cohan had also said: "I have only one request to make of you tonight . . . Please mention my name as much as possible."

Over time, Cohan's remark may have morphed into the condensed version: "There is no such thing as bad publicity."

At this point (*or* At this moment) in time

The expression may have come about with the development of space travel. In space it is not always possible to observe time measurements as they relate to an earthly clock, but in order that reports back to earth can be equated with terrestrial time-spans, a communiqué may be declared "at this point in time," referring to the time in space.

But the term caught on among people who relish orotundity, i.e., unnecessarily bombastic or elaborate speech. One such appeared to be **John Dean**, an adviser to President Richard M. Nixon. During the widely publicized and televised Watergate hearings in 1973, Dean frequently said, "at this point in time," and the term rapidly went into popular usage—sometimes in a joking way, but sometimes not.

Axis of evil

Axis is a mathematical term describing "a straight line about which a body or geometric figure rotates."

The first known use of the word axis to describe an alignment of nations was by Gyula Gömbös, the Premier of Hungary, in the early 1930s, referring to an axis that connected Fascist Italy and Nazi Germany with Hungary.

The term went into wider use when Italian premier Benito

Mussolini made a public address on November 1, 1936 saying that the Berlin-Rome line was not an obstacle but an axis (asse in Italian) around which European states with a will to collaborate could revolve.

The axis of nations was mentioned in English in newspaper reports the following day, and in time it became a familiar term during World War II as a collective description of Germany, Italy, and Japan—the Axis Powers, as opposed to the Allied Powers—Britain, United States, and Russia.

In 2002 **David Frum** was a speechwriter for President George W. Bush. He teamed the already familiar term axis with "hatred," changing it to "evil" for the President's State of the Union address on January 29 that year. Referring to countries believed to sponsor terrorism and harbour weapons of mass destruction, the President's speech declared:

> *States like these, and their terrorist allies, constitute an axis of evil, arming to threaten the peace of the world.*

President Bush's speech was widely reported and put the term axis of evil into common English usage.

Babes in the wood

The well-known tale is believed to be based on a real-life situation—two children left by their dying father with his evil brother who, wanting to get his hands on the children's inheritance, takes them into a forest and abandons them. The first known telling of the story was in a 1595 ballad: *The Children in the Wood, or the Norfolk Gentleman's Last Will and Testament*, by **Thomas Millington**.

Since then the story has appeared in dozens of versions—poems, story-books, a Walt Disney movie (which strayed from the original tale by introducing magical woodland elves), pantomimes, and a sophisticated Cole Porter song (about two "babes" who lack the innocence of the 1595 originals: "They have found that the fountain of youth/ Is a mixture of gin and vermouth . . . ").

The title phrase of the original story gradually modified the children into babes and has become a commonplace term referring to anyone who seems innocent of whatever dangers surround them.

Backseat driver

As cars became more commonplace, so too did the impulse grow for passengers to give advice to the driver. Backseat drivers were first mentioned in a newspaper in 1921 (the *Bismarck Tribune*, North Dakota) and defined as those who issue instructions, give advice and offer criticism.

The term reached a much wider international audience in 1930, when *Jeeves and the Old School Chum* by **P.G. Wodehouse** was published:

> *Quite suddenly and unexpectedly, no one more surprised than myself, the car let out a faint gurgle like a sick moose and stopped in its tracks . . . the back-seat drivers gave tongue. "What's the matter? What has happened?" I explained. "I'm not stopping. It's the car."*

Backs to the wall

On April 11, 1918, Field Marshal **Sir Douglas Haig**, Commander-in-Chief, British Armies in France, issued a "Special Order of the Day" to all ranks, containing the following:

> *Every position must be held to the last man: there must be no retirement. With our backs to the wall and believing in the justice of our cause each one of us must fight on to the end.*

The term may have been in circulation beforehand, but Haig's communiqué quickly became known as the "Backs to the Wall Order" and put the expression into common use.

(A) bad egg

A reference to a person of undesirable qualities; the image is based on the fact that an egg which looks quite acceptable on the outside may prove rotten upon closer inspection.

This image first surfaced in the 1855 novel *Captain Priest* by American author **Samuel Hammett** (writing as **Philip Paxton**). Referring to someone who appears to be utterly faultless, he says:

The perfect bird generally turns out to be a bad egg.

The term retained this negative meaning until the end of the nineteenth century when a reverse version appeared complimenting someone with admirable qualities as a "good egg."

From 1919 on, the public became acquainted with P.G. Wodehouse's character Bertie Wooster who was particularly fond of the expression "good egg," which may have been a factor in broadening its popular appeal.

Bad hair day

The expression—slang for a time when things are going badly—undoubtedly had a limited currency before it reached a wider public. In an interview on *Weekend Update*, television journalist **Jane Pauley** mentioned having invented the term herself during the 1970s. But according to the BBC, columnist **Susan Swartz** was the first person to spring the term on an unsuspecting public in print in the *Houston Chronicle* in 1988—on an unsuspecting adult public, that is. Swartz later acknowledged that she used the term quite casually, probably having heard it said by teenage girls. Nevertheless, she holds the distinction of being responsible for its first public appearance.

The really major international exposure came in the 1992 movie *Buffy the Vampire Slayer*, written by **Joss Whedon**. Buffy says to the one-armed vampire Amilyn:

I'm fine, but you're obviously having a bad hair day.

(The) balance of power

In 1734 the **Duke of Newcastle** used the term "balance of power" when writing to Horace Walpole, who repeated the phrase a few years later in a letter to his brother, Sir Robert Walpole:

The situation and conduct of the States is of that consequence to England and to the balance of power in Europe, that this place cannot be without an able and agreeable minister from England.

Five months later Sir Robert Walpole, then leader of the Cabinet, famously used the same term during a speech in the House of Commons on February 13, 1741, and thereafter it was regarded as a fundamental principle of diplomacy.

Be afraid—be very afraid

The statement, "Be afraid," goes back to antiquity—to the King James Bible, Romans 13:4: "If thou do that which is evil, be afraid." Expanding this into "be very afraid" was already occurring in the vernacular prior to its gaining major attention in the 1986 horror movie *The Fly*, in which teleportation goes wrong and a man becomes half-insect.

At a key moment during the horrific transformation, the character of Veronica Quaife (Geena Davis) says, "Be afraid. Be very afraid." The line—written by **David Cronenberg**, **George Langelaan** and **Charles Edward Pogue**—became part of the trailer advertising the movie internationally and quickly moved into common use.

In time, although usage abbreviated it to the earlier short form, "Be afraid," the connotation remained that this implied "Be *very* afraid."

(To) beard the lion in his den

In 1808, **Sir Walter Scott**'s narrative poem *Marmion* introduced the romantic character of Lochinvar, who whisked the lady he loved away from her wedding and rode off with her into the night. A line from the poem, where two aristocratic warriors confront each other, came into common usage:

On the Earl's cheek the flush of rage
O'ercame the ashen hue of age:
Fierce he broke forth—"And dare'st thou then
To beard the lion in his den,
The Douglas in his hall?"

(The) beautiful game

Known officially as Association Football, more commonly as just football, and in the United States as soccer, the game acquired a nickname when Brazilian midfield star Waldyr Pereira, known as **Didi**, coined the term joga bonito, meaning "play beautifully" in Portuguese.

In English translation it became a noun—the beautiful game—and caught on very quickly. In 1977 international football superstar Pele's autobiography was entitled *My Life and the Beautiful Game*, a feature movie *The Beautiful Game* came out in 1999, and the Lloyd Webber-Ben Elton theater musical *The Beautiful Game* played in London in 2000.

Beauty is only skin deep

Far from being a contemporary perception, the earliest known mention of beauty's superficiality came in 1613 when **Sir Thomas Overbury** wrote:

> *All the carnal beauty of my wife is but skin deep, but to two senses known.*

A few years later, John Davies of Hereford in *A Select Second Husband* (1616) tidied up the term into the form we now use it: "Beauty is but skin deepe."

Because it was there

Britain's famous mountaineer (and colorful character) **Sir George Leigh Mallory** had a passionate desire to climb to the top of Mt. Everest. After a failed endeavor in 1923, he gave lectures about the Himalayas and started to plan another attempt. Asked why he'd wanted to conquer it the first time, he replied, "Because it was there." During his 1924 attempt to reach the summit, Mallory died on the mountain.

Twenty-nine years later the Everest summit was finally reached by Edmund Hillary and Tensing Norgay. On returning, Hillary was asked virtually the same question, "Why did you want to do it?" and replied by quoting Mallory: "Because it was there." The mountaineering fraternity knew he was quoting Mallory, but journalists did not, and Hillary was sometimes erroneously credited with inventing the phrase.

In 1986 Mallory's niece Mrs. Newton Dunn wrote to the *Daily Telegraph* and explained that Mallory's sister (Mrs. Dunn's mother) had questioned his response. Mallory's impatient comment was, "Because a silly question deserves a silly answer."

Beefcake

In October 1949 an Ohio newspaper (*The Chronicle Telegram* of Elyria, Ohio) referred to a growing phenomenon in movies, namely that the moguls were beginning to realize that the female half of the population enjoyed seeing well-built men, so males with muscled chests were increasingly featured stripped to the waist. *The Chronicle Telegram* reported that cameramen had started using the term "beefcake" to describe this phenomenon. From whatever source the word arose, it came into a far wider arena after a United States coastguard named Robert Moseley made a weekend tourist visit to Hollywood and was spotted by an alert agent. Renamed Guy Madison, he appeared shirtless in his first movie in 1944, drawing thousands of letters from women and leading to a long career as a movie and television star. Hollywood historians Robert Hofler (in *The Man who Invented Rock Hudson*) and D.K. Holm (in *You'll Never Write a Book in this Town Again*) point firmly to influential show-biz columnist **Sidney Skolsky** for using the term "beefcake" to describe Guy Madison, and thus putting the term into the public arena.

See also **Cheesecake**

Been there, done that

This term of sardonic world-weariness was already in use in Australia before it reached a wider audience in 1982 when an Australian actress in America was credited with its use.

Lauren Tewes (who played cruise director Julie McCoy in *The Love Boat*) was quoted in the *Gettysburg Times* (February 22, 1982) saying that after her divorce she had no plans to remarry:

> *Using an Australian expression, she says, "Been there, done that."*

A year later the expression appeared in Australia's *Macquarie Dictionary of New Words* and has been in common use internationally ever since.

Behind the scenes

Clearly a great deal of necessary activity takes place behind the scenes/scenery in a theater, and always has. But it took **John Dryden** in *An Essay of Dramatic Poesy* (1668) to suggest that activities essential but unseen could be referred to in that way:

> *But there is another sort of relations, that is, of things happening in the action of the play, and supposed to be done*

behind the scenes. And this is many times convenient and
beautiful . . .

From there, the phrase progressed naturally into figurative use to describe the hidden machinations of those in high places.

Believe it or not

The first known use of the term was in October 1919 when **Robert Leroy Ripley** named his *New York Globe* newspaper cartoon strip featuring unusual facts. Eventually the strip was seen daily, syndicated internationally, and it grew to have a reputed 80 million readers.

There are many republished collections of the cartoon strips and the idea—and its title—gave rise to more than twenty mini-movie shorts, three television series, an animated cartoon movie series, a board game, a computer contest, and thirty-five "Believe It or Not" museums around the world.

Below the belt

Boxing as a sport has been widely practiced since at least 3000 BC. But there were no established rules in Britain until the rise of **Jack Broughton**, a former rower of passengers on the Thames who became a heavyweight boxing champion.

In 1743 Broughton drafted a set of practices that became known as the London Prize Ring Rules. These were revised in 1838 and again in 1853, stipulating that biting, head butting, and hitting below the belt were "fouls."

In 1867 John Graham Chambers revised the boxing rules under the patronage of the Marquess of Queensbury, who did not write them but under whose name they were published.

Be prepared

In his manual for Scouts, *Scouting for Boys* (1908), **Lord Baden-Powell** wrote:

> *The scouts' motto is based on my initials, it is: Be Prepared.*

Best thing since sliced bread

An effective bread-slicing machine had been developed by 1928 and within five years bakeries in America were producing more sliced bread than unsliced.

In February 1940 the *Burlington Daily Times* featured a quaint advertising campaign by the **Southern Bread** firm—an offer of *two* packs of wrapped sliced bread at a bargain price. And extolling the "Thrift Thrill Twin-Pack" was a cartoon figure representing Mother saying: "Greatest convenience since sliced bread!" The implication was that two loaves of sliced bread were better than one.

Thus the image of something being more convenient than sliced bread originated in the curious concept that the greatest convenience since sliced bread was more sliced bread!

Over time, and with some slight modifications ("greatest convenience" to "greatest thing" to "best thing"), the line came to be applied to any number of products: cell phones, Viagra, television remotes, Microsoft, Diet Coke . . .

(It's probably) better to have him inside the tent pissing out, than outside pissing in

President **Lyndon B. Johnson** had a somewhat clouded view of FBI Director J. Edgar Hoover. *New York Times* writer David Halberstam reported in October 1971 that Johnson's opinion was:

*Well, it's probably better to have him inside the tent
pissing out, than outside the tent pissing in.*

Beyond the pale

The pale here refers to a designated area within a border, either real
or theoretical, and under a different jurisdiction from the adjacent
territory. The English Pale referred to the Calais area of France
administered by England, and the Irish Pale was that section of
Ireland under English control. Beyond the Pale simply meant past
the border.

By the seventeenth century the image of a pale—an
enclosure—had acquired a metaphorical meaning, often used by
Christians referring to a defined and safe area of belief. Archbishop
Bramwell said in 1654: "We acknowledge that there is no salvation
to be expected ordinarily without the pale of the Church."

Notwithstanding the limits placed on it by church adherents—
only they themselves were within the pale—gradually the
expression came to include wider areas of acceptable behavior and
decency. Beyond the pale implied a general lack of propriety and
possibly decency. With all due respect to Archbishop Bramwell, it
was **Charles Dickens** who nailed the term into the modern
vernacular in *Pickwick Papers* (1837). Mr. Pott tells Slurk:

> *I consider you a viper. I look upon you, sir, as a man who
> has placed himself beyond the pale of society, by his most
> audacious, disgraceful, and abominable public conduct.*

(The) Big Apple

The first known connection between an apple and New York City
came by way of a rather esoteric mention in Edward Sanford
Martin's book *The Wayfarer in New York* (1909). He referred to the
perception that the people of the Midwest had of the big city and

of the proportion of the nation's wealth it attracted. An image was engendered of New York as a great tree, with its roots reaching to distant states and coasts. However, the tree's fruit showed little affection for the source of its nourishment. New York could therefore be seen as the "big apple," commandeering an unfair share of the national sap.

Referring to New York in connection with an apple is also believed to have occurred among jazz musicians referring to a booking at a prestigious venue, but "big apple" never really achieved public usage until it was heard by **John J. Fitzgerald**. He was a sports journalist who, when visiting racetracks in New Orleans, became aware not of musicians but of stable hands referring to New York as the big apple, meaning "the big time." He found the phrase evocative and, when he got back to New York, decided to use it as the title of his *Morning Telegraph* sports column. In February 1924 Fitzgerald wrote:

> *The Big Apple. The dream of every lad that ever threw a leg over a thoroughbred and the goal of all horsemen. There's only one Big Apple. That's New York.*

The term gradually came into public usage—eventually such wide public usage that in 1971 "Big Apple" became the official advertising slogan of New York City. And in tribute to John J. Fitzgerald, who helped make the term famous, the corner of Broadway and 54th Street where he'd lived for thirty years was re-named Big Apple Corner in 1997.

Big Brother is watching you

In 1949, descriptions of such concepts as closed-circuit television, Google Earth, computer scans, DNA, airport computer checks, and global Internet communication would have been considered science fiction. That year, George Orwell depicted sinister overall surveillance in his novel *1984*, with its alarming catchphrase "Big Brother is Watching You."

Over time—not necessarily in 1984—much of Orwell's projected government surveillance did eventuate. He also described government terminology and nomenclature which conveyed the opposite of the truth, and that too came to pass; the Ministry of Health, for instance, is concerned only with sickness.

(In 1999 a reality television series called *Big Brother* was launched in the Netherlands, showing a house full of people constantly being filmed. The format was copied in more than sixty countries.)

(The) bigger they are the harder they fall

The idea was put into (Latin) words as far back as the fourth century AD by Latin poet Claudian: "Men are raised on high in order that they may fall more heavily."

According to Monte D. Cox, a member of the International Boxing Research Organization, the modern version was first proclaimed by boxer **Joe Walcott** ("The Barbados Demon") who, although he was short, became the welterweight champion of the world in 1901.

The term became more widely known after Robert Fitzsimmons made a similar remark, much publicized after being reported in the *National Police Gazette* in 1902:

> *If I can get close enough, I'll guarantee to stop almost anybody. The bigger the man, the heavier the fall.*

Joe Walcott ("The Barbados Demon") is not to be confused with Arnold Cream, who called himself Jersey Joe Walcott (in honor of "The Barbados Demon") and was world heavyweight boxing champion in 1951.

Bitch goddess

The term refers to success and comes from a letter written to H.G. Wells by American philosopher and writer **William James** in 1906:

> *The moral flabbiness born of the exclusive worship of the bitch goddess success is our national disease.*

In 1928 D.H. Lawrence referred to the same matter in *Lady Chatterley's Lover*. William James's original success is sometimes misquoted as referring to fame.

Bite the dust

The idea wasn't born with Western movies. Around 700 BC Homer wrote of such an image, but it took a while to make the transition to English. Various versions filtered through, the earliest perhaps being "lick the dust," from the Book of Psalms. In 1720 Alexander Pope translated Homer's words as "bit the ground," and Cowper's translation had "press'd the dust."

But in 1748 Scottish author **Tobias Smollett** focused the varying versions of the already 2000-year-old expression in *Gil Blas of Santillane*, a novel he translated from the French:

> *We made two of them bite the dust, and the others betake themselves to flight.*

From Homer's original concept of sudden death, which it still describes, the term also came into usage in the wider contexts of defeat and failure. It can refer to political ideas, financial downturns or commercial disasters . . . even an expired romance or marriage.

(The) black dog

Referring to depression (or melancholy) as a black dog is a concept that in English dates back to at least the 1700s. The same term can also be found used in the same way by the Roman poet Horace (around 50 BC).

Samuel Johnson frequently referred to his periods of melancholy as a black dog, as in this letter to Hester Thrale (1783):

> *The black dog I hope always to resist, and in time to drive . . .*
> *When I rise my breakfast is solitary, the black dog waits to*
> *share it,,from breakfast to dinner he continues barking.*

Both Sir Walter Scott and Robert Louis Stevenson used the same image, and in more recent times the term reached a wide audience through the many references associating it with Sir Winston Churchill, who is said to have called his periods of depression his black dog. However, only one instance appears to exist of Churchill's directly mentioning his black dog; in a 1911 letter to his wife after a dinner with Lady Wimborne, Churchill wrote:

> *Alice interested me a great deal in her talk about her doctor*
> *in Germany, who completely cured her depression. I think*
> *this man might be useful to me—if my black dog returns.*
> *He seems quite away from me now—it is such a relief.*
> *All the colors come back into the picture.*

This letter wasn't published until 1998. Sir Winston's last secretary, Anthony Montague Brown, in his book *Long Sunset*, expresses doubt that Sir Winston ever actually spoke of the black dog and reports that he never heard Churchill use the expression. Other people, however, claimed he had said it to them.

Nevertheless, whether or not he used it, linking the term with the iconic figure of Churchill brought it into wider common usage.

Blood is thicker than water

Expressions of this concept—strength of kinship—have surfaced over many centuries in various cultures and languages around the world. It appeared in English in 1412 in *The Troy Book*, where John Lydgate wrote:

> *For naturally blood will be of kind.*
> *Drawn-to blood, where he may it find.*

But the saying came into more common usage, on both sides of the Atlantic, in the nineteenth century. **Sir Walter Scott** in *Guy Mannering* (1815) recounts the reading of a will that leaves the contents of the deceased's house to a young woman. The character of Dinmont, seeing his expectations disappear, exclaims in anger:

> *Weel, blude's thicker than water; she's welcome to the cheeses and the hams just the same.*

And the *New York Times*, drawing on *Harper's* magazine, reported that in 1860 the American commander Josiah Tattnall of the steamer *Toey-wan*, delivering an American consul to China, sailed into the Pei-ho River. At the time, allied British and French gunboats were attacking the Taku forts. The Chinese were returning fire vigorously, and many British ships were struck, commencing in 85 dead and 385 wounded.

Commander Tattnall ordered his own (neutral) craft into the fray to assist the wounded British admiral. Technically, this was a breach of international law.

When asked to explain his actions, Tattnall's reply to the U.S. Naval Secretary referred to Anglo-American kinship, saying simply:

> *Blood is thicker than water.*

His action was upheld.

The incident was much discussed in the United States, and as Tattnall became something of a folk hero, his use of the expression made it familiar to an American audience Sir Walter Scott might not have reached.

Bloody but unbowed

A line from the poem "Invictus" by **William Ernest Henley**. Henley suffered tuberculosis of the bone and had one leg amputated when he was a teenager. The other leg was also targeted for amputation, but Henley wouldn't allow this and remained in the hospital for three years, supervised and assisted by Joseph Lister. Henley wrote "Invictus" in the hospital, and it was published in the 1875, the year he was discharged. He went on to become a respected magazine editor.

> *In the fell clutch of circumstance*
> *I have not winced nor cried aloud.*
> *Under the bludgeonings of chance*
> *My head is bloody, but unbowed*

The poem's equally famous final line is: "I am the master of my fate, I am the captain of my soul."

Robert Louis Stevenson became a close friend of Henley's. His red beard, massive shoulders, jovial rolling laugh, and one-legged gait with his crutch was the inspiration for Stevenson's character Long John Silver.

Bloody Mary

Widely known as a mixture of tomato juice, vodka, and something spicy, the drink became popular in the early 1900s but its name was first heard in Britain nearly 400 years earlier.

Queen Mary Tudor of England, an ardent Catholic, was firmly set against the Protestant religion approved by the two monarchs who preceded her, and she set out to force the English into Catholicism—on pain of death. During her five-year reign (1553 - 1558) she had some 280 people, with whose religious principles she disagreed, tortured and burned at the stake. Hence her nickname among the populace—Bloody Mary.

The appearance of the vodka-tomato drink may be reminiscent of blood, but a Bloody Mary is a great deal less dangerous than the woman after whom it is named. (Incidentally, Mary Tudor, the original Bloody Mary, is not to be confused with Mary Queen of Scots, who never ruled England.)

Blot on the landscape

The first known use of the expression in print was in *Punch* (vol. 153, July 1917), in a somewhat unkind context. Writer **Crosbie Garstin** described the Reverend Paul Grayne, sometime curate of Thorpington Parva, as:

> . . . *a blot on the landscape; among all the heroes I have met I never saw anything less heroically moulded. He stood about five feet nought and tipped the beam at seven stone nothing. He had a mild chinless face and his long beaky nose, round large spectacles, and trick of cocking his head sideways when conversing, gave him the appearance of an intelligent little dicky-bird.*

Novelist Tom Sharpe used the expression as the basis of a 1975 comic novel about a gardener called Blott. In 1985, *Blott on the Landscape* became a successful BBC television series.

Blow the gaff

An old meaning of blow was to display something otherwise not easily seen, to expose, while gab has long referred to talk. Thus "blow the gab" referred to information being brought into the open. It has been suggested that an old meaning of gaff—a hook—came to signify a trick, a cheat, or even a device to help fake something (as, for instance, in corrupting a game of cards).

Either way, blowing the gab faded from use, and blowing the gaff became common usage and was well settled in by 1833 when it was used by **Frederick Marryat** in *Peter Simple*:

> *One of the French officers, after he was taken prisoner,*
> *axed (sic) me how we had managed to get the gun up there;*
> *but I wasn't going to blow the gaff, so I told him, as a great*
> *secret, that we got it up with a kite, upon which he opened*
> *all his eyes, and crying "sacre bleu!" walked away, believing*
> *all I said was true . . .*

Boredom

The expression "to be a bore" has been used in the sense of "to be tiresome or dull" since 1768. But until 1852 the word boredom did not exist in English.

The gap was filled by **Charles Dickens** in *Bleak House*, where we are told that Lady Dedlock:

> *. . . whose chronic malady of boredom has been sadly*
> *aggravated by Volumnia this evening, glances wearily*
> *towards the candlesticks and heaves a noiseless sigh.*

Born-again Christian

Belief in undergoing a spiritual rather than an actual rebirth—being "born again"—and thus following the edict of Jesus (John 3:3 and

Peter 1:23) had surfaced among some branches of Christianity by the 1960s. It was also sometimes referred to as being "born anew."

But the term "born-again Christian" gained wide international coverage and comment during the lead-up to the 1976 American presidential election.

Watergate conspirator Charles Colson's book *Born Again* had raised awareness of the term, and a reporter who'd read it asked the devout and clean-living presidential candidate **Jimmy Carter** if he believed in the concept of being born again.

The reply—"I am born again"—drew major attention: Colson's book went into a two-million print run, and journalist Robert Scheer interviewed Jimmy Carter for *Playboy*. The interview (in the November 1976 issue) discussed with Carter how being born again affected his life. It was the only time a presidential candidate had been interviewed by *Playboy*, and more copies were sold than of any previous issue.

Carter, who went on to become President, laid no claim to having originated the term but his use of it brought it to much wider notice than had previously been the case.

(The) boys in the back room

During the nineteenth century in both Britain and America, the term "back room" had an association with card-playing, sometimes illegally, and thus carried a faint connotation of something clandestine. It is briefly mentioned in Thomas Hardy's *Jude the Obscure* (1895).

In 1978, in the *New York Times Magazine,* American humorist Sidney Perelman wrote an appreciation of the cartoonist Tad Dorgan who had died in 1929. Dorgan had been cartoonist on the *New York Journal*—and had a gift for witty captions—one of which, Perelman pointed out, was "See what the boys in the backroom will have."

This intriguing line traveled beyond its New York audience in 1939 when it became the title of a song by **Frank Loesser**. In the movie *Destry Rides Again,* Marlene Dietrich sang Loesser's song "See What the Boys in the Back Room Will Have," and it became a memorable moment in movie history. However, it was never clear from the song just exactly who the boys in the back room were.

Three years later, in 1941, the term "back-room boys" acquired a strong connotation of unsung scientists, inventors, or strategists—anyone whose essential work on a project went largely unpublicized. This came about when Lord Beaverbrook, Britain's wartime Minister of Aircraft Production, made a speech honoring the government's researchers. Beaverbrook—who must have been a Dietrich fan—announced:

> Let me say that the credit belongs to the boys in the back rooms. It isn't the man who sits in the limelight like me who should have the praise. It is not the men in prominent places. It is the men in the back rooms.

Bread and circuses

The saying started life in the second century AD when Decimus Junius Juvenalis (Juvenal for short) wrote satirically of those Romans who had given up national pride. They were wooed by a government seeking populist political power through the provision of free grain and stadium spectaculars: "panem et circenses." (Circus referred to a round or oval-shaped open space in which spectacular entertainments took place involving chariot races or gladiatorial contests.)

In 1914 the expression moved into the English language with the publication of the book *Bread and Circuses* by prolific British-born poet **Helen Parry Eden**. The *New York Times* (July 1914) called it a "conundrum" that she had used that title for a collection of "pleasant verses"; however, she had put the expression into usage, ready to be picked up by Rudyard Kipling (*Debits and Credits*) and then Aldous Huxley (*Brave New World Revisited*).

(They) broke the mold

In literature, the Italian poet **Ludovico Ariosto** is mainly identified with his work *Orlando Furioso* (1516), a poem dealing with the knights of Charlemagne in wars against the Saracens. One line from the lengthy work has gone into common usage:

> *There never was such beauty in another man.*
> *Nature made him, and then broke the mold.*
> *(Non e un si bello in tante altre persone,*
> *Natura il fece, e poi roppa la stampa.)*

Brunch

The word conjures an image of a contemporary urban lifestyle, but in fact it came into being in nineteenth-century Britain. *Punch* reported (August 1896) that the word brunch had been:

> . . . *introduced last year by Mr. Guy Beringer, in the now defunct* Hunter's Weekly—*indicating a combined breakfast and lunch . . . probably taken just after arriving home from hunting.*

(The) buck stops here

Printed on a small sign sitting on the desk of President **Harry S. Truman**, the expression was firmly associated with the President himself, although not created by him.

The expression was first referred to in a Nevada newspaper in 1942 as a "desk slogan" of Colonel A.B. Warfield. Three years later a version had turned up at the Federal Reformatory at El Reno, Oklahoma, where it was spotted by U.S. Marshal Fred M. Canfil. He arranged with the reformatory warden that a copy be made, which he posted to President Truman in 1945. Truman placed the sign on his desk and used the phrase quite often.

It went into popular usage, even when referring to administrative hierarchies less exalted than the Presidency. One of its more unusual outings was in an unexpected context. Edward Mirzeoff's 1992 British television documentary *Elizabeth R*, celebrating the fortieth year of the Queen's reign, showed her dealing with a very large daily correspondence. Explaining her wish to see in person what people wrote to her, Her Majesty cheerfully acknowledged that "the buck stops here."

(The buck was the term used by poker players referring to the marker placed in front of the next person who was to deal—the buck stopped there. Should the player for any reason not want to deal, he passed the buck to someone else.)

Bull in a china shop

Although the expression in its current form came first from the pen of **Frederick Marryat**, the idea had been around for a long time before that—but not quite as we know it. James Boswell came close: in 1769 Boswell wrote that the "delicate and polite" Mr. Berenger had described Dr. Johnson's behavior in genteel company as being like that of "an ox in a china shop."

Sir Walter Scott retained the action but changed the animal in *The Fortunes of Nigel* (1822):

> *A person who had a general acquaintance with all the flaws and specks in the shields of the proud, the pretending and the nouveaux riches, must have the same scope for amusement as a monkey in a china shop.*

Just over a decade later, Marryat's novel *Jacob Faithful* (1834) brought the image into line:

> *Whatever it is that smashes, Mrs. T always swears it was the most valuable thing in the room. I'm like a bull in a china shop.*

(In 1936 considerable publicity was engendered by an incident in New York. Bandleader Fred Waring and actor Paul Douglas had a bet, which Waring lost. His penalty for losing the bet was to lead a full-grown bull through a real china shop and pay for any damage the bull might cause. In the event, the bull sauntered elegantly through the shop without damaging a single piece. Ironically, Waring was so nervous that *he* knocked over a table full of valuable ornaments.)

Bunch of fives

In spite of its contemporary sound, the expression bunch of fives was current in the early nineteenth century, and is first referred to in 1821 in *Boxiana*, a published collection of magazine articles on boxing by **Pierce Egan**.

Blackwood's Edinburgh Review of 1823 makes special mention of Egan's bunch of fives expression. Charles Dickens had picked it up by 1837—in *Pickwick Papers* Orson Dabbs is said to be "shaking his bunch of fives sportively as one snaps an unloaded gun."

See also **Tom and Jerry**

Burn the midnight oil

In lifestyles that often included working late, with only candles and oil lamps available, burning midnight oil was no doubt a reality and this was long before the seventeenth century; however, it was 1635 when the concept was actually seen in print.

Virtually forgotten now, English author **Francis Quarles** was secretary to the Primate of Ireland, "official chronologer" to the City of London, and father of eighteen children. Little surprise then that his 1635 poem "Emblems" included the lines:

> *We spend our midday sweat, our midnight oil,*
> *We tire the night in thought, the day in toil.*

Business before pleasure

Hardly a household name nowadays, **Letitia Elizabeth Landon** was an extremely popular and widely read writer in the nineteenth century. Remarkably, for a female writer of her time, she was able to maintain financial independence from her very prolific output: hundreds of published poems, children's stories, translations of foreign works, literary reviews, several plays, a collection of short stories, and several novels.

One of the latter, *Francesca Carrara* (1834), is now seldom mentioned, but a rare copy in the Harvard University Library shows that L.E. Landon came up with the first known use of what later became a byword of mercantile discipline:

> *Business before pleasure, I am ready to grant; but when there is none, il faut s'amuser!*

Busy as a one-armed paper-hanger

There have been various versions since (and possibly before) but **O. Henry**'s 1908 story "The Ethics of a Pig" told of a con man who buys an ordinary pig and attempts to on-sell it for exhibition as an "educated hog." In this story the ancestor of the basic image was launched into the international arena:

> *"Let me tote him in for you," says Rufe; and he picks up the beast under one arm, holding his snout with the other hand, and packs him into my room like a sleeping baby . . . And then I got as busy as a one-armed man with the nettle-rash pasting on wall-paper. I found an old Negro man with an express wagon to hire; and we tied the pig in a sack and drove down to the circus grounds.*

Later alternative versions have the tradesman busy trying to work in a gale with his trouser buttons coming adrift, or afflicted with hives. Other offshoots tell about the one-legged man in a bum-kicking competition or a dog busy burying a bone in a marble floor.

By hook or by crook

Since it first appeared in English in the fourteenth century, the exact original meanings of "hook" and "crook" have become clouded and much disputed. But the overall sense remains intact— that something will be accomplished by any means possible, no matter how difficult.

John Wycliffe in 1380 was writing his criticisms of the Catholic Church in English and not, like other scholars, in Latin. Wycliffe wanted his comments to be available to everyone:

> *They sillen sacramentis . . . and compellen men to bie alle this with hok or crok (They sell sacraments and compel men to buy all this with hook or crook).*

Call a spade a spade

Ancient writers Menander, Lucian, Aristophanes, and Plutarch all referred to the idea, as far back as 200 BC, though there is some linguistic doubt whether they were calling a spade a spade or a trough a trough.

Dutch scholar Erasmus chose spade when he wrote of the ancients, and the term came into English in 1539, translated by **Richard Taverner**. The latter's *Garden of Wysdome* (1539) says:

> *Whiche call a mattok nothing els but a mattok,*
> *and a spade a spade.*

(A mattock is another kind of digging tool.)

Charles Dickens confirmed the contemporary English version in *Hard Times* (1854) when Bounderby says:

> *There's no imaginative sentimental humbug about me. I call a spade a spade.*

One of the expression's more amusing outings occurs in Oscar Wilde's *The Importance of Being Earnest*, in a dialogue of class war between Miss Cecily Cardew and the Hon. Gwendoline Fairfax. Proud of her honesty, Miss Cardew declares: "When I see a spade,

I call it a spade," only to be squelched by the Hon. Gwen with her reply: "I am glad to say that I have never seen a spade."

Canned laughter

Laughter is generally infectious; humor is more exhilarating when enjoyed (and reacted to) by a group. In the fledgling days of American comedy shows on television, this proved to be a worry. People sitting at home in front of a box—alone or in twos and threes—lacked encouragement to feel fully amused.

Columbia Broadcasting sound engineer **Charley Douglass** invented what he called canned laughter—a method of adding pre-recorded laughter to a studio performance where no audience was present, or adding and modifying laughter where some already existed but was deemed insufficient.

The device made its debut on a no-audience situation in *The Hank McCune Show* (1949). Douglass's invention had plenty of usage over the following decades—sometimes with doubtful results, such as the same recognizable "laugh" being repeated several times within a few minutes. There was also some doubt about its use with animated cartoon shows—everyone knew there could be no audience.

Charley Douglass's canned laughter began to fade from favor toward the close of the twentieth century.

Cash register

It's a simple enough term, but someone had to be first. Back in 1879 Ohio restaurant proprietor **James J. Ritty** was concerned that some of his customers' payments were going into staff pockets. On an ocean trip he saw a device which counted the number of revolutions made by a propeller, and he reasoned that there had to be a way of adapting it to register dollars and cents. It worked and became known as "the Incorruptible Cashier."

Some years later Ritty registered a patent on his invention—now called a "Cash Register and Indicator." The term is still commonly used in regard to paying one's bill in a restaurant or bar and other environments which are virtually cash-free.

Chance would be a fine thing

In 1912, British writer **William Stanley Houghton**'s play *Hindle Wakes* was a major success. Within a year of its opening, 2000 performances had taken place in England and America. The play was made into a movie three times (1927, 1931, and 1952) and into two major television specials, by the BBC (1950) and Granada (1976).

However, mention of the play in more recent years has not drawn much response. But one of its lines survived from 1912. Fanny's parents discover that their daughter, though unmarried, has spent the weekend with a man . . .

> CHRISTOPHER: *This is what happens to many a lass, but I never thought to have it happen to a lass of mine!*

> MRS HAWTHORN: *Why didn't you get wed if you were so curious? There's plenty would have had you.*

> FANNY: *Chance is a fine thing. Happen I wouldn't have had them!*

> MRS HAWTHORN: *Happen you'll be sorry for it before long. There's not so many will have you now, if this gets about.*

Fanny's remark caught on, gradually morphing from the present indicative to the conditional: "Chance would be a fine thing."

Chariot of fire

The image appears several times in the Bible and more than once in English literature—for example, in Milton, Robert Southey, and Thomas Gray.

William Blake's poem *Jerusalem* (1804) could have taken its place as just another one of the many to use the Biblical image, but being set to music by Sir Hubert Parry in 1916 transformed the poem into a hymn sung by millions:

> *Bring me my Bow of burning gold;*
> *Bring me my Arrows of desire:*
> *Bring me my Spear: O clouds unfold:*
> *Bring me my Chariot of fire!*

Blake offered only one chariot. For some unknown reason the famous 1981 movie moved Blake's chariot into the plural—*Chariots of Fire*—which has resulted in the line often being misquoted thus.

Charm offensive

Supreme Allied Commander in Europe, General **Alfred Maximilian Gruenther**, originated the term in an October 1956 interview in the *Fresno Bee Republican*. Gruenther advised that although war was no longer just around the corner, there was a danger that democracies would relax their vigilance after the "launching of the Russian charm offensive."

Cheesecake

Curiously, the word—in connection with attractive women—was in use during the 1660s in Britain and can be found in *Poems and Songs Relating to the Late Times*, published in 1662 shortly after Oliver Cromwell died and containing the following couplet in a lament on the occasion of Oliver Cromwell's rusticating the ladies of the town.

> But ah! It goes against our hearts
> To lose our cheesecake and our tarts.

A more influential usage was launched more than 200 years later. Fast forward to 1912, when **James Kane**, a photographer working for the *New York Journal*, was posing an attractive young woman. A breeze blew her skirt, and more leg than usual came on display. Mr. Kane (who was reputed to like real cheesecake) exclaimed:

> Wow! That's better than cheesecake!

And a universal metaphor was born.
See also **Beefcake**

Che sera sera

The concept has been around at least since 1588, when Marlowe's *Faustus* included the line:

> What doctrine call you this? Che sera sera, what will
> be shall be?

Marlowe's slight linguistic confusion (in French the term would be Que sera sera; in Italian Che sarà sarà) was avoided by Beaumont and Fletcher in *The Scornful Lady* (1616). When the character of Welford importunes The Lady with his determination to kiss her, she resignedly replies in English, "What must be must be."

But the internationally famous version came in 1956 when **Jay Livingston** and **Ray Evans** wrote the song "Que Sera Sera" for Doris Day to sing in the movie *The Man Who Knew Too Much*. The gentle conversion from "Che" to "Que" tidied the phrase into acceptable French (or Spanish "Que será será") rather than muddled Italian; the song was a huge hit and its title went into vernacular use.

(An old) chestnut

When an incident or joke has been told and heard many times, it becomes a "chestnut." Playwright William Diamond used the term in his play *The Broken Sword, or, The Torrent of the Valley* at Covent Garden in 1816. In the play, a character starts to relate an incident which promises to be boring because it is already familiar. When he mentions that it happened near a cork tree, the character of Pablo interrupts him with the declaration that he had heard the story twenty-seven times before, and it had always been a chestnut tree!

The American actor **William Warren**, who played Pablo, used the word offstage in a public situation when someone started to tell a stale joke, which Warren described as "a chestnut." This incident became widely known, and the term chestnut gradually came to mean something already heard twenty-seven times or thereabouts.

Chicken feed

Regardless of the birds' ages, American vernacular morphed hens, fowls, and poultry into one word—chickens. For practical reasons, early settlers, after harvesting, kept good grain for their own household cooking and used the inferior, usually smaller, grades to feed the hens. An association grew between "small grain" (chicken feed) and "small coins." This figurative use of chicken feed was put into print by none other than **Davy Crockett** in 1834.

His autobiographical *A Narrative of the Life of David Crockett* told about traveling gamblers taking bets on the old thimble-and-pea trick, and then executing it so slickly that they were:

picking up their shillings just about as expeditiously as a
hungry gobbler would a pint of corn.

Crockett described the arrival of a crooked gambler as coming "down like a hurricane in a corn field, sweeping all before it." And Crockett stood looking on, "seeing him pick up the chicken feed from the greenhorns."

(In later years many doubted that Crockett's narratives were in fact his own work, and the assistance of ghost writer Richard Penn was revealed. This didn't alter the fact that the term chicken feed first appeared under Crockett's name.)

(A) chicken in every pot

Born in France in 1553, the Duke of Bourbon's son was four places away from the French throne. Royal deaths moved him up the list to become King of Navarre and then **Henry IV** of France in 1589. A serious king, he supported agricultural development, had roads built, created more trade opportunities, and fostered the prosperity of all citizens. His concern for the welfare of the general populace made him one of France's most popular monarchs. Historians report that his egalitarian attitude was summed up in his famous pronouncement in support of the working classes:

> *I want no peasant in my realm to be so poor that he not have a*
> *hen in his pot every Sunday (Je veux qu'il n'y ait si pauvre*
> *paysan en mon royaume qu'il n'ait tous les dimanches sa poule*
> *au pot).*

King Henry's egalitarian wish became widely quoted beyond France and, in later centuries, was appropriated by politicians elsewhere.

Chickens come home to roost

Because it is an observation of a natural happening, this fact has been universally noted and sometimes written about. Geoffrey Chaucer wrote in *The Parson's Tale* (c. 1390) of birds and nests:

> Such cursing deprives a man of the Kingdom of God, as says Saint Paul. And oftentimes such cursing returns again upon the head of him that curses, like a bird that returns again to its own nest.

> (And ofte tyme swich cursynge wrongfully retorneth agayn to hym that curseth, as a bryd that retorneth agayn to his owene nest.)

The neater version came from British historian, linguist, and poet **Robert Southey** as an inscription on the title page of his lengthy poem about the adventures of a Hindu rajah, "The Curse of Kehama" (1810):

> Curses are like young chickens, they always come home to roost.

(A) chip off the old block

Fairly obviously, a chip of wood would retain the coloring, grain, texture, and even the smell of the parent block from which it had been chipped. The similarity between fathers and sons and chips off blocks had been noticed and commented on for centuries. And as a variation on the theme, the Greek *Idylls* of Theocritus in 300 BC mention a "chip -'o- the flint."

The image appeared in English in 1621 when a sermon from **Bishop Sanderson of Lincoln** announced:

> Am not I a child of the same Adam . . . a chip of the same block, with him?

The expression has been with us ever since. It was used on one memorable occasion in 1781 in the British House of Commons when the Irish statesman and author Edmund Burke, after hearing Pitt the Younger's maiden speech, opined that young Pitt was "not merely a chip off the old block, but the old block itself."

Cleavage (formerly décolletage)

The word cleavage is a worry—it can mean rending things into separate parts and also exactly the opposite when referring to things which cling together. In terms of low-cut necklines, it somehow covers both possibilities: garments cut to show objects that are actually separate but also clinging together.

The Motion Picture Production Code was set up by Will Hays in 1930 to maintain decency in movies and was known as "the Hays code." Nudity was, of course, out of the question in movies, but décolletage must have remained modest enough to escape attention until 1945.

In that year, a British movie called *The Wicked Lady* starred two very glamorous actresses—Margaret Lockwood and Patricia Roc—as Restoration-period beauties. The two women were costumed in a style based on easily accessible contemporary depictions of Restoration fashion, including low-cut necklines: Too low for the Hollywood censors. **Joseph I. Breen**, the administrator of the Hays code, considered the necklines contravened standards of decency and invoked the previously unknown word "cleavage," defined as "the shadowed depression dividing an actress's bosom into two distinct sections."

The movie's makers were informed that the movie could not be screened to American audiences because the stars were showing more cleavage than Mr. Breen would allow. So the leading ladies were brought back to re-film several critical scenes, no doubt at great expense.

In 1946 *Time* magazine published a detailed account of the situation, bringing the word cleavage into public scrutiny for the first time ("Cleavage and the Code," August 1946). Almost overnight, the world décolletage vanished and cleavage became the norm.

Close encounters of the third kind

The well-known movie title was based on a genuine classification. Professor of Astronomy at Northwestern University in Illinois **J. Allen Hynek** was consultant to the United States Air Force for "ufology"—the official study of unidentified flying objects.

When an alien object had been sighted, Hynek was called upon to identify whether or not it was actually an astronomical body. His 1972 book *The UFO Experience: A Scientific Inquiry* introduced for the first time the concept of close encounters with aliens. These were graded as:

> *(1) Close Encounters of the First Kind—witnessing an unexplained object in the air, no more than 200 yards from a witness.*

> *(2) Close Encounters of the Second Kind—in which the UFO leaves some kind of evidence of its visit remaining.*

> *(3) Close Encounters of the Third Kind—in which any occupants of the flying object can actually be seen.*

Cold feet

In the face of major uncertainty or threat, it is common to claim cold feet. There is evidence that an analogous concept existed in old Italy, and British playwright Ben Jonson uses a similar expression in *Volpone* (1607), but referring there to being short of money.

The first known depiction of coldness in the feet in conjunction with losing one's nerve came in 1862 from the German writer **Fritz Reuter**. He depicted a card-playing scenario in which one player is at a high point, consistently winning, but thinks nervously that his luck cannot last, so decides to leave the table. His offered explanation is that his feet are cold and he must excuse himself to find some way of warming them.

The other players interpret his explanation of cold feet as actually referring to his wavering courage . . . and so has everyone else since.

(The) cold shoulder

There has been little change in the way this expression has been used since it first appeared in print. **Sir Walter Scott**'s 1816 novel *The Antiquary* offered the term publicly for the first time, amid a tangle of lost nobility, supposed illegitimacy, rescues, drownings, and haughty aristocracy.

The character of Elspeth Cheyne reports to Lord William on the behavior of his mother, Countess Glenallen:

> *Ye may mind that the Countess's dislike didna gang farther at first than just showing o' the cauld shouther—at least it wasna seen farther.*

The term may possibly have been known before 1816, but Scott's use of it here—indicating disdainful and aloof body language—cropped up again in his later writings and then spread very quickly into wider use (Dickens, Galsworthy, the Brontë sisters, Louisa May Alcott, Trollope, and Mark Twain). It remains in the vernacular, occasionally extending to more metaphorical references, such as a bank giving a cold shoulder to an application for a loan.

Cold turkey

The expression's origin is not clear. It may have grown out of the fact that cold, cooked turkey is something which can be served immediately, without further preparation. From there it acquired the meaning of simply stopping a dangerous habit without any slow lead-up. It may also refer to the pinched appearance that apparently characterizes the skin of someone in serious drug withdrawal trauma—something like the skin of a turkey.

Whatever its origin, for some time the expression was known only among those to whom it was relevant. But in 1949 a novel was published which led to the term gaining a much wider international audience. **Nelson Algren**'s brilliantly written dark story of drugs and crime, *The Man with the Golden Arm*, set in the Chicago underworld, was a critical success and won the National Book Award in 1950.

The first time "cold turkey" is mentioned in the story, the character known as Doc Dominowski lays down the law:

I'm talkin' cold turkey to you now.

Later in the story, more is made of the principal character, Frankie Machine, undergoing a gruelling cold-turkey withdrawal.

Five years later, the movie was a sensation. It took liberties with the story and softened the original book a good deal, but its focus on illegal drugs was sufficiently scandalous that a Production Code Seal of Approval was withheld.

Frankie Machine's drug-taking and spectacular withdrawal became the most talked-about feature of the movie. Screenwriters **Walter Newman** and **Lewis Meltzer** added an extra line to Frankie Machine's horrified reaction when he was confronted with the need to clear himself of his drug habit:

You mean just stop? Cold turkey? You don't understand!
The pain . . .

The movie's most harrowing scene showed the drug-addled man locked in a dark room for three days, tossing, turning, and sweating in the agonising procedure of self-exorcism. The searing cinematic images had more impact than the book.

The Motion Picture Association of America refused to certify *The Man with the Golden Arm* because it showed drug addiction. Nevertheless, the movie earned three Academy Award nominations, including one for Frank Sinatra (as Frankie Machine) for best actor in a leading role. Through Nelson Algren and the subsequent screenwriters, even the most conservative of the world's cinema-goers were introduced to the term "cold turkey."

Cold war

Now defined by *Collins English Dictionary* as "a state of political hostility and military tension between two countries or power blocs involving propaganda, subversion, threats, economic sanctions, and other measures short of open warfare."

The term "cold war" originated with **George Orwell** in a 1945 *Tribune* article, "You and the Atom Bomb." But its first publicly spoken airing as a description of post-World War II tensions between the United States and the USSR came in April 1947, when American politician Bernard Baruch used it in a speech to the South Carolina Legislature. Mr. Baruch acknowledged that the term had been provided by his speechwriter **Herbert Swope,** who had been editor of the *New York World* and had used the term in private beforehand.

Comes to the crunch

In 1939 **Sir Winston Churchill** introduced the idea of the crunch as a noun and a metaphor when he referred to political troubles in Spain depending "upon the general adjustment or outcome of the European crunch."

The image caught on and underwent a slight development with "comes to the crunch," and with alliterations like "credit crunch" and substitute synonyms such as "pinch," "clutch" and "squeeze."

Comparisons are odious

To be fair, John Lydgate in his *Debate between the Horse, the Sheep and the Goose* (c.1440) first brought the matter to attention in English, but in a structural style not perpetuated:

> *Odyous of olde been comparisonis . . .*

By 1583, the Elizabethan writer **Robert Greene** in *Mamillia* used the expression in a form closer to modern usage:

> *I will not make comparisons, because they be odious.*

Conventional wisdom

The phrase dates from 1838, introduced by prominent New York lawyer **Henry Whiting Warner** in his Inquiry into the *Moral and Religious Character of the American Government*:

> *. . . facts and principles universally known and acknowledged among us; and it will be seen that we appeal in such a case, neither to the records of legislation, nor yet to the conventional wisdom of our forefathers.*

The expression re-occurred at later intervals over more than one hundred years. Its widest international exposure came in 1958 when John Kenneth Galbraith used it in his book *The Affluent Society*.

Cooking the books

The *OED* has cooking as: "to prepare food for eating by the application of heat." In this conventional sense, cooking changes something from its original condition into a state normally considered more desirable. The metaphorical usage—that information could be cooked in order to make it seem more desirable—must have occurred to **Thomas, Viscount Wentworth** in 1636 when he wrote:

> *The proof was once clear, however they have cook'd it since.*

The use of cooked, referring to surreptitiously altered information, quickly became common parlance.

See also **Creative accounting**

(The) corridors of power

In 1956 British writer **C.P. Snow** created the term "corridors of power" in his book *Homecomings*. Sometime afterward a magazine article analyzing Snow's work plucked the term from the book and made it the article's headline.

When Snow's subsequent novel, actually called *Corridors of Power*, was about to be released, memories of the previous magazine headline somehow caused a feeling to arise that Snow had borrowed an existing term. But as Snow explained in the new book's preface:

> *The title of this novel seems to have passed into circulation during the time the book itself was being written. I have watched the phenomenon with mild consternation. The phrase (corridors of power) was first used, so far as I know, in* Homecomings.

In other words, he was being accused of borrowing a term he had himself invented.

Couch potato

When television began to be popular in America, journalists started to refer to it by the cute name "boob tube" (whereas in Britain a boob tube was a tight knitted top worn by young women), and eventually some smart alec called a person who watched a lot of TV, a "boob tuber." The Potato Museum in Albuquerque, New Mexico reports that Mr. Tom Iacino first made the connection between tuber and potato, and remarked that people watching too much TV were couch potatoes.

Illustrator **Robert Armstrong** introduced the term to a wider public when in 1976 he published an iconic cartoon that simply showed a large indolent potato lying on a couch watching a television set. Armstrong enlarged the term's exposure by registering the name Couch Potato as a trademark for his lounging potato to appear on T-shirts, etc.

Several couch potato books followed: *The Couch Potato Handbook; The Couch Potato Guide To Life* (by Dr. Spudd); and *The Couch Potato Cookbook*. The term rapidly became a standard description of anyone watching too much TV.

Countdown 5-4-3-2-1

A 1928 novel by Thea von Harbou, *Die Frau in Mond* (The Woman in the Moon), was one of many early manifestations of fascination with the notion of traveling to the moon (even Dr. Dolittle travelled to the moon). Von Harbou's novel entered another realm when it became the basis of an early German sci-fi movie. Variously known as *Woman in the Moon,* or *Girl in the Moon*, or *By Rocket to the Moon*, the 1929 German film classic had three screenwriters, headed by director **Fritz Lang**.

Created entirely from the imagination and using models, the rocket sequences were so convincing at the time that German authorities regarded the film as a possible leak of German rocket development and had the movie banned (one good copy survived). Another of its remarkable features was Lang's treatment of the rocket launch—he is credited with inventing the reverse countdown.

Instead of the previously universal "1-2-3-Go," his rocket was launched after "3-2-1-Go." Fritz Lang's idea was taken up in real life and has now become standard practice, not only for space mission launches but also for talent quests, raffle winners, or beauty contests—any situation where the tension of announcing a winner is enhanced by a reverse lead-up.

Count your blessings

The phrase has become familiar mainly because of Irving Berlin's song "Count Your Blessings" (instead of sheep) from the movie *White Christmas* (1954) and the recordings by Bing Crosby, Rosemary Clooney, and Eddie Fisher.

But the line had first been heard in the hymn originally called "When Upon Life's Billow" by **Johnson Oatman Jr.**, published in 1897, but later known as "Count Your Blessings"—for obvious reasons:

> *Count your blessings, name them one by one,*
> *Count your blessings, see what God hath done!*
> *Count your blessings, name them one by one,*
> *And it will surprise you what the Lord hath done.*

Creative accounting

A development arising from the original seventeenth-century reference to information being "cooked." Creative accounting refers to the presenting of financial information in such a way that it influences whoever peruses it toward a contrived conclusion and possibly hides some unwelcome facts. The term crept into being during the 1960s, but was given international prominence by **Mel Brooks** in his script for the movie *The Producers* (1968).

The accountant Leo Bloom (Gene Wilder) tells the Broadway producer:

> *Under the right circumstances a producer could make more money with a flop than he could with a hit . . . If he was certain that the show would fail, a man could make a fortune . . . It's simply a matter of creative accounting.*

See also **Cooking the books**

Credibility gap

The difference between a statement of claim, and the reality that is perceived to exist. During the presidency of Lyndon Johnson the American involvement in Vietnam was presented by officialdom as limited. But the American public formed a strong and growing impression that the American involvement, far from being limited, was actually escalating.

In May 1965 journalist **David Wise** wrote for the *New York Herald Tribune*, commenting on the government's "credibility" and the "gap" between its actions and its words. The headline to Wise's article put the two words together. Thereafter, credibility gap exemplified the difference between stated policy and a growing awareness that the stated policy simply wasn't true.

(In 2003, writer Chris Appy in *The President's Global Credibility Gap* described how the Vietnam-era "credibility gap" later became a Grand Canyon.)

Cried all the way to the bank

If a boxing match is "fixed," the loser may suffer apparent shame but still earn a substantial fee. Such was said to be the situation in September 1946 when a charismatic American boxer known as Belloise lost his match.

The *Wisconsin State Journal* reported that Belloise's manager **Eddie Walker** was miserable—he "cried all the way to the bank."

Eight years later, piano-playing entertainer Liberace, after being savaged by a music critic, picked up the expression and used it to great effect.

Crocodile tears

Crocodiles can't cry. Apparently there is some basis for the belief that sometimes small drops of fluid are exuded from crocodiles' eyes, possibly to aid their chewing as they trickle down, or possibly activated by the movement of their jaws, or triggered by the heat of the sun. But whatever the cause, it is a physical reaction not an emotional one.

These "tears" may have caused the belief that crocodiles weep as they demolish their victims. The thought was first seen in English when **Sir John Maundeville**'s book *Voyage and Travail* appeared in 1400. Sir John wrote:

> *There be great plenty of Cokadrilles—These serpents slay men, and then weeping, eat them.*

The image of emotion falsely displayed, based on Maundeville's crocodiles being sorrowful over lunch, has been with us ever since.

Curate's egg

The term arose from a cartoon in *Punch* in November 1895 by **George du Maurier**. A high-ranking member of the Church of

England clergy is lunching with a younger member and exclaims, "I'm afraid you've got a bad egg Mr. Jones."

The young curate replies: "Oh no my lord, I assure you! Parts of it are excellent!"

Over time, the words in the cartoon caption have become condensed into the notion of the curate's egg, indicating that something seemingly attractive may on closer examination have serious flaws.

(The) cure is worse than the complaint

The thought of seventeenth-century "cures"—like garlic, leek, and onion soup for a cold—may have been on **Francis Bacon**'s mind when he wrote, in *Of Seditions and Troubles* (1625), that:

> . . . *the remedy is worse than the disease.*

This gradually evolved, so that by the nineteenth century it was in the form we know it now: "The cure is worse than the complaint."

(The) customer is always right

The expression started out the other way around, and in French. In 1908 the Swiss hotel proprietor **César Ritz** coined the phrase, "Le client n'a jamais tort"—"The customer is never wrong."

The wording underwent a change in English, possibly with the help of H. Gordon Selfridge, whose London store opened in 1909 and used the Ritz slogan in English—and back to front.

Cut off your nose to spite your face

Paparazzi and gossip columnists aren't new. News sheets, pamphlets, and satiric poems have been handed around populations for centuries, often stridently attacking the establishment.

In late seventeenth-century France, no high-profile figure was safe from the chatty but vicious observations of French gossip **Gédéon Tallemant des Réaux.** His targets included the King, the Cardinals, the aristocrats, and the military brass. His acerbic *Historiettes* were completed around 1659 but not published until well after his death. They contained references to a policy which King Henry IV was contemplating, but of which Tallemant disapproved. He commented that if the King followed his plan:

Se couper le nez pour faire dépit a son visage.

He would be "cutting off his nose to spite his face."

Cut to the chase

In early cowboy movies there were frequent scenes of frantic travel on horseback—often good guys chasing bad guys. Within the rhythm of movie-making, such scenes usually alternated with more static dialogue-based scenes that served to advance the plot and explain why the goodies were chasing the baddies. So among the scriptwriters and directors the instruction "cut to the chase" indicated to the film editor it was time to cut into the film and add some more footage of the galloping horses.

The term went public in 1929 when journalist, screenwriter, novelist, and comicstrip writer **Joseph P. McEvoy**'s novel *Hollywood Girl* was published. As part of the novel, a short section of a (fictional) screenplay was shown:

Jannings escapes . . . Cut to the chase.

Gradually, the term shifted from its original absolutely literal meaning and became a metaphor instead, referring to ditching the preamble and getting straight to the point of any discussion.

Cyberspace

Although fans of technology speak of cyberspace, it of course doesn't actually exist as distinct from "space." Strictly, the word cyberspace refers to a system rather than a place. A great number of signals pass through space (radio and television signals, for instance), but so do rain, wind, sound, and light. To this still uncrowded highway, add satellite signals, cell-phone messages, and wireless Internet communications.

The first of the cyber words was cybernetics, derived from the Greek word kubernetes, meaning "a steersman," which crept into French in the 1800s as "cybernétique."

In 1948, American mathematician Norbet Wiener, wanting to describe the control of automated decision-making in machines, announced, "We have decided to call the entire field of control and communication theory, whether in the machine or in the animal, by the name cyber-netics."

Over thirty years later, in 1982, the word cyberspace was invented by science fiction writer **William Gibson** in a story called "Burning Chrome." Its use expanded in his 1984 novel *Necromancer* and gradually went into universal vernacular, spawning derivatives: cyberpunk, cyberhippy, cyberjunky, and cybercafé.

See also **Virtual reality**.

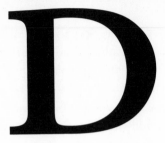

Damned if you do, damned if you don't

Starting around 1800, an enthusiastic and very eccentric preacher began touring the United States, often on horseback, attracting large crowds with his declamatory style and bizarre appearance. Unkempt, far from clean, he yelled and postured, flattered, fascinated, and challenged.

Lorenzo Dow died in 1834, and in 1836 his writings were published as *Reflections on the Love of God*. During his many speeches he had made a point of attacking clergymen who drew attention to the inconsistencies and contradictions within the Bible. This argument appeared in his writings as:

> . . . those who preached it up to make the Bible clash and contradict itself, by preaching something like this: "You can and you can't—You shall and you shan't—You will and you won't—And you'll be damned if you do—And you'll be damned if you don't —"

It is possible that Lorenzo Dow may have influenced the usage of other similar expressions like "Between a rock and a hard place," "Between the devil and the deep blue sea" and "A no-win situation."

Darby and Joan

Envisaged universally as the quintessential devoted old couple, Darby and his wife Joan were real people who died sometime around 1730. John Darby was a printer who lived at Bartholomew Close in London. Mr. Darby had an apprentice whose poetic talent had been encouraged by Alexander Pope.

In 1735, shortly after John Darby is believed to have died, a ballad appeared in *The Gentleman's Magazine*. There is no solid evidence as to who wrote the poem, but the UK National Dictionary of Biography names the author as that apprentice printer of John Darby's, one **Henry Woodfall**. Entitled "The Joys of Love Never Forgot," the poem told of a loving married couple in their late years. They were depicted as old-fashioned and not welcoming change; no attempt was made to glamorize them:

> *Old Darby, with Joan by his side,*
> *You've often regarded with wonder:*
> *He's dropsical, she is sore-eyed,*
> *Yet they're never happy asunder.*

The poem was an immediate success and its title has been quoted ever since, evoking an image of a married couple whose family have flown the nest, leaving the old people comfortably alone.

Besides figuring in the vernacular, the old couple's names are commemorated in dozens of Darby and Joan Clubs.

Dark side of the moon

There is no actual dark side to the moon. It revolves around the earth and, while doing so, is also revolving on its own axis. So one half of it appears to be dark—just as half of the Earth is always dark.

We only ever see one side of the moon. Astronauts who photographed the far side of the moon proved that it isn't dark. But a vague impression of mystery and possible danger clings to the term.

The concept of the moon having a dark side dates back to 1928 when **Hugh Lofting**'s *Dr. Dolittle in the Moon* was published. The good doctor, wearing dinner jacket and top hat, climbs on the back of a giant moth and flies to the moon. There he becomes very bouncy because of the lack of gravity, learns to talk to the insects and plants, and explores "the dark side of the moon."

Davy Jones' locker

There is no clear explanation as to why the deepwater monster whose locker is at the bottom of the sea is named Davy Jones. But he first reached the attention of the general English-speaking public in **Tobias Smollett**'s novel *The Adventures of Peregrine Pickle* (1751), in which the fiend that presides over all the evil spirits of the deep is described as follows:

> I'll be damned if it was not Davy Jones himself. I know him
> by his saucer eyes, his three rows of teeth, his horns and tail,
> and the blue smoke that came out of his nostrils . . .

Dead as a dodo

The dodo is definitely dead. Nobody has seen one since 1662 and we only have a vague idea of what they might have looked like based on skeletal reconstruction and paintings done long after they were gone. Lewis Carroll brought the dodo fancifully back to life on the pages of *Alice's Adventures in Wonderland* (1865) and this reminded people that the bird was extinct.

But its first use as a metaphor for something lifeless had to wait a few more years. **Michael Davitt** was a prominent Irish labour leader, journalist, social activist, and member of the Irish Republican Brotherhood (which was active in ostracizing land agent Charles Boycott). The Brotherhood's leader was British MP Charles Parnell, from whom Davitt eventually became alienated.

In July 1891, the *New Zealand Tablet* newspaper reprinted a report that Michael Davitt and his wife had sailed for San Francisco on board the *Polynesian*. When interviewed, Mr. Davitt had said:

> *After the next election Mr. Parnell will have only four*
> *followers. Except as a private Member of Parliament,*
> *Mr. Parnell is as dead as the dodo.*

Dead as a doornail

Although the theory is not entirely proven, it is believed that the nail referred to was the kind hammered through a thick door then "clenched" on the other side, thus rendering it useless if salvaged. To be dead as a doornail was certainly an expression known in France around 1200, when it appeared in a French poem "William of Palerne." The authorship is unknown, and neither do we know who translated the work into English around 1350.

But we can thank **Humphrey de Bohun**, Earl of Hereford and Lord High Constable of England, who commissioned the translation telling of William's battle with the Steward of Spain at the fatal end of which:

> *He bar him down to the earth, as ded as dornayl.*

(The) dead parrot

Originally entitled "The Pet Shop," this sketch was first broadcast in December 1969 and became one the most famous comedy items in British television history. Scripted and performed by Monty Python's **Michael Palin** and **John Cleese**, it presented theater of the absurd in an irresistibly accessible way, with a script that seemed to use every known adjective, euphemism, idiom, metaphor, symbol, and synonym for death.

It became universally known as the dead parrot sketch, and that name gradually moved into general usage to refer to anything utterly beyond resuscitation.

In full confidence that the public would understand, a failed political movement, struggling business, or unpopular theory could be dismissed as a dead parrot. In the vernacular, the parrot that had reached such a profound end could be compared with a politician's popularity that had "joined the choir invisible," or with an unsuccessful parliamentary proposal that was "bereft of life," or had "expired and gone to meet its maker."

Deep Throat

The term was coined by an experienced writer/director of pornographic movies, **Gerard Damiano**. His 1972 movie *Deep Throat* about a young woman with an unusual appetite was an underground sensation as well as an above-ground headline story when twenty-two U.S. States banned showings within their jurisdictions.

Two years later the phrase moved into an entirely different area of publicity with the release of the book *All the President's Men* by Bob Woodward and Carl Bernstein. This backgrounder to the Watergate scandal was a major sensation. It told of the informant within official circles who gave secret information about the level of involvement of the President. This person was identified only by a code name borrowed from the blue movie—"Deep Throat."

(In 2005, the former Associate Director of the FBI, W. Mark Felt, revealed that he had been the Deep Throat who gave information to Woodward and Bernstein.)

The 1972 movie had certainly given the expression a certain (somewhat clandestine) public awareness. Their use of the term implies that Woodward and Bernstein recognized this. But the ructions about Watergate propelled the term deep throat into wide—even international—usage. Boosted by its intriguing connection with a secret whistle-blower inside U.S. government circles, the term came to be used to describe any anonymous informant.

But none of this would have happened without Gerard Damiano.

Desperate times call for desperate measures

The expression originated with woodcutting. In 1500, the Dutch scholar Desiderius Erasmus published the woodsmen's saying about protecting tools used on an obdurate part of the tree:

> *Malo nodo malus quaerendus cuneus*
> *(A hard wedge must be sought for a hard knot).*

In 1539, British scholar **Richard Taverner** published a version he described as "Englished," meaning that he had replaced the forestry imagery with a medical one:

> *Stronge disease requryeth a strong medicine.*

Legend has it that in 1605, when Guy Fawkes failed in his attempt to blow up King James I and his Protestant lords, he offered his version of the 1539 expression to his captors: "A desperate disease requires a desperate remedy."

Over time the expression moved beyond wood-cutting and illness into a wider field. Crime novelist Lucy Malleson (under her nom-de-plume **Anthony Gilbert**) in *She Shall Die* (1961) came closest to the now-common contemporary version:

> *She'd have sold the roof over her head sooner than have you know. Desperate situations require desperate remedies.*

Diamonds are forever

The original line was "A diamond is forever." This simple statement was dreamed up in 1947 by New York copywriter **Frances Gerety** on behalf of De Beers Consolidated Mines. It became part of a brilliant advertising campaign, and in 1999 won an award as "advertising slogan of the century." One aspect of the slogan's success was its not-so-subtle implication that diamonds never deteriorate, matching their appeal to the desire for a permanent symbol of love and marriage.

Ian Fleming moved the slogan into another sphere in 1956 when he used the phrase, with a subtle change into the plural, as the title of a James Bond novel.

Did you feel the earth move?

In *For Whom the Bell Tolls* (1940) by **Ernest Hemingway**, the character of Robert Jordan makes love to Maria and feels

> . . . *the earth move out and away from under them.*

He asked Maria, "Did thee feel the earth move?"

The title *For Whom the Bell Tolls* comes from John Donne's Meditation XVII, and literary scholarship has found further traces of Donne's influence. The same text (Meditation XVII) presents an image of the earth as being driven by erotic tension.

Die Hard

The expression became famous as the title of a 1988 movie starring Bruce Willis, followed by two sequels.

But it had been in use over a century and a half earlier. Britain's National Army Museum in Chelsea, London, reports on the gallantry of the 57th Foot (West Middlesex) Regiment and their formidable commander Lieutenant-Colonel **Sir William Inglis** during the Peninsular War in 1811.

A battle at Albuera in Spain found the British troops under determined attack by French troops. Inglis was shot and badly wounded, but remained in command, encouraging his soldiers to:

> *Die hard—my men, die hard!*

Only one of the 24 officers survived, and 168 of the 584 troops. Subsequently, the 57th Regiment and the various military groupings descended from it became widely known as the Die Hards, a designation that has persisted for 200 years.

Different strokes for different folks

The genesis of the expression is unknown, though accredited to the southern states of the U.S. Strokes may refer either to the sport of rowing, or to a recreation of a more intimate kind. The term was brought into the open in 1966 when boxing star Muhammad Ali was reported in the Kansas newspaper the *Great Bend Daily Tribune* to have used it. But a greater impact came two years later with the release of the number-one hit single *Everyday People* by **Sly and the Family Stone** with its catch line: "Different strokes for different folks."

Distance lends enchantment

From Scottish poet **Thomas Campbell**'s *Pleasures of Hope* (1799):

> *'Tis distance lends enchantment to the view,*
> *And robes the mountain in its azure hue.*

Doc Martens

In 1945 in the German town of Seeshaupt, **Doktor Klaus Maertens** damaged a foot in a skiing mishap. To facilitate the healing, he made a pair of shoes with trapped air built into the soles, which assisted walking.

Maertens was persuaded to produce more of them, and they found a ready market with elderly women having foot troubles. The designs were patented and the shoes sold throughout Germany, until 1960 when a British firm was contracted.

Doktor Klaus Maertens' name was anglicized to Doc Marten and the shoes became one of the most recognized brands in the world (also sometimes known as Doc Martins).

(The) domino effect

During the 1950s, American journalist Joseph Alsop wrote a column entitled "Matter of Fact," which often referred to the dangers of Communism and the dangers of it spreading from one country to another by the "falling domino" effect: if one country embraced Communism, others in the same region would follow.

At a presidential press conference in 1954 the relevance of Communism in South East Asia was a topic. **President Dwight Eisenhower** drew on Alsop's domino image and said:

> . . . *you have broader considerations that might follow what you would call the falling domino principle. You have a row of dominoes set up, you knock over the first one, and what will happen to the last one is the certainty that it will go over very quickly. So you could have a beginning of a disintegration.*

Eisenhower's statement received wide publicity and Alsop was rapidly sidelined. The abbreviated form became known as Eisenhower's "domino theory," or the "domino effect." Soon it was applied to any situation, political or not, where a single action could instigate a succession of related, and usually unfavorable, events.

Don't call us—we'll call you

Believed to have originated in show business (where it remains a dreaded alternative to "You've got the part . . . ") the expression was exposed to a wider audience by American journalist **Dorothy Killgallen**, whose column in the Massachusetts paper the *Lowell Sun* (March 1944) featured a "Fable from the Forties," telling of a (fictional) heroine for whom:

> *Audition after audition left her with nothing but "Sorry" and "Not the type" and "Don't call us we'll call you" and a heart that was close to breaking.*

The expression remained part of show business but in time also came into use in almost any sphere where someone is being euphemistically dismissed.

Don't panic

The BBC television series *Dad's Army* began broadcasting in 1968 and ran for a decade. From it arose a parallel radio version, a feature movie, and a theater show. Throughout the series—written by **Jimmy Perry** and **David Croft**—the character of Lance-Corporal Jack Jones (actor Clive Dunn) used the catchphrase "don't panic."

The same catchphrase showed up when *The Hitch-Hiker's Guide to the Galaxy* began as a radio serial in 1968, later growing into a cult classic spawning five published books, a television series, a full-length movie, comic books, a computer game, and stage shows.

Down memory lane

Like some other expressions in vernacular use, down memory lane seems to have arisen from a song.

In 1924, songwriters **Buddy De Sylva**, **Con Conrad**, and **Larry Spier** provided the song "Memory Lane" for the Broadway show *Betty Lee* starring comedian Joe E. Brown. The song was popular and surfaced again in high-profile company as a sometime theme for the *Voice of Firestone* radio show, which ran from 1938 to 1956. It was also a featured song in the Abbott and Costello movie *In Society* (1944).

Gradually, the song title seemed to morph quite naturally into "*Down* Memory Lane," and appeared thus as the title of a collection of Mack Sennett comedy movies in 1949.

Down the tubes

A variation on "down the pan," "down the drain," or "down the gurgler." The first known public use of the tubes version came from **William "Parry" O'Brien**, an American who twice won gold as an Olympic shot-put champion. He broke the world record seventeen times. Besides his eminence in sporting achievements, O'Brien left a lasting memento in the language.

After his gold medal-winning feat in the 1952 Olympics, he was told that an earlier record from his university days had been broken by a younger athlete. O'Brien told the *Charleston Daily Mail* that because of this he had visions of all his records "going down the tubes."

He needn't have worried. He was flag-bearer for the U.S. Olympic team in 1964 and inducted into the American Track and Field Hall of Fame, the American Olympians Hall of Fame, and University of South Carolina's Athletic Hall of Fame.

Do your own thing

Not as 1960s as it seems, the line originated over a century earlier with **Ralph Waldo Emerson** in his *Essay on Self Reliance* (1841):

> *If you maintain a dead church, contribute to a dead Bible Society, vote with a great party either for the Government or against it . . . Under all these screens I have difficulty to detect the precise man you are . . . But do your own thing, and I shall know you.*

In later printings of Emerson's line, busybody do-gooders changed the word "thing" to "work," but the original still stands.

(The) dreaded lurgy

A lurgy is an unspecified illness or infection, at its worst referred to as "the dreaded lurgy."

A German firm specializing in metal and chemical processing, named Metallurgische Gesellschaft, was founded in 1897. The firm used five letters of its name—lurgi—as its cable address, and it was split into various companies in 1919, one of which concentrated on gaseous products and was actually named Lurgi.

The name Lurgi was well known to industrial chemists and because the company was involved in metal manufacture, the word was printed on containers, including the containers which held poisonous gases. So, among the Allied military in both wars, there was an association made between the word lurgi and poisonous gas.

In 1951, Britain and the Commonwealth were somewhat startled to hear a new radio program called "The Goon Show." The Goons specialized in creative lateral thinking and wrote and broadcast such icons of appealing nonsense as "The Legend of the Phantom Head Shaver," "The Affair of the Lone Banana," and "The Dreaded Batter Pudding Hurler of Bexhill-on-Sea."

In November 1954 they broadcast a story called "Lurgi Strikes Britain," which was about a mysterious and somewhat ridiculous disease. The word lurgy entered the language almost immediately (because it was initially only heard spoken on radio, it emerged in print with various spellings). It has been used ever since to mean any unidentified illness.

Several of the Goons had strong military associations, so it is likely they knew of the German metallurgische, or there is a faint possibility they made a deliberate corruption of allergy. Either way, the lurgy went into wide English usage because of the Goons.

(The) Eagle has landed

In July 1969, as the Apollo 11 space mission craft touched down on the moon, **Neil Armstrong** announced: "The Eagle has landed." Apparently, no official announcement had been prepared, and the way Armstrong phrased the remark was a surprise to everyone concerned.

The eagle is a national symbol in America and the spacecraft was named *Eagle*, so the announcement was completely logical. The rhythmic neatness of the remark caught the public's imagination as well, and the line reappeared for decades afterwards in various guises.

Jack Higgins' novel *The Eagle Has Landed* (1975) used the expression but shifted the action to World War II, as did the movie of the same name the following year. Heavy metal musicians Saxon released their *Eagle Has Landed* album in 1982. A punning version also appeared—the ego has landed—referring pejoratively to a person's over-confidence. In 1999, British pop star Robbie Williams used the term, in deliberate self-deprecation, as the title of his *Ego Has Landed* album.

Ear candy

Australian singing star **Helen Reddy** had spectacular successes during the 1970s, selling 15 million albums, appearing in movies and on the Broadway stage, and starring in her own television series. Her 1972 recording "I Am Woman" was greeted with enthusiasm among feminists and won that year's Grammy Award for Female Pop Vocal Performance. At the televised ceremony, after accepting her award, Helen Reddy gained worldwide attention by thanking God "because She makes everything possible."

While Reddy's rich singing voice and charismatic presence continued to drive her career, there was occasional comment about her choice of easy-listening repertoire. Recording company **Capitol** guessed ahead when settling on a title for Reddy's 1977 album, and with just two words captured an ironic reference to any comment which might arise about its pleasant and elegantly sung list of items. The album was called *Ear Candy*.

If the term had been used prior to 1977, few people noticed. But the Reddy album's name soon went into the vernacular referring to music perceived as having an attractive sound and pleasing appeal, but little lasting quality.

See also **Arm candy**

Eat my hat

This declaration of certainty (or failure—it depends on the circumstances) may or may not have appeared in Homer's works, but it came into English as a deliberate parody of his style as part of Thomas Brydges' *Homer Travestie: Being a New Burlesque Translation* (1747), a work which is justifiably obscure:

> For though we tumble down the wall
> And fire upon their rotten boats and all
> I'll eat my hat if Jove don't drop us
> Or play some queer rogue's trick to stop us.

Eating one's hat was given far more prominence in 1837 when **Charles Dickens'** creation Mr. Pickwick was depicted seeking new accommodation. He was visiting a very unpromising room which had the added disadvantage of "chummage" (in modern terms, roommates). Dismayed by the lack of comfort and unwilling to accede to the eccentric requirements of the others, Mr. Pickwick wondered aloud if he could break the agreement and go to live elsewhere. At that, one of the "chummers" (a rather dodgy cleric) announced:

> *If I knew as little of life as that I'd eat my hat and swallow the buckle.*

Economical with the truth

A way of referring to a delicate conveying of information that may possibly skip over some salient points—in other words, a softened description of lying. The expression has been employed for several centuries: Edmund Burke wrote "in the exercise of all virtues, there is economy of the truth," (1769) and Rudyard Kipling in 1904 described a character being "by temperament, economical of the truth."

But its leap into common usage came in 1986 when the expression surfaced during a colorful court case. The British government attempted to prevent publication of the book *Spycatcher* by former spy Peter Wright. At one widely publicized point, the British Cabinet Secretary **Sir Robert Armstrong** attempted to differentiate between a lie, a misleading impression, and "being economical with the truth." The television program *Four Corners* reported that journalists covering the case "all but ran out of the court with their notes burning in their hands." And the expression became common parlance.

Egg on your face

The origin of the expression has never been satisfactorily pinned down. It could be a simple description of remnants of yolk left around the mouth after eating a soft-boiled egg, or possibly the result of a very real protest aimed at old-time actors (or politicians) in the form of a thrown egg. Rural America believes the blame lies with farm dogs who, after a tasty snack in the hen-house, carry the evidence plain to see around a furry snout.

Whichever of these versions is true, the meaning is always clear: you've done something foolish, maybe said something you regret, and the consequences of your action have rebounded on you in an unwelcome form.

While not unfamiliar in America, where it was heard on a 1950s television series (*Front Page Detective*), the term came to prominence in Britain in 1972 when former Labour minister **Lord Chalfont** wrote somewhat scathingly in *The Times*:

> *There is something reassuringly changeless about the capacity of the highest military authorities for getting egg on their face.*

Eight days a week

Drummer **Ringo Starr** was fond of using this colorful Liverpudlian term meaning "hard work." Lennon and McCartney decided it would be a good title for a song (1964), and it was, although the eight-day week of the song referred to loving rather than manual labor.

The French sometimes refer to a week as huitaine—eight days; whether or not Liverpudlians picked up the eight-day concept from France isn't clear.

Elementary, my dear Watson

Sherlock Holmes never said it in any of Sir Arthur Conan Doyle's books. Doyle died in 1930, and nine years later a movie was released called *The Return of Sherlock Holmes*, which contained the line, "Elementary, my dear Watson."

The scriptwriters were **Garrett Fort** and **Basil Dean.**

Elephants never forget

It is acknowledged that elephants are highly intelligent and do remember certain things such as traditional jungle pathways, burial locales, other related elephants, and certain taught behaviors.

British writer **H.H. Munro** (aka Saki), was born in Burma (Myanmar) where his father was an inspector-general of police, and young Munro later spent two years in the Burmese police himself. He was very familiar with elephants.

In 1904, Saki's fictional character Reginald first introduced English readers to the concept of elephants having good memories. His story "Reginald on Besetting Sins" told of an unnamed woman who had an unwelcome habit of always telling the exact truth, and once told Miriam Klopstock what she thought of her dress. Then she went to the kitchen and reprimanded the cook for drinking too much. The result:

> *The cook was a good cook, as cooks go; and as cooks go she went. Miriam Klopstock came to lunch the next day. Women and elephants never forget an injury.*

Elvis has left the building

In 1954, when Elvis Presley was just starting out, he sang on the *Louisiana Hayride* radio program. He came across as an appealing singer, minus the wriggling and sneering that had yet to develop.

Teenage girls began to take notice, and Presley's continuing performances on the show rapidly acquired an audience.

Over the next couple of years, the Presley phenomenon far outgrew the twenty-eight states to which *Louisiana Hayride* program was broadcast. Aiming to conquer audiences nationwide, Elvis gave his last performance for the show on December 15, 1956. His broadcast had a fairground audience of 10,000 excited teenagers, who screamed all the way through, and continued screaming for more when he left the stage.

Attempting to dampen the hysteria and get on with the rest of the show, announcer **Horace Logan** said: "Elvis has left the building," little knowing his spontaneous remark would go into show-business history.

The term was subsequently widely used to signal that Elvis had left a concert venue when he'd finished performing, but, curiously, its meaning reversed. That first time in Louisiana, Horace Logan wanted the audience to stay so the show could go on. But over the years, when Elvis had finished performing solo concerts, it was said to encourage audiences to *leave* . . . Elvis would not be returning to the stage.

In time, the term became a catchphrase which no longer referred to Elvis personally. It came to mean that the excitement is over; the proceedings (of whatever kind) have come to an end.

Eskimo pie

In 1919, a Danish immigrant to the U.S. came up with the idea of coating an ice cream bar with melted chocolate, then refreezing it. In 1920, Christian Nelson sold the first "I-Scream-Bar."

Russell Stover, a chocolate manufacturer, went into business with Christian Nelson to manufacture and patent the confection, but he didn't like the name. Russell's wife **Mrs. Stover** came up with the name Eskimo Pie, which was patented and franchised. The first advertisement carrying the name Mrs. Stover had invented appeared in 1921, and within two years there were more than 1,000 franchises offering the chocolate ice cream bar.

(In 2009, an Inuit tourist in New Zealand bitterly criticized the continuing use of the name Eskimo Pie, which she said was offensive to her people.)

(The) Establishment

As a verb, "establish" has been around since the fourteenth century, referring to the action of making something permanent or stable—a group, a business, a skill, an organization, etc. Gradually, a noun developed that had a special aura when referring to an upper echelon with power over nominated groups, e.g., a literary establishment or art establishment, meaning the eminent literary and artistic figures whose opinions made or broke the reputations of those less well placed.

In 1935, when Ford Madox Ford wrote of "the establishment," he was referring to the literary elite. The term had moved closer to meaning the governing classes when historian A.J.P. Taylor reviewed William Corbett's biography in the *New Statesman* in 1953 and used the term (with an uppercase E), but without actually defining it.

But in 1955, the British government was in some confusion about the high-profile spies who had defected from Britain to Russia. In September of that year, journalist **Henry Fairlie** in the *Spectator* retained the uppercase initial, and redefined the term in a sense that rapidly became commonplace. Fairlie wrote:

> By the "Establishment," I do not mean only the centers of official power—though they are certainly part of it—but rather the whole matrix of official and social relations within which power is exercised.

This was perceived to mean those individuals and organizations with a strong interest in maintaining the status quo, and the clout to do so—the ruling elites, generally perceived to be a combination of the financial sector, the Church, the civil service, the Crown, and the military.

The term also came to be used in a narrower context, for instance when a person seeking advancement within a political party could be said to require the approval of the Establishment within just that group.

Eureka!

In essence, "heureka" is the first person singular of the Greek word heuriskein—to find—and thus means "I have found." Its most famous utterance is attributed to the Sicilian mathematician **Archimedes**, who invented various military devices, and also the water screw.

Legend tells that around 270 BC King Hieron of Syracuse delivered some pure gold to a goldsmith in order to have a new crown made. When it was finished, the king suspected the gold in his new crown had been corrupted with other metal, the craftsman having kept the leftover gold for himself. The king asked Archimedes to test it. This posed a problem—Archimedes didn't know how to do that.

Both the crown and the original supply of gold were the same weight. But one day, stepping into his (full) bath, Archimedes noted that a quantity of water spilled over the edge. It dawned on him that the volume of water that overflowed would be equal to the volume of his body; therefore, the *bulk* of an object could be measured by the amount of fluid it displaced. Shrieking "Eureka" and jumping from the bath, Archimedes supposedly ran naked through the streets, hastening to test how much water would be displaced by the king's crown.

Archimedes knew that a portion of gold weighed more than

portions of other metals of the same size. So, all he had to do was place the crown in water, measure how much water it displaced, and then find a piece of gold which displaced exactly the same amount of water. When he compared the weights, if both were pure gold they should both weigh the same.

But they didn't. The crown turned out to be lighter in gold than it should have been. History does not relate what happened to the goldsmith, but Archimedes and his cry of Eureka! have been part of folklore for more than 2,000 years.

With its connotation of discovering gold, the word Eureka was incorporated into the Great Seal of the State of California in 1849 and became the State's official motto in 1963.

Everybody's doing it

The genesis can be traced to a Mozart opera of 1790, commissioned by Emperor Joseph II of the Holy Roman Empire and said to be based on a much gossiped about real-life incident in Vienna.

Mozart's librettist **Lorenzo da Ponte** entitled the story *Cosi Fan Tutte*—which translates as "Everybody's doing it" (though purists will point out that "tutte" can be seen as the feminine of "tutti," and thus only *women* are "doing it").

In 1912, **Irving Berlin** brought the term into everyday English (with any doubt about gender removed). *Everybody's Doing It*, published in 1912, meant that everybody was doing the dance called the Turkey Trot.

Everybody talks about the weather but nobody does anything about it

An abbreviated form of the original statement in the *Hartford Courant* newspaper in 1897: "A well-known American writer said once that while everybody talked about the weather nobody seemed to do anything about it."

It has been assumed that the American writer referred to was Mark Twain, but there is no evidence that Twain ever said it or wrote it. The favored candidate is **Charles Dudley Warner**, the then editor of the *Hartford Courant* and a friend of Mark Twain's, who *may* have been reporting something Twain said.

Whatever its ancestry, a version of the expression emerged as the name of a song ("Everyone Complains about the Weather") in the 1953 movie (and 1961 theater musical) *Calamity Jane*.

Every man has his price

Recording the *History and Proceedings of the House of Commons* (1734), Sir William Wyndham wrote that, "It is an old maxim that every man has his price—if you can but come up to it."

But alas, it was when the term was used by the more famous **Sir Robert Walpole**, Earl of Orford (whom Wyndham disliked) that it went into the vernacular. Walpole had been Prime Minister of England, Chancellor of the Exchequer and First Lord of the Treasury. In 1798, historian William Coxe published *Memoirs of the Life and Administration of Sir Robert Walpole, Earl of Orford*, in which he quoted a statement of Walpole's that, although it was a repeated version of Wyndham's, became the basis for common usage in English.

Regarding the declarations of men whose patriotism he questioned, Walpole said:

All those men have their price.

Walpole had been referring to a specific group, rather than mankind in general. But when the remark went into general usage, its meaning was distorted by the word "those" customarily being left out.

The abbreviated version became even more firmly entrenched with the publication of a play in 1869 written by Sir Edward Bulwer-Lytton, a three act comedy in rhyme called *Walpole—or Every Man Has His Price*. By that time (and thereafter), Walpole was credited with the remark, despite it having been "an old maxim" he had employed in reference to a particular group of people.

Extraterrestrial

In its meaning of something from outside or beyond the earth, the word extraterrestrial was first used by **H. G. Wells** in his 1898 novel *War of the Worlds*. The narrator tells of arriving at a pit where a mysterious cylinder has fallen to earth and a small crowd has gathered. The narrator is convinced that " . . . the Thing had come from the planet Mars," and reports:

> . . . *the yellowish-white metal that gleamed in the crack between the lid and the cylinder had an unfamiliar hue. "Extra-terrestrial" had no meaning for most of the onlookers.*

(The later abbreviation of extraterrestrial to E.T. is credited to L. Sprague de Camp in 1939.)

Fall on your feet

The first known use of the expression comes from **Anthony Trollope** in *Barchester Towers* (1857):

> *It is well known that the family of the Slopes never starve: they always fall on their feet, like cats.*

(The) family that prays together stays together

Irish-born Patrick Peyton was ordained a Roman Catholic priest in the United States in 1941. At that time of trouble, Father Peyton developed a strong belief in the power of rosary prayers. In 1942, he initiated a Family Rosary Crusade to promote the praying of the rosary by families as a move towards encouraging stronger faith. The crusade became widespread, aided by modern technology—Father Peyton was one of the earliest evangelists to make use of the mass media.

In 1947, **Al Scalpone**, a young advertising executive, came forward and offered to help. An experienced writer of advertising copy, his initial contribution to the crusade was the slogan:

> *The family that prays together, stays together.*

This added greatly to the success of Peyton's crusade, which gathered wide support throughout Catholic America and then internationally.

Scalpone eventually became Vice-President of CBS-TV, and his slogan went into common usage (although sometimes with variations its author may not have expected).

Famous for being famous

While fame is sometimes a tribute to the worthy and the honorable, sometimes it is not. "Famous for being famous" has become a pejorative expression describing someone with no discernible talent or quality, but who becomes the focus of consistent publicity.

The term originated from an assessment written by eminent American sociologist, historian, and Pulitzer Prize winner **Daniel Boorstin**, whose 1961 book *The Image—a Guide to Pseudo Events* contained the lines:

> *A celebrity is a person known for his well-knownness.*
> *Celebrities intensify their celebrity images simply by*
> *being well-known for relations among themselves.*
> *By a kind of symbiosis, celebrities live off each other.*

Over time, popular usage condensed the concept into "famous for being famous."

Boorstin had little sympathy for those celebrities he saw as "counterfeit people" who had little connection with reality. And with impressive foresight he scorned events that would be staged and scripted as a "counterfeit version of actual happenings," although by 1961 the entertainment industry had yet to invent "reality" television shows.

(Another epigram attributed to Boorstin: "Some are born great, some achieve greatness, and some hire public relations officers.")

Famous for fifteen minutes

In 1968, **Andy Warhol** wrote a catalogue for an exhibition of his work in Stockholm, and included the sentence:

In the future, everyone will be world-famous for fifteen minutes.

Various paraphrases developed by media have been at variance with the original, e.g., "In the future fifteen people will be famous" and "In fifteen minutes everybody will be famous." Sometimes the variations came from Warhol himself, apparently tired of being queried about the 1968 original (in 1979 he said that his 1968 prediction had come true—everyone *was* famous for fifteen minutes).

In usage, Warhol's original sentence has been shortened to "Famous for fifteen minutes." The term is customarily used, rather scathingly, in the sense that Warhol intended—that the attention some personalities or incidents attract is fleeting.

Condensed to "They've had their fifteen minutes," the expression is immediately understood as a put-down—someone's time in the sun has now become time in the shade.

(In recent times the original Warhol statement has started to show signs of moving with the times, becoming "Fifteen megabytes of fame.")

Far from the madding crowd

This started life in William Drummond's sonnet "Dear Wood" (1614):

Far from the madding worldling's hoarse discords.

Perhaps the word worldling seemed a little clumsy to **Thomas Gray**, whose "Elegy in a Country Churchyard" (1751) produced an echo of William Drummond's line with:

Far from the madding crowd's ignoble strife . . .

The term was later taken up by Thomas Hardy as the title of a novel (often misquoted as " . . . the *maddening* crowd"). The archaiac word "madding" means "frenzied."

Fast and loose

Old-time fairs featured a test of skill called "Fast and Loose," in which a displayed rope appeared to be tied up in a complex series of knots and loops. A punter would attempt to thread a stick through a group of loops in such a way that the stick would remain in place.

But cunning knotting by the proprietor often ensured that wherever the stick was placed it could not remain firm. Hence the name of the game became a synonym for something being treated with rather too broad a view of what is honest and reliable.

In 1557, **Richard Tottel** put the term into print in his *Songs and Sonnets*, telling of:

> *. . . a new maried studient that plaied fast or loose.*

Fasten your seat-belts—it's going to be a bumpy night

A memorable and oft-repeated line written by **Joseph L. Mankiewicz** and spoken by Bette Davis playing the fading star, actress Margot Channing, in the 1950 movie *All About Eve*.

The line is often misquoted as "bumpy ride," but Margot Channing said it at an evening occasion when she knew there were going to be ructions later that night.

Fate worse than death

Referring to the rape of both married and unmarried women in ancient Rome during the sackings of Rome by Goths and Huns, **Edward Gibbon**'s *Decline and Fall of the Roman Empire* (1781) declared that:

> *The matrons and virgins of Rome were exposed to injuries more dreadful, in the apprehension of chastity, than death itself.*

This could be seen as the precursor to various other versions of the expression that surfaced several times over the following century, albeit with minor variations in the wording. But by the time Edgar Rice Burroughs wrote *Tarzan of the Apes* (1914) it had settled into its current form. A disgruntled ape at odds with his tribe captures Jane Porter, throws her across his shoulders and carries her back into the jungle to "a fate a thousand times worse than death."

She is of course rescued by Tarzan.

Fellow traveler

Literally, it just means a companion on your travels. But in 1924, **Leon Trotsky**'s book *Literature and Revolution* picked up a Russian word that had been in informal use since 1917—popútchik.

Its meaning in this context had to do with people who sympathized with the policies of a political group, without actually being formal members. Popútchik can be translated as "walk part of the way," so when Trotsky's writings were circulated in English, the term "fellow traveler" took on a new significance—describing non-Communists who nevertheless were inclined to agree with some Communist principles.

(The) female of the species is more deadly than the male

From **Rudyard Kipling** (1911):

> *When the Himalayan peasant meets the he-bear in his pride,*
> *He shouts to scare the monster, who will often turn aside.*
> *But the she-bear thus accosted rends the peasant tooth*
> *and nail.*
> *For the female of the species is more deadly than the male.*

Few and far between

Often heard in weather reports as an adjunct to, or substitute for "scattered showers." But originally the line had nothing to do with intermittent rain or sunny patches—it concerned contact with heavenly hosts.

The original idea may have come from Robert Blair's 1743 poem "The Grave":

> *" . . . visits, like those of angels, short and far between."*

But the form we and the weather presenters are familiar with comes from the Scottish poet **Thomas Campbell**, who wrote in 1840:

> *What though my winged hours of bliss have been*
> *Like angel visits, few and far between.*

(Campbell also created another phrase that later became widely used: "Distance lends enchantment.")

First catch your hare

Commonly misattributed to either one of two famous cooks—

Isabella Beeton or Hannah Glasse. The latter came closer, in *The Art of Cookery Made Plain & Easy* (1746), where her instructions for making hare soup began: "Take your hare when it is cased (meaning 'skinned')."

A century later **William Makepeace Thackeray** gave us the line, in *Rose and Ring* (1855), but it had nothing to do with cooking: rebel troops, determined on usurping a Prince, track him to a tavern and demand his sword. The Prince—who clearly had misheard Hannah Glasse—announces:

> *First catch your hare. Ha!*

First Lady

When the United States became independent of British rule, British titles and honorifics were abandoned as well and the Americans began to establish their own honorifics, e.g., Representative, Congress Person, Oscar Nominee, Senator, Colonel (attached to men who had never been in an army, e.g., Harlan Sanders and Andreas van Kuijk, aka Tom Parker)—and Mr. President. But despite the logicality of "Mr. President," there was some uncertainty about how his consort should be described.

Mrs. President was tried, and Presidentess, but neither seemed particularly graceful. Then in 1849, during the tenure of the twelfth President **Zachary Taylor**, Dolley Madison, the popular wife and widow of the fourth President, died. In his speech at Dolley Madison's funeral, Taylor is reputed to have said:

> *She will never be forgotten because she was truly our first lady for a half-century.*

The term First Lady has been in use ever since.

Fish and visitors go off in three days

The elegantly artificial prose style of sixteenth-century writer **John Lyly** made him famous at the time. His best-known work *Euphues— the Anatomy of Wit* is commemorated today in the English word euphemism—a gentler way of referring to something considered unpalatable.

But in 1579 Lyly abandoned the softly-softly approach, when he wrote bluntly:

> *Fish and guests in three days are stale.*

Benjamin Franklin's adaptation "Fish and visitors stink in three days" came in 1733.

Float like a butterfly, sting like a bee

Associated with, and widely used by, boxer Muhammad Ali, the line was created for him by his assistant trainer and long-time companion **Drew "Bundini" Brown**. When Brown's adult son Drew Brown III set out to be a speaker on the subject of motivation, Muhammad Ali wrote in a testimonial for him:

> *Motivation is in Drew Brown's blood. His father Drew "Bundini" Brown motivated me to become one of the greatest boxers of all time. Drew Brown speeches are doing the same for both young and old. His timely message is exactly what is needed in today's ever-changing society. His dad's slogan of "Float like a butterfly; sting like a bee," motivated me to be a champion.*

Flogging (beating) a dead horse

The landlubber's version may have originated in an old seagoing term. Admiral Smyth's *Sailor's Word Book* explains this as the time when a seaman ashore is paid in advance for a month's work and immediately spends it, then for the first month at sea feels he is working for no pay—it is a "dead horse" month. At the end of his prepaid month when normal wages ensue, the crew makes an effigy of a horse, drags it around the deck and casts it into the sea. The dead horse has been flogged.

The expression came ashore and into public awareness when it surfaced in the British Houses of Parliament. John Bright was a radical MP, a Quaker and a renowned orator (he coined the phrase "Britain is the mother of Parliaments"). In 1867, Parliament's dealing with the Reform Bill seemed to be becoming bogged down, and Members of Parliament appeared to be showing a lack of interest. **John Bright** attempted to ignite the Members to more vigorous action and announced in a speech that trying to get the matter activated was like flogging a dead horse and trying to make it pull a load.

(A year later, John Campbell Colquhoun used the term in describing "Popery" as a "dead horse".)

Fools rush in where angels fear to tread

In times past, the word "fool" implied simple lack of judgement rather than foolhardy risk-taking. **Alexander Pope**'s *Essay on Criticism* (1711) was a sounding-off against literary critics, rather than a finger-wagging at people whose courage exceeds their common sense:

> *No Place so Sacred from such Fops is barr'd,*
> *Nor is Paul's Church more safe than Paul's Church-yard:*
> *Nay, fly to Altars; there they'll talk you dead;*
> *For Fools rush in where Angels fear to tread.*

Foreign muck

British writer **Johnny Speight**, creator of the enormously popular television series *Till Death Us Do Part* (first seen in 1965), put the words into character Alf Garnett's mouth, and thus eventually into the front line of current expression.

The concept wasn't new—people were often suspicious of foods with which they were unfamiliar in their own culture. The attitude can be found in 100 AD when ancient Roman writer Juvenal expressed dislike of everyone and everything not of his own immediate circle.

Alf Garnett (and later his American spin-off Archie Bunker) specialized in shock-value put-down phrases spoken out loud on television. Alf referred to dark skinned people as *coons*, called his wife a *silly old moo* and his son-in-law a *randy scouse git*.

Most of these shock phrases were clever adaptations by the scriptwriter of expressions already in existence. In Garnett's view, foreign muck included avocados, lemon grass, tandoori chicken, lasagne, sushi, and aubergines.

People who lived in England as long ago as the 1920s report that although the phrase foreign muck was well within the common vernacular, it was still shocking to hear actor Warren Mitchell announcing it loudly on television whenever anyone mentioned pasta or pizza.

Fresh as a daisy

Because many daisies close their petals at night and open up again in daylight, they gained a reputation for being "fresh." In 1834, Captain **Frederick Marryat** put the expression into English in *Jacob Faithful*:

> *Rouse a bit, wash your face with old Thames water, and in half-an-hour you'll be as fresh as a daisy.*

From cradle to grave

In essence, the concept—from birth to death—has been around since antiquity. The more idiomatic "cradle" version surfaced as a translated saying of Islam founder Muhammad ("Seek knowledge from cradle to grave"), but it has been in English in its own right since 1857.

In *Tom Brown's Schooldays*, **Thomas Hughes** writes:

> *After all, what would life be without fighting, I should like to know? From the cradle to the grave, fighting, rightly understood, is the business, the real highest, honestest business of every son of man.*

Dickens used it later (in *Somebody's Luggage*), as did both Edgar Rice Burroughs and E.M. Forster. The expression achieved prominence in Britain during 1948 when it was cited as part of the creed of the newly established National Health Service.

(In 1931, a story was published by American writing team Colin Campbell Clements and his wife Florence Ryerson, entitled "From the Cradle to the Shave.")

Gentrification

Berlin-born Ruth Lazarus (later Glass) moved to London in 1932 when she was twenty. By 1943, she was conducting surveys for Planning and Regional Construction, and became a respected urban sociologist.

In the early 1960s, she identified a trend in which the shabby Victorian dwellings of working-class areas of London were being bought and renovated by young people perceived as "gentry." In 1964 **Ruth Glass** published her article "Aspects of Change" in which she coined the word gentrification:

> *Once this process of "gentrification" starts in a district it goes on rapidly until all or most of the original working-class occupiers are displaced and the whole social character of the district is changed.*

Get a life

During the 1980s, the growth in popularity of video games and computers resulted in many young people hovering over machines for hours at a time. Keyboards and screens seemed to be taking over their lives—hence the exhortation to "get a life"—meaning to take part in "real" life and leave fantasies behind.

The term had major public exposure in 1987 when actor **William Shatner**—Captain Kirk in *Star Trek*—appeared in a comedy skit on *Saturday Night Live*. This was a satiric send-up involving *Star Trek* fans, who were depicted as fanatics wearing pointy ears and asking absurdly trivial questions (e.g., "What was the combination of the safe Captain Kirk opened in episode 38?").

At the end of the sketch, Shatner told the besotted trekkies they should "Get a life." His remark was given wide coverage and is believed to have kick-started the term's popularity.

Get off my back

The actual authorship of *A Thousand and One Nights* is lost in Middle-Eastern antiquity. It appeared in French in 1717, with several English versions following. Among the tales with which Scheherazade regales the Caliph is the story of Sinbad the sailor, who gives a poor old man a ride on his shoulders. The old man clamps his legs around Sinbad's neck, shoulders and back, and for several days refuses to get off.

Unlike earlier translations with their rather elaborate Victorian style, **Sir Richard Burton**'s 1850 version was in easily accessible English. After telling of Sinbad begging the old man to "dismount," Burton has Sinbad saying:

> But he would not get off my back.

From that literal beginning grew the metaphorical concept of some relationship or other issue proving difficult to dislodge from one's life.

Get someone's back up

Everyone's seen an angry cat do it, and that was doubtless the image behind the original use of the term. This was in the play *The Provok'd Husband* (1728) by architect and dramatist **Sir John**

Vanbrugh, and **Colly Cibber**, showing the character of Jenny relishing the fact that she is to marry a Count, giving her a higher rank than her mother. Jenny's comment on the matter:

> *Oh Lud! How her back will be up then, when she meets me at an assembly!*

Ghostwriters

For many centuries it has been common practice for someone in a back room to write well-crafted prose for someone else to speak or publish. The names of popes, prelates, presidents, stars of stage, screen, and sports field have all been linked to words they themselves did not create.

The back-room writer is sometimes credited ("as told to"), but often remains unknown. In other areas, the back-roomer is widely known but faintly disguised with an alternative job description: communications coordinator, press secretary, or information officer.

While ghostwriter carries a slightly pejorative air, speechwriter does not—and countless politicians and public figures employ (and do not hide) speechwriters (who are never referred to as ghostwriters, though that is what they are).

Initially, the practice was somewhat clandestine and was known simply as "ghosting." Then, in 1921, an entrepreneurial American called **Christy Walsh** enlarged the concept and coined the term "ghostwriter." Walsh formed an organization that arranged ghostwriting for many major sports stars, and there was no secret about it. *Observer* writer Tim Adams ("The Honorable Tradition of Ghostwriting") quoted Christy Walsh's first rule about sports stars' so-called autobiographies:

> *Don't insult the intelligence of the public by claiming these men write their own stuff.*

Ginormous

This combination of "giant" and "enormous" was known among British military personnel during World War II, but it was only in limited public usage. Then a minor incident in the U.S. helped bring the term first into public print, then gradually into wider use.

In Muskingum County, Ohio, in May 1951, the *Zanesville Signal* newspaper interviewed a helicopter operator called **Carl Agar**. He worked for the Okanagon Air Service, British Columbia and when asked the size of the service for which he was a pilot he replied: "It's ginormous."

The term had surfaced from somewhere in Mr. Agar's background, possibly through military connections. But his remark (despite being reported in a provincial newspaper) gradually spread the usage across the U.S. and eventually into the Merriam-Webster dictionary and the English-speaking world at large.

Glittering prizes

The Education of Henry Adams was written by Boston author and well-respected historian **Henry Adams** about himself. Initially, it was only printed privately in 1907, and contained the following:

> *Among all these, Clarence King, John Hay, and Henry Adams had led modest existences, trying to fill in the social gaps of a class which, as yet, showed but thin ranks and little cohesion. The combination offered no very glittering prizes, but they pursued it for twenty years with as much patience and effort as though it led to fame or power.*

Since this book was at first self-published and distributed only among friends, Henry Adams might not have been considered as the first person to put the term before the public eye. But after he died in 1919, the book was published commercially and put on the open market. The following year it won the Pulitzer Prize.

Whether or not Britain's Lord Birkenhead had read *The Education of Henry Adams* is not known but, making a speech as Lord Rector of Glasgow University in November 1923, he advised the students that there were still "glittering prizes" to be had, rewarding "stout hearts and sharp swords."

Global village

Predicting the effects of growth in electronic technology long before the explosion of the Internet, **Marshall McLuhan** coined the phrase global village in his 1962 book *The Gutenberg Galaxy*:

> *The new electronic inter-dependence recreates the world in the image of a global village.*

He mentioned the term again in his *The Medium is the Massage* (1967).

Go ahead, make my day

In the 1983 movie *Sudden Impact*, Clint Eastwood as (Dirty) Harry Callahan walked into a coffee shop being held up by some violent characters. He told them that "we" weren't going to let them escape—"we" being "Smith, Wesson, and me."

The resulting shootout left just one man holding a waitress hostage, and a gun pointed at Harry. With his own gun pointing straight at the robber, Harry spoke the memorable taunt:

> *Go ahead, make my day.*

The line was written for him by **Joseph Stinson**. It is now included by the American Film Institute as number six in their one hundred all-time most memorable film quotes.

Gobbledygook

Although gobbledygook can now be used to indicate any kind of nonsensical language, its original application was a dismissive reference to the unfathomable kind of jargon that tends to come from official sources.

American **Maury Maverick** was elected to Congress in 1934 and grew to dislike long-winded euphemistic language. During World War II, he worked for the Office of Price Administration, the Office of Personnel Management, the War Production Board and the Smaller War Plants Corporation. In the middle of all that, he rebelled against the over-inflated, convoluted and pompous way information was distributed. In 1944 he invented a word to describe it—gobbledygook—based on the meaningless "gobbling" noise of turkeys when make by a human "gook."

Fittingly, Maury Maverick was a grandson of Samuel Maverick, who inspired the word maverick, meaning one who goes against the tide. In later times gobbledygook widened its meaning to include other kinds of confusing wordiness, and the official kind became known as corporate-ese.

Gobsmacked

Gobsmacked is a dialect expression, long familiar in the Northern counties of England, usually referring to slapping the hand over the mouth in astonishment. The term reached prominence in 1991 when, as the *Independent* newspaper reported, the Chairman of the Conservative Party heard of Labour's claim that its poll-tax replacement would save the average household £140.

The Conservative Chairman **Chris Patten** (former Governor of Hong Kong) declared himself "gobsmacked." The comment made headline news and quickly went into widespread popular usage.

God helps those who help themselves

It sounds as if it comes from the Bible, but it doesn't. The clue is in the plural—the original expression is: "The gods help them that help themselves." It can be found in the fables of Aesop—several centuries BC—and from an ancient Greek culture which worshipped many gods.

British historian **James Howell**, a glass-factory administrator who became a secretary to the Privy Council, is believed to be the first British writer to earn a living writing solely in the English language. In 1659 he introduced Aesop's maxim into English as:

God helps him who helps himself.

In successive centuries it quietly slid back to its original non-gender-specific form as "God helps them (or those) who help themselves."

Go down like a lead balloon

The idiom originated in 1924 with American cartoonist **Loren Taylor**, whose character Pop excitedly bought shares in a mothball company. But when he visited the Stock Exchange, he saw the shares "go up like a lead balloon."

While the failure of a lead balloon to "go up" is obvious, in ensuing decades the "go up" has sometimes been replaced with "go over" or "go down," both theater expressions that indicate an audience didn't "get" a joke or dramatic twist.

Going for a song

In current times, going for a song indicates that something of great value is available, or has been procured, for a mere fraction of its true worth. The expression's origin indicated exactly the opposite.

Edmund Spenser's poem *The Faerie Queene* was written to honor Queen Elizabeth I. Thomas Fuller in *Worthies of England* (1662) reported that Good Queen Bess—who was never one to turn her back on flattery—ordered that Spenser's effort be honored in return with £100, an enormous sum in the 1590s.

On hearing about the Queen's wish, **William Cecil** (Lord Burghley, the Lord High Treasurer) exclaimed petulantly, "What? All this for a song?" His remark was widely repeated and went into common usage, meaning a high payment for something of low value. Over the centuries the term became both shortened and overturned in meaning.

Going-going-gone!

In 1777 **Richard Brinsley Sheridan**'s successful play *The School for Scandal* played at Drury Lane Theatre, London. An auctioneer's closing statement, this may have been in use before, but Sheridan's play was its first known use before the public, and in print.

In the story, Charles Surface expresses a wish to sell off his own family, and after much banter and bargaining a sum of £300 is agreed, whereupon the auctioneer calls "Going-going-gone!" Auctioneers have been doing it ever since.

(Sheridan would have known about auctions. Auction laws were first passed in England, and licenses granted c.1500 during the reign of Henry VII. Sotheby's was established in 1744 and Christies in 1766.)

Golden handshake

A generous one-off payment, over and above their salary, made to someone leaving a business at retirement, or possibly to persuade them not to make a fuss about something.

The term golden handshake was coined in Britain c.1965 by the city editor of the *Daily Express*, **Frederick Ellis**. It was so apt and immediately successful that it was followed by the imitative forms golden hello, golden boot, and golden parachute.

(Frederick Ellis was knowledgeable about city finances—most of the time. In 1964, he publicly and strongly advised readers not to invest in the Beatles' publishing company Northern Songs. Some years later the company sold for $47 million.)

Goldfinger

The combined talents of Ian Fleming, Sean Connery, and Shirley Bassey made the name Goldfinger known internationally. What wasn't widely known was that this megalomaniac force of evil was deliberately named after a genuine living person.

Enrö Goldfinger was a London architect whose tower block designs were the subject of much attention and some controversy. Goldfinger's wife Ursula had a cousin, John Blackwell, with whom **Ian Fleming** played golf. Fleming heard Blackwell mention the architect's name, liked it, and without asking, allocated the name to a totally fictional evil character in a novel he was working on. In 1959, information filtered through to Enrö Goldfinger that a depiction of a world-class villain was about to be published, with his unusual but real surname.

The fictional Goldfinger (born in Latvia) was a brutal egotist planning to steal all the gold from Fort Knox. Enrö Goldfinger (born in Hungary) was himself no shrinking violet, and demanded that the publisher provide him with a proof copy. Having read it, he threatened to sue, on such strong grounds that the publishers were concerned they might have to pulp an entire edition.

But a settlement was reached out of court, which included a requirement that every single time the name Goldfinger was mentioned in the book, it must be preceded by the character's first name—hence, not just Goldfinger, but Auric Goldfinger (Au is the chemical symbol for gold).

Fleming was so angry he threatened to change the character's name to Goldprick. But this did not happen.

Golliwog

For a century golliwogs were a common toy for children. But eventually a growing awareness of insensitivity to black Americans sidelined the woolly-headed doll. Although inspired by American imagery, the golliwog and its name were actually invented in London. Englishwoman **Florence Upton** and her mother **Bertha** had lived in New York for some years, and on returning to Britain, they produced a children's story: *The Adventures of Two Dutch Dolls and a Golliwogg* (1895).

Florence, an accomplished illustrator, was responsible for the golliwogg's appearance. Popularity was immediate, and sequels followed. The final "g" got lost along the way, and the golliwog received further major exposure when his image joined the label of a popular jam.

The golliwog later became a springboard for Enid Blyton's tar babies Golly and Woggy. But during the 1990s Blyton's tar babies and the Uptons' black doll themselves faded to black.

(As children, C.S. Lewis and his brother created and wrote, around 1916, about the mystical world Boxen, which included the characters of King Bunny and Golliwog.)

Gone with the wind

The Pulitzer Prize-winning novel (1937) sold 30 million copies, and the blockbuster movie (1939) is still regarded as one of the all-time Hollywood classics. The expression gained front-line attention. Author Margaret Mitchell had plucked one line from a poem published more than forty years before, and she made that line world famous.

The poem (1896) by British poet **Ernest Dowson** has the forbidding title "Non Sum Qualis Eram Bonae Sub Regno Cynarae," but contains the more accessible line:

> *I have forgot much, Cynara! Gone with the wind . . .*

Besides being Mitchell's title, the line occurs in the novel when Scarlett O'Hara is wondering if her home Tara is still standing. Mitchell had reputedly considered several other titles: *Bugles Sang True, Not in Our Stars,* and *Tote the Weary Load.* In hindsight it's easy to agree *Gone with the Wind* was the best choice.

Cole Porter was also apparently a fan of the same Dowson poem. In Porter's show *Kiss Me Kate* the characters of Bill and Lois sing "Always True to You Darling in My Fashion," echoing a sentiment from "Non Sum Qualis" in which Cynara is told repeatedly: "I have been faithful to thee Cynara! in my fashion."

(Incidentally, MGM's highly publicized search to find a screen Scarlett O'Hara culminated in the choice of Vivien Leigh, one of the great beauties of the time. This decision was at quixotic variance with writer Margaret Mitchell's opening line: "Scarlett O'Hara was not beautiful . . .")

(A) good career move

This remark, in spite of its rampant cynicism, contains a grain of truth. The industries which have grown around celebrity deaths have been notably prolific (largely due to a financial benefit which the aforesaid celebrities can no longer enjoy). In their book *Live from New York* Tom Shales and James Andrew Miller recount how the expression first arose, as reported by respected movie director John Landis.

On August 16, 1977, Landis was in a discussion with *Saturday Night Live* comedy writer **Michael O'Donahue** when a secretary came in with the news that Elvis Presley had been found dead. Upon which O'Donahue remarked, "Good career move." The remark rapidly went into show-business folklore and was at various times alleged to have been originated by John Lennon, or Presley's manager Tom Parker. But Landis dismisses these and firmly pins it on O'Donahue because, as he says: "I was there."

The term has since been recycled following the deaths of celebrities who died young: Kurt Cobain, Andy Warhol, Princess Diana, Freddie Mercury, and Heath Ledger. Of the later uses of O'Donahue's remark, one of the most publicized was seven years after Elvis died, when Gore Vidal repeated the line—this time about the death of Truman Capote.

(A) good innings

Obviously connected to cricket—an innings being the period the batsman has his turn at batting. So, a good innings is one in which many runs are clocked up. The expression remained in cricket parlance until 1837, when **Charles Dickens** in *Pickwick Papers* used it in another context referring to someone making a success of an opportunity. Sam Weller says:

> *It's my innings now gov'nor, and as soon as I catch 'old of this here Trotter, I'll have a good 'un.*

The term then went into wider general use signifying a period of success—or a long rewarding life.

(A) good man is hard to find

However much a cliché it might now seem, the observation didn't enter the language in that concise form until 1918 when legendary American jazz musician **Eddie Green** put it into a song, and also into the language—Green's song garnered more than one hundred cover versions.

A risqué expression (which might have been devised by Mae West) based on the song's title inverted became almost as well known as the original.

(A) good time was had by all

Though not in vernacular use, the term was common in old-fashioned newspaper reports of genteel social functions, church fêtes, and birthday gatherings. British novelist and poet **Stevie Smith** eased it into common usage by using the term as the title of her published collection of poetry (1937).

(*The Book of Hollywood Quotes* credits film star Bette Davis with remarking about an unnamed starlet: "She's the original good time that's been had by all.")

Google

The well-known Internet search engine was invented in 1998 by **Larry Page** and **Sergey Brin**. They invented the name Google because the word suggested the similar word googol—a mathematical term denoting a figure followed by one hundred zeros. This association evoked an image of the Google search engine sweeping through hundreds of thousands of search options. (It is also believed that Page and Brin, in coming up with the name Google, had in mind to tease the CEO of Yahoo, whose name was Koogle.)

The Google search engine has no known connection with the term googly, which like googol is also a real word—describing in cricket "an off break bowled with a leg break action."

Go the whole hog

To act wholeheartedly and without reservation; to supply anything to the fullest possible level.

In centuries past, hog may or may not have meant shilling, and spending all of it may or may not have engendered remarks about 'the whole hog'. But there is no uncertainty that, all along, hog also meant pig.

Americans regard the expression "whole hog" as having originated in the butchery trade in Virginia where meat for sale was charged by its trimmed weight. An entire beast provided a great deal of meat, which worked out at a cheaper cost per pound. Groups of neighbors could economize by buying a whole hog.

The first person to refer to the whole hog in print definitely meant a genuine pig.

In 1779, British poet **William Cowper** wrote "Hypocrisy Detected" about Muslims conferring over a cooked pig, and attempting to follow the religious law that allowed only one part of a pig to be eaten. However, they couldn't remember which part. So by a process of hunger-influenced reasoning, they arrived at the inevitable conclusion:

> But for one piece they thought it hard
> From the whole hog to be debarr'd
> And set their wit at work to find
> What joint the prophet had in mind.
> Thus, conscience freed from every clog
> Mahometans eat up the hog.
> With sophistry their sauce they sweeten
> Till quite from from tail to snout 'tis eaten.

The first time the expression is known to have moved from the butcher's shop into more general application was in 1828 when Andrew Jackson was running for President. Massachusetts Senator

Daniel Webster wrote that Jackson: "Will either go with the party as they say in New York—or go the whole hog, as it is phrased elsewhere."

Grace under pressure

F. Scott Fitzgerald received a letter from **Ernest Hemingway** in 1926 in which Hemingway mentioned the concept of grace under pressure (reprinted in *Ernest Hemingway—Selected Letters.*)

The term came to wider notice when Hemingway was interviewed by Dorothy Parker for the *New York Times*, ("The Artist's Reward," November 1929). She asked him, "Exactly what do you mean by 'guts'?" Hemingway replied: "Grace under pressure."

Grandfather clock

Until 1876 tall clocks were always called long-case clocks and, in the antique trade, they still are. Legend has it that their cases were made by coffin makers during slow seasons. One such tall clock stood in the foyer of the George Hotel in Piercebridge in the English county of Yorkshire. The hotel was run by the two Jenkins brothers and their clock was notable for the consistency of its timekeeping. This was slightly unusual, since floor clocks of the era weren't always accurate.

The clock's reliability started to fail when one of the Jenkins brothers died; gradually it began to fall behind until a whole hour of each day was lost. The surviving Jenkins brother reached the age of ninety, and then he too died.

At the time the clock was fully wound, but it stopped completely and never worked again. The hotel's new management respectfully left the clock in the foyer, standing silent with its hands at the position they were in when the second brother died.

In 1875, American songwriter **Henry Clay Work** came to stay at the George Hotel. Mr. Work heard the story of the silent clock standing in the foyer and was intrigued. Back in America, he remembered the clock which stopped with the death of its owner and, adding a few fanciful variations, he wrote a song.

Henry Work condensed the two Jenkins brothers into a fictional grandfather whose faithful clock had been bought on the day of his birth, had celebrated his marriage, and then stopped short, never to go again, when the old man died.

Work's song *My Grandfather's Clock* was published in 1876 and the sheet music sold over a million copies. The song became so well known that it changed the name of the long case clock—but minus Mr. Work's apostrophe. The grandfather's clock became just a "grandfather clock."

Granny Smith

Mrs. Maria Smith (née Sherwood) was a pioneer orchardist in Australia. During the 1860s, Mrs. Smith bought a crate of "French" crab apples, grown in Tasmania, and later their remains were thrown in a heap by a small river. From the heap, there grew an unusual tree. The tree was later defined as a "fixed mutation"—a hybrid, which retained its hybrid qualities into future generations.

It produced apples with notable qualities: a strong and beautiful green skin; excellent properties for cooking as well as eating; slow to oxidize and turn brown, and therefore good for slicing into salads; and able to resist bruising during travel.

In 1868, Mrs. Smith invited nearby orchardists Edwin Small and his father to examine her tree and its crop. By then Maria was sixty-nine years old and a grandmother, so she referred to her new fruit as "Granny Smith's apples."

Mrs. Smith died before her new apple became an industry—widely grown by other orchardists, exhibited in agricultural shows, and taking prizes for cooking. In 1895, the New South Wales

Department of Agriculture pronounced "Granny Smith's seedlings" as being suitable for export. The bright green apple went on to become one of the most recognizable fruits in the world, and the Beatles used it as a company logo for Apple Records.

Grassroots

Apart from its obvious literal meaning, grassroots came to mean the essential foundations of society at a local level. This metaphor was first seen in print in **Rudyard Kipling**'s *Kim* (1901). The old holy Teshoo Lama tells the young Kim:

> *Then I was shaken in my soul: my soul was darkened, and the boat of my soul rocked upon the waters of illusion. Not till I came to Shamlegh could I meditate upon the Cause of Things, or trace the running grass-roots of Evil.*

(The) great unwashed

There are traces of this expression in the Bible ("washed" referring to "cleansed of sin") and in Shakespeare (meaning literally "not washed"). But referring to the great unwashed as a social distinction may have originally crept into English when used in private by the upper classes to indicate a certain contempt for the lower classes.

It didn't appear in the public arena before being seen in print in 1830. By then the expression great unwashed had come to include not only the lower orders, but also was used to dismiss any group that didn't agree with whoever was holding a certain opinion.

The novel *Pelham—The Adventures of a Gentleman* by prolific British writer Baron **Edward Bulwer-Lytton** was published in 1828. The author was less than pleased when the fictional character of Pelham came in for some censure from one or two critics of the day.

After waiting two years to hit back, in 1830 Bulwer-Lytton published the novel *Paul Clifford*, which included an "Epistle of Dedication" to an unnamed friend. In the epistle he mentioned the earlier criticism, finding it completely unwarranted and totally misinterpreting the intended characterisation of Pelham. In disparaging tones Bulwer-Lytton dismissed the critics as "the Great Unwashed." Whether or not Bulwer-Lytton invented the phrase, this appears to be the first time it was seen in print (suggestions that Edmund Burke said it earlier are difficult to substantiate).

(Incidentally, Bulwer-Lytton's fictional character Pelham was a society fashion plate who drew attention to himself by not wearing colorful clothes at evening functions, instead dressing all in black. Bulwer-Lytton himself followed the same principle, declaring that a person "must be very distinguished to look well in black." British society men followed his lead, which is said to have given rise to the customary black dinner suit now considered the norm in Britain.)

See also **It was a dark and stormy night**

Gridlock

A familiar (and dreaded) term, originally coined to describe the situation where the flow of traffic through a grid of intersecting streets is locked into immobility. In a city this happens when the lights change at an intersection but the number of vehicles trying to get across is greater than the time allotted, and those which can't get through back up across the intersection. Those wanting to cross the intersection at right angles can't get through, and the grid is locked.

The word first came to light in public during a 1980 transit strike in New York. The Chief Engineer of the New York Department of Transportation, **Sam Schwartz**, described the traffic congestion as gridlock in several prominent contexts, and was quoted in newspapers. He didn't claim to have invented it, but later explained that the word had already been used among his staff.

Shortly after, in 1980, the *New York Times Magazine* defined gridlock as "a panic inside a nightmare inside a worst case. Instead of going with the traffic flow, everything stops and every frenzied driver leans on his horn."

Soon the expression moved beyond traffic problems and is now applied to other similarly jammed situations: overloading of a telephone exchange; heavy Internet usage; or too much legislation facing Congress. There is even "vocal gridlock," when several people on a television or radio panel talk at the same time and none of them can be heard clearly.

Grin like a Cheshire cat

The first publication to mention this eccentric image was the work of satirist **Peter Pindar** (pseudonym of **John Wolcot**), who wrote *A Pair of Lyric Epistles* (1795) containing the line:

> *Lo, like a Cheshire cat our court will grin!*

Seventy years later William Makepeace Thackeray in *The Newcomes* also referred to the infamous grinning cat:

> *Mr. Newcome says to Mr. Pendennis in his droll humorous way, "That woman grins like a Cheshire cat."*

Then in 1865 Lewis Carroll's *Alice's Adventures in Wonderland* brought the Cheshire cat to center stage. Carroll didn't invent the image, but he certainly brought it wide international awareness and usage.

(There are various theories as to why Cheshire cats are described as grinning. Round Cheshire cheeses with semi-circular "smiles" impressed on them is one possibility. But when Alice asks the Duchess why the cat has a grin, she replies, "It's a Cheshire cat, and that's why." With that we have to be satisfied.)

Grotty

Meaning unpleasant and unattractive, this slang version of "grotesque" may have been in use prior to the rise of the Beatles. But in 1964 **Alun Owen**'s script for the movie *A Hard Day's Night* showed George Harrison being asked an opinion on the fashion appeal of some trendy shirts. Harrison described them as "dead grotty, yeah," and the word came into wider use. (After the movie's premiere, Princess Margaret asked what the word meant.)

In 1976, British television viewers were introduced to a variation on grotty by the character Reginald Perrin, for whom writer **David Nobbs** introduced the word "grot" for goods and gifts which were of absolutely no use or value (e.g., tiny drinking glasses for canaries to put their false teeth into).

Guinea pigs

Despite the name, Guinea pigs come from South America, not Guinea. But it is true that from the mid-1800s guinea pigs were used for medical experiments because their immune systems and their inability to synthesize Vitamin C mirror the human condition.

In contemporary times we accept the term guinea pig as a metaphor for experimental treatments performed on humans rather than little animals.

The University of Texas Health Science Center survey of *Twentieth Century Milestones in Clinical Research* records that in 1913 **George Bernard Shaw** was the first person to refer to human research subjects as "guinea pigs."

Halcyon days

The term is used in Aristophanes' *The Birds* (414 BC), meaning a calm and stress-free period, so its significance was recognized by the public at that time. But it was the Roman poet Publius Ovidius Naso, known as **Ovid** (43 BC to AD 17 or 18), who told the whole story in his *Metamorphoses*.

In Greek mythology, the daughter of Aeolus, god of the winds, was Alcyon (the "h" was added later), and she married a mortal man. The couple angered Zeus, who threw a thunderbolt at a ship in which the husband was sailing and he drowned.

Distraught, Alcyon threw herself into the sea to end her life. Zeus, however, in a fit of pity, turned them both into shining kingfisher birds which could skim along the water and make their nests on the sea's surface. The birds were named after Alcyon (and still are). Alcyon produced kingfisher eggs, and because her father was god of the winds he calmed the seas so she could safely hatch her chicks. This gave rise to a legend that told of the seas staying calm for fourteen days a year so the two birds could safely breed.

Ovid wrote:

> *Sev'n days sits brooding on her floating nest:*
> *A wintry queen: her sire at length is kind,*
> *Calms ev'ry storm, and hushes ev'ry wind.*

Arthur Golding translated Ovid's *Metamorphoses* into English in 1567, in time for Shakespeare to include the phrase in *Henry VI, Part I* (c. 1599), as spoken by Joan La Pucelle.

The expression has remained in English consistently, although its origin has a curious flaw: kingfishers do not float their nests on the sea—they nest in holes they have burrowed into banks.

Happy ever after

This traditional ending to many stories, usually after trials and tribulations have been suffered, owes its ancestry to **William Makepeace Thackeray**. He first used the phrase privately in a letter to his fiancée Isabella in 1834, then appeared to take a liking to it, using it publicly several times afterward in his literary output. An early example can be found in *History of Pendennis* (1850):

> *And we will send the money to Pen, who can pay all his debts without hurting anybody and then we will live happy ever after.*

With a subtle change from adjective to adverb, Thackeray's vision of a blissful future eventually became a cliché and a subject of satire.

Have a nice day

It was far from being the irritating ploy it later became when Kirk Douglas said the line for the first time publicly in the 1948 movie *A Letter to Three Wives* based on a novel by **John Klempner**.

A variation occurred five years later in 1953 when the Californian advertising agency Carson/Rogers designed a sketched caricature smile accompanied by the slogan "Have a Happy Day," then extended the slogan to their switchboard. Operators were instructed to answer calls "Carson/Rogers—have a happy day!" But only until noon; the theory was that if callers weren't having a happy day by noon, the joyous greetings weren't going to help it happen. Carson/Rogers dispersed the slogan on letterheads, towels and tie pins.

Over the next twenty years "happy day" morphed back into the 1948 original "nice day," and gradually crept into the daily vocabulary of people in service occupations, such as supermarket checkout staff, often repeated in an uncaring monotone.

One punter, objecting to the formula, would snap back defiantly, "I won't."

Head over heels

It started out as "Per caputque pedesque" around 60 BC, when Roman poet **Gaius Valerius Catullus** in his poem *Carmina* told of someone that he would like to see go "over head and heels" into mud. Usage over several centuries rearranged the words slightly but retained the image.

The expression came into English the same way, but had become inverted by 1771 when Herbert Lawrence in *The Contemplative Man* wrote about someone receiving:

> *Such a violent involuntary kick in the Face,*
> *as drove him Head over Heels.*

Hear no evil, see no evil

It's doubtful that anyone ever said it in English before the end of the seventeenth century. The concept of "See not evil, hear not evil, speak not evil" related back as far as Confucius in China, several hundred years BC, and then traveled to Japan, where it was known for centuries as a moral maxim. By a trick of the Japanese language, the maxim eventually became known worldwide. "Kikazaru, Iwazaru, Mizaru" actually means "See not evil, hear not evil, speak not evil," but the Japanese suffix for "not" (zaru) sounds very much like the Japanese word for monkey (saru). So, gradually, an association grew between avoiding the proscribed evils, and monkeys.

A stone carving of three monkeys appeared in Japan during the sixteenth century. But it was one hundred years later that the most famous visual image appeared—showing monkeys not seeing, hearing or speaking.

The spectacular Toshogu Shrine near the town of Nikko took 15,000 craftsmen over two years to build and then decorate with two million sheets of gold leaf. Its elaborate stable for the emperor's sacred horse features wall designs by the celebrated carver **Hidari Jingogo** in 1636, including his famous depiction of three monkeys who avoid evil by not seeing it, speaking it or hearing it.

The popularity of the three wise monkeys quickly spread. By the end of the nineteenth century they had become an established image in Western decor. An international hobby group estimates that they have been created in over 20,000 different versions as ornaments, and in every conceivable substance.

Miniatures are made in gold and set with jewels; they can be shelf-size in brass; or right up to life-size wise monkeys made of concrete for garden decoration. They can be found in porcelain, alabaster, plaster of paris, wood, bronze, nickel, and pewter. They adorn door knockers, cigarette boxes, bookends, paperweights, wine bottles, and toasting forks. The three wise monkeys are everywhere.

Here comes the bride

The attractive bridal chorus melody from *Lohengrin* (1850) is probably the most widely recognized of all Wagner's music. But it was not the composer's intention that it be associated with a bride's arrival at her wedding. In the opera, the chorus is sung *after* the wedding. It has nothing to do with the religious ritual of marriage, but rather its physical consummation: the ladies-in-waiting sing the chorus as they lead the now-married bride to the honeymoon suite, where her new husband awaits her.

Their words ("Treulich geführt ziehet dahin, wo euch der Segen der Liebe bewahr") hint at joys to come.

The music stayed safely within its opera until Queen Victoria's daughter Princess Victoria married a Prussian prince in 1858. She used the Wagner music (instrumental only) during the ceremony, initiating a trend that spread through the entire English-speaking world and still survives.

In 1881 the New York-published *Franklin Square Song Collection* presented a version of English words:

> *Guided by us, thrice happy pair*
> *Enter this doorway, 'tis love that unites.*

Then in 1912 *The Victor Book of the Opera* offered this translation:

> *Faithful and true, we lead thee forth*
> *Where love triumphant shall crown thee with joy.*

Those versions adhere to Wagner's words—not a sign of "Here Comes the Bride."

The film industry was still in its infancy at the time, but nevertheless a great many movies were being made. One particularly prolific writer of film scenarios and scripts was **Shannon Fife**. Between 1912 and 1929 Fife wrote eighty-three movies, and it was she who penned the title of a 1915 movie and, against all indications from Wagner, came up with *Here Comes the Bride*. The movie was of course silent, so no song lyrics were required—just the evocative title.

Shannon Fife's title almost instantly became the point of reference for Wagner's melody, and it was open slather. *Here Comes the Bride* cropped up as the title for a Broadway play, a musical, and several more movies. At least four other sets of lyrics to accompany

Wagner's tune arose, all competing in triteness:

> *Here comes the bride, friends by her side,*
> *Wedding bells ring loud, the door opens wide . . .*

and

> *Here comes the bride, all dressed in white*
> *Sweetly, serenely, in soft glowing light.*

Wagner's melody remains a fixture at many weddings—but in general, only as an instrumental—still referred to by Shannon Fife's title. Any suggestion of words to the famous tune generally brings a ribald response.

He's just not that into you

In the television series *Sex and the City* an episode called "Pick-A-Little, Talk-A-Little" went to air in July 2003. In that episode, the character of Miranda was upset because phone calls she had hoped for from a certain man had not eventuated. Berger told her bluntly, "He's just not that into you." The line was written by **Julie Rottenberg** and **Elisa Zuritsky**. Comic Greg Behrendt, who was engaged as a consultant, had reputedly explained such a possibility to one of the writers, who was attempting to understand an incident in her own life.

A year later Behrendt co-authored with Liz Tuccillo the bestselling book *He's Just Not That into You* (2004), which became the basis of a full-length feature movie in 2009.

He who can does, he who cannot teaches

It has the feel of an ancient proverb, but the line dates back only to 1903: **George Bernard Shaw**'s *Man and Superman* (Appendix 2— "Maxims for Revolutionists").

He who hesitates is lost

This started life in 1713 when British commenter on manners and morals **Joseph Addison** presented his play *Cato*. Addison's words for the character of the dutiful Marcia included:

> *When love once pleads admission to our hearts,*
> *(In spite of all the virtue we can boast),*
> *The woman that deliberates is lost.*

Over the following centuries, usage modified the verb and eventually reversed the gender, but the essence remained when the expression became "He who hesitates is lost."

Hit the nail on the head

It has a crisp, modern no-nonsense sound, but doesn't seem modern when you look at its first appearance in English:

> *I xal so smytyn ye nayl on ye hed.*

This was written in 1438 by **Margery Kempe**. Mrs. Kempe was a very religious woman who made arduous journeys from Norfolk to Jerusalem, Rome, Germany, and Spain besides mothering fourteen children. Her *Book of Margery Kempe* is considered to be the oldest surviving autobiography in English.

Ho ho ho

The image of Santa Claus was invented almost entirely by poet Clement Moore in his 1822 poem "A Visit from St. Nicholas" ("Twas the night before Christmas . . . "). Over the following decades, folklore added considerably to the myth of Mr. Claus, moving him from Turkey (where the real St. Nicholas came from) to the North Pole. But prior to the change of address, author

Frank Baum (who also wrote *The Wizard of Oz*) made his own contribution, now inseparable from Santa Claus in America.

In a 1902 children's book called *The Life and Adventures of Santa Claus*, Frank Baum had Santa living in the Valley of Hohaho, and singing:

> *With a ho ho ho, and a ha ha ha,*
> *And a ho ho ha ha ha he,*
> *Now away we go o'er the frozen snow,*
> *As merry as we can be.*

And ever since Santa's catchcry has been "Ho ho ho."

Hold the fort

The expression began as an instruction during the American Civil War. In 1864 General Corse and his troops were in a fort at Allatoona. The general had been painfully wounded and had lost a large number of his troops when a message arrived from General William Sherman: "Hold out, relief is coming."

Some time later, American poet **Philip Bliss** attended a YMCA meeting in Rockford, Illinois, at which Civil War officer Major Whittle told the story of the Allatoona battle and Sherman's message. Hearing about the incident had a great effect on Bliss. Inspired by Sherman's line, and noting its similarity to Revelations 2:25 ("But that which ye have already, hold fast till I come."), he sat up that night writing the words and composing the music for a new hymn. His words modified Sherman's original instruction slightly, and became:

> *Hold the Fort for I am Coming, Jesus signals still.*

The hymn was a great success and became a standard of the American evangelists Moody and Sankey, who led its singing throughout America and Britain. Soon the term "hold the fort," moving away from its literal meaning, became a common expression for keeping everything as normal as possible under difficult circumstances.

Hollow men

The title of a reflective and pessimistic 1925 poem by **T.S. Eliot** (which also refers to the world ending "Not with a bang but a whimper"). The term acquired wide and somewhat unexpected attention when used by Donald Shepherd and Robert F. Slazer as the title of a searing biography of Bing Crosby—*The Hollow Man* (1982)—whose uncompromising dark side came as an unpleasant surprise to those who had cherished the charming and amiable public persona.

Hollywood

Harvey and **Daeda Wilcox** moved from Kansas to Los Angeles in 1883. Harvey set up as a real estate developer and bought a considerable area of land. In 1886 Daeda went back to Kansas for a visit, and returned to Los Angeles by train. On the train Mrs. Wilcox had a conversation with an unknown woman who said she had named her summer home "Hollywood."

Daeda found the name attractive, and back in Los Angeles she suggested their property could be called the same. On February 1, 1887, Harvey Wilcox filed with the county recorder's office a prepared map of a subdivision to be called Hollywood—the first official registering of what has since become one of the most famous towns in the world.

(In an attempt to give the area some connection with its name, Mr. Wilcox imported holly bushes from England. But sunny California was not to their liking and the planting project was abandoned.)

Home James and don't spare the horses

There is a wonderful story—which has to be apocryphal—that Queen Victoria had a carriage driver whose name was James Darling. In that period, aristocrats called servants by their surnames, but it was clearly inappropriate that a Queen should address a footman as Darling so she called him James, and occasionally issued the command: "Home James."

Whatever truth there is in that tale (probably none), the saying "Home James" was known in the nineteenth century, though not necessarily in connection with horses. "Home James" turns up as a movie "short" title in 1918 and again in 1921, and about the same time is a caption on a Felix the Cat cartoon as Felix heads home riding on an elephant's trunk.

The full expression—Home James and don't spare the horses— became widely known as the result of a song composed by musical comedy actor and prolific song composer **Fred Hillebrand**. Previously, his songs had been inclined towards the minstrel type, or had South American rhythms. But in 1934 he came up with the jaunty number "Home James."

In Britain, a celebrity singer of the time—Elsie Carlisle, known as "Radio Sweetheart Number One"—recorded "Home James and Don't Spare the Horses" with Burt Ambrose and the Mayfair Hotel Orchestra. The recording was a major success and put "Home James" into nationwide use, this time with the horses included.

Even though the use of carriage and horses faded, the saying remains as a jocular admonition to get moving, even in a car.

Elsie Carlisle's performance of the song was reissued in 1966 in an Ambrose compilation (AMG-R-263315, Pearl Flapper).

Hot under the collar

Possibly having heard the expression among the London writers he knew, expatriate American poet **Ezra Pound** was the first notable to mention being hot under his collar. He used the expression (to John Quinn) in 1918 when giving vent to his feelings about literary editors:

> *After years of this sort of puling imbecility one gets hot under the collar and is perhaps carried to the extreme.*

How's your father

In the early 1900s, music hall comic **Harry Tate** may have been using an existing piece of Cockney rhyming slang: "How's your father"(= lather). But the phrase attained much wider familiarity as a result of Tate's comedy performances and took on a new connotation. If one of Tate's monologues was leading toward anything too suggestive to declare outright, Tate would suddenly break off and address someone in the audience he supposedly recognized, with the query, "And how's your father?"

This was done with such comic effect that the phrase developed a strong connection with sexual activity, and also as a way of avoiding mention of anything too complex or boring (as in, 'I went to the Ministry and there were forms to fill in and that kind of how's your father.")

The British Library shows that the phrase was familiar enough for it to be the title of two songs and one dance, published between 1915 and 1922. And incidentally, Harry Tate, who died in 1940, is believed to have been a pioneer of the personalized number plate: His car had the plate T8.

How the other half lives

The concept of one socio-economic group being unaware of how another group lives was in French consciousness at least as early as the sixteenth century (Rabelais mentions it in 1532). Bishop Joseph Hall brought the matter into English with his *Holy Observations* in 1607:

> *One half of the world knowes not how the other liues: and therefore the better sort pitty not the distressed . . . because they knowe it not.*

But to American pioneer photojournalist **Jacob Riis** goes the honor of launching the more concise and currently recognizable form. *How the Other Half Lives* was the title of his 1890 study of the squalid tenement areas of New York and the levels of poverty and crime among them—though the buildings were mainly owned by the absent rich. The term quickly went into common usage, referring not only to the rich observing the poor, but also exemplified by glossy magazines that enable the poor to spy on the rich.

Humble abode

A simple enough coupling of two words, but somebody had to think of it first. And that somebody was **Jane Austen** in *Pride and Prejudice* (1813) when the obsequious Mr. Collins explains to Mr. and Mrs. Bennet his close friendship with Lady Catherine De Bourgh:

> *The garden in which stands my humble abode is separated only by a lane from Rosings Park, her ladyship's residence.*

I can see Russia from my house

During the 2008 American presidential campaign, Sarah Palin, the Governor of Alaska and runningmate for John McCain, described Russia as a neighbor to Alaska and added, "You can actually see Russia from land here in Alaska, from an island in Alaska."

This is perfectly true—the Alaskan island of Little Diomede is only a few kilometers from the Russian island of Big Diomede, behind which the coast of mainland Russia can clearly be seen.

But in a later widely reported television appearance, comedy actress **Tina Fey**, dressed and made-up to resemble Mrs. Palin, changed her words to, "I can see Russia from my house." Fey was so convincing that many people believed they'd heard Sarah Palin say it, which she hadn't.

I couldn't care less

It is used informally as a dismissive statement expressing lack of interest. The phrase surfaced publicly in 1945 when BBC war correspondent Stewart MacPherson commented on a commando operation in which the British gave the impression they were going on a picnic:

They just couldn't care less.

But much wider public exposure came internationally in 1946, when former Air Transport Auxiliary man **Anthony Phelps** published an informal memoir of his World War II experiences, entitled *I Couldn't Care Less*, described as "The humor, thrills and pathos, the hardships and fun that Ferry Pilots alternatively endured and enjoyed. Incidents in their daily work are recounted in an easy-flowing style."

(For unknown reasons, American usage has reversed the term into "I could care less," though quixotically its meaning remains exactly the same.)

I did it my way

French musician Jacques Revaux composed the tune with words by Gilles Thibaut and Claude François. Their song was called "Comme d'habitude" (As Usual), a sad song about the singer's low-spirited loneliness and feelings of defeat at the failure of a romance.

While holidaying in France during 1967, Canadian singer-songwriter **Paul Anka** heard the song, liked the tune, and sought to obtain the rights. Two years later fifty-four-year-old Frank Sinatra told Anka he was considering retirement, and Anka abandoned the original depressing words to "Comme d'habitude" and invented an entirely different set of English words with the opposite meaning.

Set to the French tune, Anka's anthem of defiant self-confidence was retitled "My Way." Sinatra recorded the song in 1969, and far from retiring, he continued singing it for the next twenty-five years. Cover versions by Elvis Presley, Brooke Benton, Rod McKuen, Dorothy Squires, Sid Vicious, Robbie Williams, and Greta Keller helped cement the phrase from which the title comes into common usage.

If I'm not in the obituaries, I get up

In 1959 veteran British actor **A.E. Matthews** was ninety years old and still appearing on stage at London's Aldwych Theatre in *How Say You* with Derek Nimmo. During this period he said:

> *I pick up* The Times *every morning and look in the obituary column—if I'm not in it I get up and go to work.*

He died soon after (1960), but the line lingered on and has been "borrowed" by other aging celebrities ever since.

If it ain't broke, don't fix it

Variously described as an old saying from Sweden, or an old saying from Texas, the expression was seen in the *Wall Street Journal* in October 1976 in the form: "If it ain't broke let's don't fix it."

The expression sprang into greater prominence during Jimmy Carter's presidency. The President's Director of Office Management and Budget was **Bert Lance**, who in May 1977 was quoted in *Nation's Business* as saying, "If it ain't broke, don't fix it." The words have become a favorite warning of the cautious against anything new and untried.

(An interesting variation came from New Zealand writer Colin Hogg, commenting on a public organization which appeared to be running smoothly and then, without warning, changed to something else. Hogg said their policy seemed to be: "If it ain't broke—break it.")

If it looks like a duck, walks like a duck, and quacks like a duck, then it's probably a duck

An early version of this reasoning is found in the works of American poet **James Whitcombe Riley,** who sometime prior to 1916 wrote:

*When I see a bird that walks like a duck and swims like a
duck and quacks like a duck, I call that bird a duck.*

The term became more prominent in a rather more elaborate
form in 1950. Richard Immerman's book *The CIA in Guatemala:
The Foreign Policy of Intervention* quotes **Richard Cunningham
Patterson Jr.**, United States ambassador to Guatemala in 1950,
referring to the possibility of Communism:

> *Suppose you see a bird walking around in a farm yard. This
> bird has no label that says "duck." But the bird certainly looks
> like a duck. Also, he goes to the pond and you notice that he
> swims like a duck. Then he opens his beak and quacks like a
> duck. Well, by this time you have probably reached the
> conclusion that the bird is a duck, whether he's wearing a label
> or not.*

A later abbreviated version was famously used by President
Ronald Reagan in 1967:"If it walks like a duck and quacks like a
duck, then it must be a duck."

If the mountain won't come to
Muhammad then Muhammad must go to
the mountain

The legend tells that the power of the prophet Muhammad was
put to the test when he tried to summon Mount Safa. When the
mountain didn't budge, Muhammad explained to his followers that
if the mountain had obeyed and come to him, it knew that its
weight would crush him and everyone with him.

Therefore, he should go to the mountain and give thanks for
its wisdom in sparing them all. This story came into English in
1625, as reported by **Francis Bacon** in *Essays*.

If you can't beat them, join them

Before it became internationally popular, the notion existed in various formats:

> *If you can't whip 'em, jine 'em*

or

> *If you can't lick 'em, jine 'em.*

In a 1932 edition of the *Atlantic Monthly*, Frank R. Kent wrote that the latter version was one of the Indiana Senator **James Eli Watson**'s favorite phrases. Watson's usage helped popularize the saying, which underwent some further refinement over the years. It appeared in Quentin Reynolds' *The Wounded Don't Cry* (1941) as an "old adage":

> *If you can't lick 'em join 'em.*

"Lick" being a peculiarly American usage, in time the saying became: "If you can't beat them, join them."

If you can't stand the heat, get out of the kitchen

Harry S. Truman apparently enjoyed saying it, but there is evidence. He had heard it from someone else years before he became U.S. President. Truman's biographer Robert Ferrell reports that in 1931 Truman took the oath of office as presiding judge in Jackson County. The *Independence Examiner* newspaper of January 1, 1931 tells that during the same ceremony, another judge was sworn in—**E.I. "Buck" Purcell**—who remarked that as a judge he expected there would be occasions when the heat was applied, "But if a man can't stand the heat, he had better stay out of the kitchen."

Truman went on to use it on various occasions himself over the years of his presidency, as also did his Presidential Military Aide, General Harry Vaughan.

Ignoramus

As part of the Latin verb ignorare, the word ignoramus (meaning we do not know) was once used only by the legal profession. It was written on documents to indicate that the matter therein was of imperfect reasoning or doubtful validity.

The word was launched into a much wider public arena in 1615 when playwright **George Ruggle**'s new work was staged, portraying the legal profession as imbued with both arrogance and ignorance. The main character—and the play's title—was *Ignoramus*.

I have a cunning plan

In 1983 British TV viewers were introduced to Blackadder, an accident-prone prince of doubtful lineage, played by Rowan Atkinson and surrounded by an ensemble cast of magnificently eccentric characters. **Rowan Atkinson**, **Richard Curtis,** and **Ben Elton** were the scriptwriters, providing Blackadder with apparently insoluble crises to which his ramshackle dogsbody servant Baldrick would suggest possible solutions of tangential absurdity.

As delivered by actor Tony Robinson, these invariably began with the line:

I have a cunning plan . . .

which was greeted with ever more despairing groans from the others, through four series, five specials, and numerous guest appearances. The line became a widespread jocular introduction whenever someone was about to outline perfectly mundane arrangements.

I have a dream

Notably said by Baptist minister **Martin Luther King** in Detroit in June 1963, then again with tremendous effect at the Lincoln Memorial, Washington, in August 1963.

The expression is simple and could have been used previously by others at other times—there is an echo of Stephen Sondheim's words ("I had a dream") introducing Ethel Merman's hit number "Everything's Coming Up Roses" in the show *Gypsy* (1959), but such was the impact of the Lincoln Memorial speech there is little doubt that when the phrase is used nowadays, Martin Luther King comes to mind first.

I kid you not

Its quasi-archaic inversion, combined with the informal "kid" draws attention to the fact that the speaker is being definite about something.

The expression may have been in use prior to 1951, but made a notable debut in print when **Herman Wouk**'s *Caine Mutiny* was published and became a Pulitzer Prize winner. The book introduced the character of Lt. Commander Queeg, who said:

> *I am damn well responsible for anything that happens on this ship.*
> *From here on in, I don't intend to make a single mistake . . .*
> *I won't tolerate anybody making any mistakes for me, and I kid you not.*
> *And, well, I think you get the idea without my drawing you a picture.*

Soon after, Wouk's *Caine Mutiny* was adapted into a Broadway play, followed by a 1954 movie (five Oscar nominations) starring Humphrey Bogart as Queeg.

Clearly the expression "I kid you not" had received widespread coverage by 1956. More was to come.

In 1957 Jack Paar became host of the television show *Tonight*. For six years, before large audiences of viewers, Paar made a catchphrase of "I kid you not," and became closely associated with it. His 1960 book used the expression as its title. Sometimes Jack Paar is credited with coining it, which is not the case. But he certainly helped make it very widely known.

In a nutshell

A supposed observation from the Roman orator and statesman **Cicero** (106–43 BC) was later commented on by Pliny the Elder in his *Naturalis Historia* (AD 77). It referred to Cicero's contention that Homer's *Iliad* had been copied in such small writing that the whole work could fit inside a walnut shell. Since the *Iliad* has over 15,000 verses, this was no mean feat—if it were true.

Nevertheless, the image remained and still does, having passed down through centuries and languages. Although Cicero was apparently describing an entire work that was simply of small size, the effective metaphor is that a large amount of information can be reduced to its essence in just a few words.

In a rut

A truly rural statement indicating the situation of a carriage driver with a wheel stuck in a groove in the road. **Thomas Carlyle** used the term metaphorically in *Essay on Chartism* (1839), indicating any situation that allows for little change or development.

The metaphor rapidly took over from the literal meaning, among business and professional people in cities who had perhaps never seen a real rut.

In one ear and out the other

The expression dates back, more or less intact, to 1387 in **Geoffrey Chaucer**'s *Troilus and Criseyde*, when Pandarus is comforting Troilus for the loss of his loved one, though the words of comfort are simply not being taken in. The Penguin Classics edition presents Nevill Coghill's setting of the original Chaucer in contemporary English:

> *He spoke whatever came into his head*
> *To help his friend, and following his brief*
> *He did not care what foolishness he said*
> *So long as it might bring him some relief.*
> *But Troilus, so nearly dead for grief*
> *Paid little heed, whatever it was he meant*
> *In at one ear and out the other it went.*

Inside every fat man there is a thin man

The concept came originally from British novelist **George Orwell** in his 1939 novel *Coming Up for Air*.

> *Has it ever struck you that there's a thin man inside every fat man, just as they say there's a statue inside every block of stone?*

Orwell's original line has been recycled and adapted many times. In 1944 Cyril Connolly expanded the original line into "Imprisoned in every fat man a thin man is wildly signalling to be let out" (*The Unquiet Grave*). And one of the line's more unusual adaptations was screenwriter Stephen Schiff's remark that "it's not true that in every terrific book there's a terrific film wildly signalling to be let out."

An amusing use of the line surfaced in the British TV series *Absolutely Fabulous* when actress Jennifer Saunders, complaining about being overweight, said to her screen mother (June Whitfield), "Inside this fat woman there's a thin woman screaming to get out." Miss Whitfield replied, "Just the one, dear?"

(To be) in someone's black books

At least as early as 1175 there were various official books—bound in black leather and actually called Black Books—containing straightforward matter concerning the Exchequer or the Admiralty. But the term gained its connotation of someone being out of favor in the reign of **King Henry VIII**.

During the 1530s he was anxious to shed Queen Catherine for the more youthful charms of Anne Boleyn. But the Pope refused him an annulment, and Henry went looking for news of murky doings in the strongholds of the Church in England—corruption in the monasteries, abuses of privilege and breaths of scandal.

Henry didn't write the assertions himself, but ordered that all damaging information found be recorded in black-bound books. So black books referred quite literally to records of censure.

From there, black books acquired a metaphorical sense. Being in someone's black books didn't necessarily mean anything was written in an actual book, just that disapproval existed. That same aura of censure carried over to the later term "black list." By the nineteenth century, black books had also developed a parallel but slightly softened version—bad books.

Insomnia

The condition of sleeplessness is known as far back as history relates and is alluded to by writers in various terms: Chaucer's "endure without sleep and be in sorrow"; Charlotte Brontë's "restless pillow"; F. Scott Fitzgerald's "worst thing in the world is to try to sleep and not to."

The word insomnia had been in English from the seventeenth century, but not in everyday use. A poem by **Dante Gabriel Rossetti** brought the term into prominence. Rossetti, after a ten-year courtship, married and then suffered the death of his wife only two years later. His sleeplessness became critical and his poem "Insomnia" was published in 1881, only a month before his own death.

> *Thin are the night-skirts left behind*
> *By daybreak hours that onward creep,*
> *And thin, alas! the shred of sleep*
> *That wavers with the spirit's wind . . .*

These, and the disturbing (to an insomniac) lines that follow, brought the formal word insomnia into common recognition.

In the doghouse

Although many dogs live indoors with the rest of the family, a doghouse, or kennel, is a common enough feature of thousands of back yards. And sometimes even an indoors dog who is in disgrace may be sent out to the doghouse.

Steam locomotives had a small windowed alcove built above the engine tender to house the brakeman. Not the most comfortable place to live, it was sometimes known as a "doghouse."

But deep in the psyches of generations of theater patrons, cinemagoers and television audiences is the real doghouse of the Darling family in *Peter Pan*, created by **J.M. Barrie** and first introduced to the public in 1904. The family's dog Nana is indeed nanny to the Darling children, and their father Mr. Darling sometimes chained her up.

When the children are whisked away by Peter Pan to Neverland, Mr. Darling feels so contrite (Nana, chained at the time, couldn't save them) that he takes up residence inside Nana's kennel, vowing to stay there until the children return. In disgrace, he is literally "in the doghouse."

The situation became firmly entrenched in the vernacular to describe someone being punished (usually by the withdrawal of otherwise familiar comforts) and attempting to atone for sins committed.

(Mr. Darling didn't do things by halves—he remained in the doghouse during the working day. It was carried out and taxied to and from his office, people asked for his autograph, newspapers interviewed him and he was even invited to dinner—and expected to arrive inside the doghouse.)

In the lap of the gods

Beyond the control of normal earthly forces. It's no surprise that it's an English translation from a line in the *Iliad* of **Homer** and has been in use as a common expression since around 800 BC.

"Lap" is a convenient version of a Greek word that is closer to "knees," and has two connotations. A practice of the time is thought to be the placing of gifts on the knees or laps of statues of seated gods, in the hope that wishes would be granted. It was thought that a person's fate was controlled by the threads of life, spun and woven on the laps of gods, and could be twisted or even severed at any moment.

Iron curtain

At first the phrase had no political implications, being merely the name for the fireproof safety curtain found in traditional theaters. Used metaphorically, the term was seen in the diary of Lord Munster in 1819, and then again in H.G. Wells' *Food of the Gods* in 1904. But neither use had any connection with political isolation.

However, in 1914 **Queen Elisabeth** of the Belgians used the term specifically referring to a political barrier between Belgium where she lived, and Germany where her family lived. Born in Bavaria, a daughter of Duke Karl Theodor, she announced:

> *Between [Germany] and me there is now a bloody iron curtain which has descended forever.*

Used in its political sense, the term appeared again in English in Ethel Snowden's book *Through Bolshevik Russia* (1920): "We were behind the Iron Curtain at last." Nazi propaganda minister Joseph Goebbels used the expression several times before 1945.

In 1946 Winston Churchill, addressing Westminster College in Missouri, used the term Iron Curtain referring to the barrier of secrecy created by Communist countries after World War II.

The term had been in use for over a century and there was never a suggestion that Churchill claimed it as his own invention, but after the Missouri occasion it became closely associated with him.

I shall lose no time in reading it

Benjamin Disraeli's reply when receiving unsolicited books sent by authors anxious for his endorsement (quoted by Wilfred Meynell in *Disraeli*).

The faintly disturbing irony of the remark has an echo in the later (possibly apocryphal) practice attributed to Noel Coward, who when he found a performance indifferent but was obliged by protocol to visit backstage afterward, would exclaim: "Marvellous isn't the word!"

I smell a rat

Generally assumed to be derived from the notion of a cat smelling a nearby rat, but unable to see it. The term first turns up in 1601 in an anonymous play *Blurt, Master Constable*, published in London a year later: "Printed for Henry Rockytt, and are to be solde at the long shop under S. Mildreds Church in the Poultry, 1602."

The play is usually attributed to **Thomas Middleton** and **Thomas Dekker,** and during its action an old courtier called Curvetto exclaims: "Rat? Me! I smell a rat, I strike it dead!"

A more colorful use of the phrase arose when the Irish Parliament was enlivened during the period 1777–1801 by speeches from MP **Sir Boyle Roche**.

Among his more convoluted policy statements:

> *It would surely be better, Mr. Speaker, to give up not only a part, but, if necessary, even the whole, of our Constitution to preserve the remainder!*

One of his much talked about mixed metaphors contained the fragment that helped propel the rat into permanent English usage:

> *Mr. Speaker, I smell a rat; I see him forming in the air and darkening the sky but I'll nip him in the bud.'*

It goes with the territory

In **Arthur Miller**'s 1949 play *Death of a Salesman* the lead character Willy Loman has a neighbor named Charley. Willy is not notably successful in his work, but Charley is very successful in his. And while there is a certain level of friendship between them, there is also envy on Willy's side and compassion on Charley's. He feels Willy would be better off in some other job, and he tells Willy's son Biff:

> *A salesman is got to dream, boy. It comes with the territory.*

Lifted out of the play, the expression fitted many other situations and was used accordingly, though since 1949 popular usage has gradually turned "comes" into "goes."

It's a great life if you don't weaken

The first known use of the expression is in *Mr Standfast* (1919) by **John Buchan**. The character of Mr. Brand explains that after a demanding walk he planned to make around the lochs, he would then go back to work in Glasgow. Brand's companion Gresson remarks:

> *It's a great life if you don't weaken.*

It's all part of life's rich pageant

British writer, broadcaster, panellist, journalist, reviewer, and monologist **Arthur Marshall** sometimes performed comedy skits based in the confined world of all-girls' schools. His 1937 recording of a monologue called "The Games Mistress" included the line:

> *What, knocked a tooth out? Never mind, dear, laugh it off, laugh it off; it's all part of life's rich pageant!*

In later years Peter Sellers, as Inspector Clouseau in the movie *Shot in the Dark*, stuck to Marshall's original wording, but custom and usage have sometimes varied "pageant" with "tapestry," "fabric," or "pattern."

It seemed like a good idea at the time

In 1931 a collection of short stories by **John Monk Saunders** was gathered into his book *Single Lady* about a group of World War I pilots visiting Paris and Lisbon for recreation. Soon after, the book became the basis of the movie *The Last Flight*, for which Saunders also wrote the screenplay.

During the story the free-spirited character of Nikki (believed to be based on Saunders' wife Fay Wray) is asked why she painted her toenails red, and she replied that it "seemed like a good idea at the time."

Later her line is revisited to sombre effect when one of the men is seriously gored after jumping into a Portuguese bullring. When reporters ask his friends why he did such a thing, the character of Cary thinks for a moment and then repeats Nikki's line:

It seemed like a good idea at the time.

(British actor Archie Leach appeared in a Broadway stage version of the story, and in the character of Cary spoke the line in question. After that, he adopted the character's name for himself, and became Cary Grant.)

It's the thought that counts

Repeated countless times as an excuse for inadequate or inappropriate gifts, this expression first surfaced in **Rosamond Lehmann**'s 1936 novel *The Weather in the Streets*. The rather pretentious Mrs. Curtis is discussing with her two daughters a suitable wedding present for Dolly Martin, who is about to marry a missionary in China. Somewhat doubtfully they ponder whether a cake-basket or cruet set would be suitable at a mission house in China, but are assured by Mrs. Curtis that "it's the thought that counts."

It was a dark and stormy night

It is the opening line from the novel *Paul Clifford* by acclaimed nineteenth-century MP and prolific writer Lord **Edward Bulwer-Lytton**.

It was a dark and stormy night; the rain fell in torrents, except at occasional intervals, when it was checked by a violent gust of wind which swept up the streets (for it is in London that our

*scene lies), rattling along the housetops, and fiercely agitating
the scanty flame of the lamps that struggled against the
darkness.*

Lord Bulwer-Lytton's writing might have faded into obscurity
but for a whim of cartoonist Charles Schultz. Starting in 1965,
Schultz's character—the engaging dog Snoopy (in "Peanuts")—
frequently sat on the roof of his kennel hammering out yet another
novel on his toy typewriter and always beginning with "It was a
dark and stormy night . . . "

The phrase has become associated with overwriting, and
became the focus of the annual Bulwer-Lytton Fiction Contest
sponsored by the English Department of San Jose State University,
in which the worst and most extreme examples of "dark and
stormy night" writing are recognized.

As reported by Associated Press, the 2008 winner David
McKenzie wrote:

> *Folks say that if you listen real close at the height of the full
> moon, when the wind is blowin' off Nantucket Sound from
> the nor'east and the dogs are howlin' for no earthly reason,
> you can hear the awful screams of the crew of the Ellie May, a
> sturdy whaler captained by John McTavish; for it was on just
> such a night when the rum was flowin' and Davey Jones be
> damned, Big John brought his men on deck for the first of
> several screaming contests.*

See also **(The) great unwashed**; **Purple prose**

Ivory tower

Mentions of ivory in the Bible refer to a house, and to a woman's
neck, so neither of those is the origin of the term "ivory tower" as
we use it now. Living in an ivory tower refers to people of position

who are aloof from common life and may be able to observe it without being affected by it.

That frame of reference came to light in 1837 in the work of French poet **Charles Augustin Saint-Beuve**. In his poem "Thoughts of August," the ivory tower image served as a critical comment on the lifestyle of poet Alfred de Vigny, whom Saint-Beuve regarded as too concerned with romanticism. The tower made of ivory formed a charmed retreat in which a poet isolated himself from society, not necessarily to the advantage of his poetry.

The term still carries that pejorative connotation, indicating a failure to connect with the everyday world and a perceived condescension on the part of the tower dweller.

I want to be alone

The line was written by a man, although the process began with Austrian author Vicki Baum, who, after she had worked as a chambermaid, wrote *People in a Hotel* published in 1929. The book became a successful play first in Berlin, and then New York.

In the play's English translation the ageing ballerina Grusinskaya speaks the line, "But I wish to be alone." For the famous 1932 movie version *Grand Hotel*, in which Greta Garbo played Grusinskaya, screenwriter **William A. Drake** modified the line to: "I want to be alone."

Spoken in Garbo's distinctive husky voice the line went into history, but with some confusion. Inability to recognize the difference between a character speaking lines from a script, and the actor playing the role, caused the saying to become attached to Garbo herself.

For the rest of her life she denied having said she wanted to be alone. There is a widespread belief (but little real evidence) that she explained the confusion by having once said that she, Garbo, wanted to be *let* alone.

Jack of all trades

In medieval times a jack was just an ordinary man, and one who traveled around able to turn his hand to anything (i.e., "of all trades"), which wasn't necessarily a liability. In 1618 **Geffray Mynshal** wrote *Essays and Characters of a Prison* and gave the first exposure to:

> *Some broken citizen who hath plaid Jack-of-all-trades.*

The term now sometimes carries an aura of disapproval—perhaps the Jack in question knows a little about a lot, but not a useful amount about any one thing.

Jumbo

Long before jumbo shrimps, mushrooms, and jets, London welcomed a huge elephant bought from the Paris zoo. He had been born in Africa in 1861 then taken to France. The London zoo bought him in 1865 and he became enormously popular—and enormous.

His **keeper** gave him the name Jumbo. The word wasn't new; it could have been derived from the term mumbo-jumbo, which had been heard in Britain since the eighteenth century, and had acquired the meaning of mysterious (or nonsensical) verbiage.

Amidst great controversy, Jumbo was sold to American showman P.T. Barnum in 1882, and the huge elephant became an A-list celebrity in the U.S. Advertisers rushed to feature him in posters and packages helping sell everything from baking powder to laxative (one advertisement showed Jumbo feeding the Castoria laxative to a baby elephant).

His name caused much discussion. Was it simply an African word for elephant? Could it be a version of the Swahili word for chief (which seems likely)? Or hello (which doesn't)? Barnum, unimpressed by semantics, made energetically sure that whatever its origin, the word Jumbo meant big. By the time Jumbo died in a train accident three years after he arrived in America, his name was in the English language to stay.

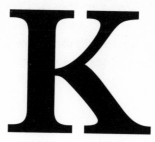

Keeping up with the Joneses

This expression could have had us keeping up with the Smiths but was changed by its creator at the last minute.

In 1913 American cartoonist **Arthur Momand** realized that in his neighborhood people seemed over-conscious of conspicuous prosperity, and a certain sense of competition prevailed. He devised a comic-strip that showed characters living up to—or beyond— their means, in order to keep pace with a community that appeared to be more wealthy than it actually was.

He planned to name the cartoon strip "Keeping Up with the Smiths," but after consideration changed the family's name to Jones because it flowed better. The cartoon strip ran for twenty-eight years across the U.S.

Kettle of fish

In earlier times, kettle meant a large deep vessel—and an oval-shaped kind evolved especially for cooking fish. The earliest known reference in print comes from **Thomas Newte** in *A tour of England and Scotland in 1785* (published in 1791).

Mr. Newte described a Scottish custom whereby landed gentry held a gathering by a river bank and amid a garden-party-type atmosphere, lit a fire and cooked freshly caught salmon in an appropriate vessel. The gathering took on the name of the cooking vessel and became known as "a kettle of fish."

In later centuries the term developed two separate meanings: it can refer to (a) an entirely new subject (a *different* kettle of fish), or (b) a difficult situation (a *pretty* kettle of fish).

King Kong

Edgar Wallace wrote 175 novels and 24 plays. Over one hundred movies have been based on his stories. But it would be fair to say that people who have never heard of Wallace, or any of the books or plays he authored, would undoubtedly recognize the name King Kong.

Wallace and **Draycott Dell** came up with the name for their fictional giant ape, first heard of in their short story about him in 1933.

Knee high to a grasshopper

Referring usually to those who are short, small, or very young, the term has seen many variations. They all arise from a short person being compared to a toad. The American newspaper *Portsmouth Oracle* carried the first known printed version of this term in 1814:

As Farmer Joe would say, knee high to a toad.

Since then, the toad has been replaced by a frog, a mosquito, a splinter, a duck, a bumble bee and, eventually, a grasshopper, which outlived all the others.

Knock off (work)

There is a belief—for which no substantial evidence exists—that the expression arose in ancient times when some seagoing vessels had teams of oarsmen whose rhythm was maintained by a leader beating a drum. The signal for a work break, or change of shift, was a special knock that the rowers recognized.

That story may not be accurate, but the expression knock off, referring to work or activity, is certainly not new. It first occurs in a novel by British/American novelist **William Clark Russell**, and although Russell was also a seaman, and the novel *An Ocean Tragedy* (1881) has a marine setting, it has nothing to do with rowing or oars. The men attempt to salvage supplies from a wrecked vessel:

> *Then they waded back to us and the four of us heaved together, and in this way, as I have said, we saved an abundance of useful things.*
> *There was plenty yet to come at, but we were forced to knock off through sheer fatigue.*

Know the ropes

The term refers to a person having knowledge of a particular system. It did not necessarily arise among sailing ship crews, though its first known occurrence in print does concern a sea captain. In *Two Years Before the Mast* by **Richard H. Dana** (1840):

> *The captain, who had been on the coast before and "knew the ropes," took the steering oar.*

Dana's use of quotation marks around the expression indicates that it was known before 1840, but his book put the term into the public arena and it has been commonly used ever since.

(To) know what's what

Sometimes said of society matrons who understand perfect etiquette and the science of dinner-table seating. Or pundits who know political gossip and the status of the financial market. The term first appears in *Hudibras* by **Samuel Butler** (1663):

He knew what's what, and that's as high
As metaphysic wit can fly.

(Memorably quoted by Mae West when a lifejacket was named after her:

"I've been in Who's Who *and I know what's what, but this is the first time I've been in a dictionary."*)

(The) Lady with the Lamp

In November 1854, only a few months after the start of the Crimean War, Florence Nightingale arrived in the Constantinople district of Scutari with thirty-eight nurses. To begin with, the doctors were resistant to the women's presence but they soon proved themselves invaluable.

Besides acting as head nurse, Florence also wrote letters home on behalf of injured soldiers, helped them with their pay and arranged for reading material. Eventually, she was treated with enormous respect. She was unswerving in her care of the wounded and often remained with them long after the rest of the hospital staff had gone to bed.

She was first connected with a lamp in a report from **John Cameron Macdonald** in *The Times*:

> *She is a 'ministering angel' without any exaggeration in these hospitals, and as her slender form glides quietly along each corridor . . . she may be observed alone, with a little lamp in her hand, making her solitary rounds.*

The war ended in 1857 and Florence returned to England to considerable fame and a long campaign to upgrade the qualities of and respect for the nursing profession. By then several drawings of her had been published, showing her night-time tours holding a lamp.

That same year, American poet **Henry Wadsworth Longfellow**'s poem *Santa Filomena* was published in the Atlantic Monthly. St. Philomena is thought to have been a thirteen-year-old medieval Greek princess who on declining to marry the Emperor of Rome was tortured, saved by angels, and died a martyr. There is no connection at all between Florence Nightingale and Philomena, who in her thirteen troubled years was never known to have nursed soldiers. But in spite of Longfellow's poem being named for Philomena, it was widely perceived as having been inspired by the reports of Florence Nightingale.

> *The wounded from the battle-plain,*
> *In dreary hospitals of pain,*
> *The cheerless corridors,*
> *The cold and stony floors.*
>
> *Lo! in that house of misery*
> *A lady with a lamp I see*
> *Pass through the glimmering gloom,*
> *And flit from room to room.*

The legend of the Lady with the Lamp was set for all time.

(Strangely, for one so associated with curing the sick, after her return to London from Turkey, Florence Nightingale went to bed and stayed there for fifty years!)

Lame duck

In 1761 the Earl of Orford, Horace Walpole, wrote to the British Envoy in Tuscany, Sir Horace Mann, saying:

> *How Scipio would have stared if he had been told that he*
> *must not demolish Carthage, as it would ruin several*

aldermen who had money in the Punic actions! Apropos –
do you know what a Bull, a Bear and a Lame Duck are?
Nay, nor I either—I am only certain they are neither
animal nor fowl!

This indicated that the expressions, later famous in the financial sector, were being used at the time, even if Walpole didn't understand them apart from recognizing a vague connection with people who had money invested.

The usage was clarified a decade later when David Garrick's play *Foote's Maid of Bath* made its debut (1771). In the Prologue, Garrick referred to financiers who frequented Exchange Alley (the Stock Exchange) and classified them as:

. . . gaming fools are doves, knaves are rooks, Change-Alley
bankrupts waddle out lame ducks.

The term went into use referring to brokers who defaulted on debts, and remained in use to describe those with financial problems, but grew to include anyone deemed ineffectual. When the "lame duck" term traveled to America it assumed the feathers of politics and waddled into the arena of elected officials whose term of office was nearing an end.

(As) large as life (and twice as natural)

Pre-photography, portraits were painted, and while head and shoulders was the norm, the grand and the wealthy were depicted full length—and as large as life. Canadian historian, agriculturalist and humorist **Thomas Haliburton** in *The Clockmaker* (1837) extended the image and made a subtle put-down of it:

He marched up and down afore the street door like a
peacock—as large as life and twice as natural!

More than sixty years later, Lewis Carroll picked up the idea and has the King's messenger say it about Alice.

(The) last laugh

The person with the last laugh is the one who appeared initially to be failing in some way, but ultimately is proven correct and successful. The modern version is a variation on "Hee laugheth best that laugheth to the end," found in *The Christmas Prince* (anon, 1607) and later in Vanburgh's *Country House* (1715).

There is a version in German, "Wer zuletzt lacht, lacht am besten" (He who laughs last, laughs best), and a character of Sir Walter Scott's (in *Peveril of the Peak,* 1822) refers to the old French proverb: "Rira bien, qui rira le dernier" (He laughs best who laughs last).

The abbreviated English version came into popular usage during 1937 as a result of songwriters George and **Ira Gershwin** and their amusing song "They All Laughed" with its refrain, 'Who's got the last laugh now?" Gershwin's lyrics refer to historical figures whose theories were mocked (Christopher Columbus, Marconi, the Wright Brothers) but who eventually had the last laugh.

It was composed for the 1937 movie *Shall We Dance* and sung by Ginger Rogers, who was later joined by Fred Astaire for a spectacular dance routine built around the song. Astaire later sang the song himself many times, and subsequent recordings by Frank Sinatra, Chet Baker, Ella Fitzgerald, Louis Armstrong, and André Previn helped the term achieve wider recognition.

Last, loneliest, loveliest

From *Song of the Cities*, in which **Rudyard Kipling** gave poetic impressions of his 1891 visits to Bombay, Calcutta, Madras, Rangoon, Singapore, Hong Kong, Halifax, Quebec, Montreal,

Victoria, Cape Town, Melbourne, Sydney, Brisbane, and Hobart, finishing at Auckland:

> *Last, loneliest, loveliest, exquisite, apart—*
> *On us, on us the unswerving season smiles,*
> *Who wonder 'mid our fern why men depart*
> *To seek the Happy Isles!*

Laugh on the other side of one's face

The basic idea (the reaction to unwelcome contrary news) has been around for several centuries, surfacing in Italian (Torriana) and French (Molière), usually as laugh "on the other side of one's mouth."

French author Alain-René Lesage used the mouth version in *Histoire de Gil Blas de Santillane* in 1715 and that was how it arrived in English in the 1809 translation by Benjamin Malkin:

> *We were made to laugh on the other side of our mouth by an unforeseen circumstance.*

By 1837 when **Thomas Carlyle** wrote his fictional *Diamond Necklace* (based on an incident concerning Marie Antoinette), he had moved from the mouth to the face:

> *Thou laughest there; by-and-by thou wilt laugh on the wrong side of thy face.*

From there, the wrong side gradually became the other side.

(A) legend in his own lunchtime (or lunch hour)

In 1976 a book called *Testkill* was published in Britain, co-written by well-known cricket captain Ted Dexter, with an experienced sports editor called Clifford Makins, who was known among his colleagues for his *bon vivant* lifestyle and gravitation toward wine bars.

Reviewing the book in the *Observer* on June 20, 1976, journalist **Christopher Wordsworth** commented that Makins was "a legend in his own lunchtime."

Wordsworth's dig was clearly a play on "legend in one's own lifetime," first seen in Lytton Strachey's description of Florence Nightingale in *Eminent Victorians* (1918):

> She was a legend in her lifetime, and she knew it.

Custom and usage added the word "own" in later years, presumably for greater emphasis.

Let sleeping dogs lie

In the early 1300s the French were saying "N'esveillez pas lou chien qui dort" (Wake not the sleeping dog). It drifted toward **Geoffrey Chaucer** some years later (*Troilus and Criseyde*, c.1374) and the English language was enriched with

> It is nought good a slepyng hound to wake.

Over centuries, the advice gradually shifted its focus from negative to positive, and by 1824 in *Redgauntlet* **Sir Walter Scott** phrased it in the familiar modern form. The character of Wandering Willie (who likes to whistle Corelli sonata melodies) is asked whether the laird has ever been a soldier. He replies:

> I'se warrant him a soger. But take my advice and speer as little about him as he does about you. Best to let sleeping dogs lie.

Let them eat cake

The line is referred to as an already familiar expression in **Jean-Jacques Rousseau**'s *Confessions* written between 1766 and 1770. He wrote "brioche," which is usually a bun-shaped, slightly sweet, soft pastry, though this has been interpreted in English as "cake."

The expression was known long before Rousseau's *Confessions*—and he had written that particular section before Marie Antoinette even arrived in France. After Rousseau, other people quoted the line and it became a common saying.

Marie Antoinette could quite possibly have heard the phrase after she'd arrived in France (1770), and there is doubt that she ever said it. But if she did, she was quoting Rousseau.

(A) license to print money

By 1955 television in Britain was starting to develop from being a service into a business. In 1957 a commercial television company opened in Scotland, with **Roy Thomson** (later Lord) as CEO. In *Roy Thomson of Fleet Street* biographer Russell Braddon highlighted Thomson's description of a commercial television network as "a license to print money."

The term quickly went into the vernacular referring to any organization making a sure profit.

(A) lick and a promise

Familiar enough as a reference to doing something in a hurry and fairly inadequately, but with the intention of completing the job later. The meaning hasn't changed since the 1812 *Critical Review of the Annals of Literature* makes a snide remark about nurses delivering only "a lick and a promise" when feeding babies.

But in *The Modern Cook* (1845), **Elizabeth Acton** went out on a limb and nailed the expression down for all future use when she advised her readers:

> *You ought not to do anything by halves. What you do, do well. If you clean, clean thoroughly, having nothing to do with the "slut's wipe," and the "lick and a promise."*

Lie back and think of England

The line and its various versions ("close your eyes and . . . " or " . . . and think of the Empire") have absolutely no verifiable provenance. The remark was purportedly advice given by Lady Hillingdon to young women apprehensive about sexual activity. The source is said to be her 1912 diary.

But there is absolutely no proof (and even the name varies, from Hillingdon to Hillingham). There was a genuine baroness, Lady Hillingdon (1857–1940), but neither her diary nor any other statement of advice from her on sexual matters has ever been seen.

Other sources claim that Mrs. Stanley Baldwin thought "of the Empire," but nobody knows exactly who first said what, or when, but it has become too popular an expression to be laid aside for lack of provenance.

Life begins at forty

In 1932 American psychologist and writer **Walter B. Pitkin** created the phrase as the title of his book on the subject.

Pitkin opined that in previous eras the American male was worn out at forty. From seventeen to twenty-four were the years of apprenticeship to social life. Then from twenty-four to forty the responsibilities of employment, home and family left no energy for anything else in the years following. Pitkin was himself fifty-four when he wrote the book, and pointed out that in view of new standards of living, better technology, and increased opportunities for leisure, life after forty could become enjoyable, productive, profitable, and exciting.

Life Begins at Forty was the bestselling nonfiction book in America for 1933, and its title became a byword for a new, more positive attitude to aging.

In successive decades, Pitkin's argument that improved living conditions would extend our active years proved to be true, and the forty of his original estimate was occasionally informally upped to fifty, or even sixty.

(Pitkin's expression became extremely popular as the title of a song Sophie Tucker recorded in 1936 when she was actually fifty-two (Parlophone F-621), and sang for the next twenty years.)

Like a bear with a sore head

The afflicted bear has at times been called "cross" or just "sulky," but maritime novelist Captain **Frederick Marryat** in *Kings Own* (1830) settled for:

As savage as a bear with a sore head.

Like a house on fire

Indicating great speed or the rapid progress of intimate understanding, the term first appeared in English in the book *A History of New York, from the Beginning of the World to the End of the Dutch Dynasty* by **Washington Irving** (as Diedrich Knickerbocker) in 1809, when writing of a nation or a community:

In proportion does it rise in grandeur—and even when sinking under calamity, makes, like a house on fire, a more glorious display than ever it did in the fairest period of its prosperity.

Like it or lump it

In earlier times the word lump carried a meaning of sulking, possibly as a result of having to swallow something disagreeable. Although known beforehand, the expression "like it or lump it" was first set before a wide audience by **Bernard Blackmantle** in *The Punster's Pocket Book* (1826).

The term appears here as an awful pun in a little dialogue between a hostess and an unfavored guest, who is handed an unsweetened cup of tea. The guest explains that this is not to her taste, upon which she is handed a bowl of sugar cubes with the line:

Well, ma'am, if you do not like it, you may lump it.

American author John Neal in *Down Easters* (1833) used the term in a more straightforward way:

Bear it like a man Mr. Potipher . . . git naite-ralized right away, and let 'em lump it if they don't like it, an' squirm their hides off; that's none o' your look out is it?

Little grey cells

The term "grey matter" has long been found in genuine medical writings, referring to the cortex of the brain—the part responsible for processing information. The reason why it is referred to as grey matter even in a clinical context is quite simple—when viewed it does literally look grey.

The scientific name for grey matter is cinera, and it is made up of neutrons—otherwise known as cells.

In 1920 **Agatha Christie** invented a Belgian detective named Hercule Poirot, whose command of English, though informative, was occasionally slightly eccentric. Bypassing cinera, or neutrons, or even grey matter, M. Poirot frequently acknowledged that his "little grey cells" were what led him to conclude who had done the murder.

Agatha Christie's books have sold over two billion copies, of which thirty-nine titles and fifty-one short stories featured Poirot, plus nine movies, five TV specials, and two television series. One result has been that Dame Agatha single-handedly caused the term grey matter to be virtually sidelined in popular usage for the brain, while the phrase little grey cells has become the more commonly used term for intelligence, reasoning, and the processing of information.

Live fast, die young, and leave a beautiful corpse

The expression was first seen in 1947 in the novel *Knock on Any Door* by American writer **Willard Motley**, about a law-breaker whose life's end was inevitable. The novel became a movie of the same name in 1949, and actor John Derek spoke the line:

> *Live fast, die young, and leave a beautiful corpse.*

In 1958 the line itself became the title of another movie. And in later years Willard Motley's image was applied to reality, summing up in macabre fashion the tragic lives and early deaths of James Dean, Marilyn Monroe, Kurt Cobain, Marc Bolan, Princess Diana, Janis Joplin, James Morrison, River Phoenix, Buddy Holly, Freddie Mercury, and Heath Ledger.

Lock, stock, and barrel

Meaning "everything," and referring to the sum of parts of a musket, the expression surfaced in 1838 when John Gibson Lockhart's *Life of **Sir Walter Scott*** included a letter of Scott's written in 1817, using the phrase:

> *Like the High-landman's gun she wants stock, lock and barrel to put her into repair.*

Over time, the lock and the stock became reversed.

Lock the stable (or barn) door after the horse is stolen (or has bolted)

The basic idea is found in *Asinaria* by Plautus (c. 200 BC):

Ne post tempus praedae praesidium parem.

In English, the concept arrived with **John Gower**'s *Confessio Amantis* (1390):

Whan the grete Stiede Is stole, thanne he taketh hiede,
And makth the stable dore fast.

Over time the horse was variously stolen, lost or simply broke loose, but eventually settled into having bolted.

Long hot summer

Some of the elements in William Faulkner's 1940 book *The Hamlet* became the basis of a famous movie, but the movie's simple evocative title was the result of a small alteration of Faulkner's original. The movie rights for *The Hamlet* were bought in 1955 and it was quickly decided that its title had to change to avoid confusion with the other Hamlet. Screenwriters **Irving Ravetch** and **Harriet Frank** took one section of Faulkner's book, entitled "The Long Summer," and added the word hot.

With its magnetic teaming of Paul Newman and Joanne Woodward, the 1958 movie was received with critical acclaim and commercial success, and its title went into the vernacular.

Publishers Signet Books reissued Faulkner's original story, but now with the movie's title. Following the movie came a TV series in 1965, and a remake TV series in 1985.

Loose cannon

In practice, a loose cannon was one inadequately lashed in place on the deck of a ship, which caused havoc by rolling dangerously and unpredictably. The first known image of an unlashed rolling cannon occurs (in French) in Victor Hugo's 1874 novel *Ninety Three*. But within a year English writer **Henry Kingsley** in his book *Number Seventeen* (1875) narrowed the expression down into the form we now know it—but again in its literal sense:

> *At once, of course, the ship was in the trough of the sea, a more fearfully dangerous engine of destruction than Mr. Victor Hugo's celebrated loose cannon.*

It was another decade before the term became metaphorical—referring to an unpredictable or unreliable person or situation—when the Texas newspaper *Galveston Daily News* referred to the potential influence of the African-American vote as "a loose cannon."

Lounge lizard

A "lounge lizard" is, or was, a well-dressed man of good appearance and sleek manners, very much at home in circumstances where there are also unattached women. His actual employment may be vague and his social motives suspect.

The term was in use in America in the early 1920s. It was brought to public attention in 1923 when *The Washington Post* reported that an Anti-Flirt Club had been organized in Washington, DC. Its president was **Miss Alice Reighly** and the club was composed of "young women and girls who have been embarrassed by men in automobiles and on street corners."

On February 18, 1923 the *Post* published the code of guidance for members of the Anti-Flirt Club. Besides advising members against smiling at strangers, getting too close to elderly men taking a "fatherly" interest, and accepting rides from flirtatious motorists, the code included:

> *Don't fall for the slick, dandified cake eater—the unpolished gold of a real man is worth more than the gloss of a lounge lizard.*

American researcher Joe Manning ascertained that Miss Reighly died, unmarried, at eighty-one.

Lunatic fringe

President Theodore Roosevelt's opinion of the Progressive Party in 1913:

> *Every reform movement has a lunatic fringe.*

(The) lunatics have taken over the asylum

In the earliest days of cinema, neither the actors' nor the director's names were displayed or advertised. That anonymity gradually gave way to the star system, but there was still a feeling at the administration level that actors and directors were just staff.

In 1918, three of the greatest stars—Charlie Chaplin, Mary Pickford, and Douglas Fairbanks, together with director W.D. Griffith—founded a movie studio of their own to be called United Artists. When this news reached the head of Metro Pictures **Richard Rowland**, his reaction was: "The lunatics have taken over the asylum."

(Metro Pictures later teamed with Samuel Goldwyn and Louis Mayer, became MGM, and eventually bought United Artists.)

British Prime Minister David Lloyd George was of a similar opinion, albeit on a grander scale: "The world is becoming like a lunatic asylum run by the lunatics."

Mad as a hatter

Originally the expression is believed to have been "mad as an adder," meaning "angry as a snake." However, in the Canadian writer **Thomas Haliburton**'s *Clockmaker* serial (1836), the adder became a hatter and mad could mean loopy as well as angry.

By then it was known that mercurous nitrate caused mental instability among hatters, who used the substance in brushing fur pelts. But contrary to perception, the character in Lewis Carroll's *Alice in Wonderland* (1865) is not actually named the Mad Hatter.

Make a hash of it

Most uses of the word hash derive from the French "hacher"—to cut up (e.g., the # key, which resembles "cross-hatching" as practised by draughtsmen). By 1662 in English it had come to mean chopped up foods. **Samuel Pepys** recorded:

> *After oysters, I had at first course, a hash of rabbits, a lamb, and a rare chine [backbone] of beef.*

(This was followed by a roasted fowl, a tart, then fruit and cheese. Pepys observed, "My dinner was noble and enough.")

By association with chopping and mixing, hash came to refer to any job or project which has collapsed into mess and disorganization.

ke haste slowly

When Emperor Augustus ruled Rome, from 27 BC, one of his favorite maxims was "Festina lente" (make haste slowly). The term first came into English through **Geoffrey Chaucer** in *Troilus and Criseyde* (c.1385):

> *He hasteth wel that wisly kan [knows how to] abyde.*

Making a mountain out of a molehill

The Greek satirist Lucian (AD 120–200) in his work *Ode to a Fly* reflects on the concept of magnifying a small problem out of all proportion to its actual size. Other languages have their own versions: To make an elephant (or a stallion) out of a mosquito, to make a camel out of a flea, or to make an ox out of a fly.

Thomas Becon was chaplain to Archbishop Cranmer, and around 1563 his "Catechism" brought the matter into English:

> *They make of a fly an elephant and of a mole-hill a mountain; making such a stir in the house as though heaven and earth should go together.*

Male bonding

The concept may have existed ever since the invention of cricket, football or bar-rooms. But in his book *Men in Groups* (1969) American anthropologist **Lionel Tiger** analyzed the particular way in which men befriend each other, establish camaraderie, and share activities and time together, leading to a feeling of mutual comfort.

The phrase he created—male bonding—went into common use almost immediately.

Many happy returns

In 1776, Miss Hester Mundy married Sir Roger Newdigate. The novelist George Eliot lived nearby, and the character of the aristocratic lady in Eliot's *Mr Gilfil's Love Story* is modeled on George Eliot's acquaintanceship with Hester, Lady Newdigate. When Hester died, she was commemorated by a beautiful white marble urn that still stands in Harefield Church.

Lady Newdigate's other claim to fame is that she was the first person known to use the expression "Many happy returns." In 1789 Hester was away from her home, and on Sir Roger's birthday she wrote to him:

> *I am just come from Church my dear love, and at the Altar have implored for Blessings on your head—and for many happy returns of this day . . .*

The same term appeared in another of her letters on their wedding anniversary, indicating an annual celebration for various notable occasions. But during the nineteenth century the application of the expression narrowed to birthdays alone.

Marches to a different drum

The contemporary usage is a condensed version of a thought from American writer **Henry David Thoreau**. As an exercise in self-reliance, he had spent two years living in a rustic cabin in the woods. His resultant work *Walden; or, Life in the Woods* was published in 1845 and admired as a work of philosophical non-fiction.

Thoreau's desire was to experiment with simple living and to focus on self-sufficiency. This period of self-imposed rural solitude was considered somewhat eccentric by his acquaintances, but in Chapter 18 he outlined a relevant point of view:

If a man does not keep pace with his companions, perhaps it is because he hears a different drummer. Let him step to the music which he hears, however measured or far away.

The sentiment became widely quoted, and over time was paraphrased and contracted into various shorter versions, though the basic image remained the same.

(The) medium is the message

Although there are conflicting reports as to when he actually originated the term, there is no doubt that Canadian commentator on communications **Marshall McLuhan** was creator of the phrase. One version has him voicing the idea at an academic cocktail party before including it in a lecture in 1958.

McLuhan was a Professor in the University of Toronto's Centre for Culture and Technology, and his most famous expression reached print in his 1959–60 report *Project on Understanding the New Media* written for the United States Department of Health, Education and Welfare. In a radio interview he summarized the concept as:

> *The dominant fact in any art form is the medium being employed.*

In 1967, when his original remark had become known internationally, McLuhan (perhaps with tongue in cheek) co-authored *The Medium Is the Massage* with Quentin Fiore and Jerome Agel.

Metrosexual

In the early 1990s a concept of maleness emerged that did not confine itself to football, beer, and bawd. The new type of man was politely perceived as having a heightened aesthetic sense. In 1994, writing in the *Independent*, journalist **Mark Simpson** in his article "Here Come the Mirror Men" invented a term to describe this new development:

> *Metrosexual man, the single young man with a high disposable income, living or working in the city (because that's where all the best shops are), is perhaps the most promising consumer market of the decade. In the Eighties he was only to be found inside fashion magazines such as GQ, in television advertisements for Levi's jeans or in gay bars. In the Nineties, he's everywhere and he's going shopping . . . A metrosexual is a clotheshorse wrapped around a dandy fused with a narcissist. Like soccer star David Beckham, who has been known to paint his fingernails.*

Mark Simpson's word survives as the first description of the quiet social phenomenon now known as the metrosexual.

Middle Earth

From 1936 on, **J.R.R. Tolkien** certainly made the term famous, and he invented the setting, the language, the characters, and the stories. But the name had been around a long time before that. The term middle earth dates back to ancient Scandinavian mythology, perceived of as a mystic place somewhere between heaven and hell.

By the eighth century, an English version of the name existed—*middangeard*—and is mentioned in one of the oldest pieces of English writing, *Beowulf*, a work with which Tolkien as a professor of Anglo-Saxon studies was very familiar.

Shakespeare, too, mentions it in *The Merry Wives of Windsor* when someone speaking of Falstaff says, "Smell a man of middle-earth," implying that it was not at that time seen as a very desirable place.

So although the name already had an impressive pedigree, it was

Tolkien who gave it a whole new life in the popular imagination.

Midnight cowboy

The term "midnight cowboy" has no distinct definition, but various strong if ill-defined connotations of shady sex. Real cowboys ride by day; midnight cowboys "ride" late at night, probably requiring payment, and perhaps "on top."

While watching rehearsals of his own play *A Streetcar Named Desire* in 1948, **Tennessee Williams** saw Marlon Brando playing Stanley Kowalski. Brando biographer Darwin Porter reports that Williams described Brando as an "earthy proletarian male," and a "regular midnight cowboy."

Williams' friend James Leo Herlihy liked the latter phrase, remembered it and later used it as the title of his 1965 novel, which became an Oscar-winning film (1969).

(The) Mile-High Club

An experienced daredevil American aviator, **Lawrence Sperry**, invented an early prototype of the autopilot (his father was co-inventor of the gyro-compass). In 1916, Lawrence Sperry was giving flying lessons to a **Mrs. Waldo Polk**. They were flying together in a biplane over the district of Babylon near New York when Sperry apparently decided to give the newly invented autopilot a rather stringent test. Mrs. Polk agreed, and Sperry set the plane onto auto before abandoning the controls in favor of less mechanical activities.

Something went wrong and the small plane crashed into a bay below (Sperry later mentioned having bumped a lever with a knee when his hands were busy elsewhere). Duck hunters rescued the two passengers—both naked. The shock of crash-landing, they explained, had shaken their clothes off, which some newspapers obligingly reported (though perhaps with tongue in cheek).

One paper was less coy. Rhiannon Guy's book *Travellers' Companion* recounts that the headline in the *New York Daily Mirror* read:

> *Aerial Petting—Ends in Wetting.*

Lawrence Sperry and Mrs. Polk did not create the term "Mile-High Club," and few would have had the opportunity to do so before 1916. But it's fair to say that their widely publicized amorous pleasures were an inspiration to their adventurous imitators, through whose highjinks (literally) the name evolved.

Mince your words

Usually expressed as *not* mincing your words. It is commonly acknowledged that less tender cuts of meat can only be made more palatable if they are finely minced. Matters that demand honesty but have not been couched in gentler terms could be compared to meat which hasn't been minced.

This analogy between cheap meat and blunt words was not lost on the Rt. Reverend **Joseph Hall,** Bishop of Norwich, the first known user of the mince metaphor. In 1649, when referring to messages from God in his *Resolutions and Decisions of Divers Practicall cases of Conscience*, he wrote that:

> *It is not for an herald of heaven to be out of countenance, or to mince aught.*

(The) moment of truth

A Spanish term—*hora de la verdad*—used in bullfighting. In theory it refers to the decisive moment in the battle in which the fate of the bull and the fighter is determined: who will win and who will die?

(This is, of course, illusory since the bull *always* dies, either in the fight, or afterward because he killed the matador.)

The term came into English in 1932 in **Ernest Hemingway**'s *Death in the Afternoon.*

Monarch of all I survey

The character of Robinson Crusoe (inspired by the real-life adventures of Alexander Selkirk) was written about in prose by Daniel Defoe in 1718.

William Cowper followed in 1782 with "Verses Supposed to be Written by Alexander Selkirk" (1782), which began with the lines:

> *I am monarch of all I survey,*
> *My right there is none to dispute . . .*

Mondegreen

Lyrics have been misheard as long as there have been songs. There was the child puzzled by a hymn about "Gladly, the Cross-eyed Bear," or the people who sang "My Body Lies Over the Ocean" and followed it up with "God Rest Ye Married Gentlemen."

Until 1954 this phenomenon didn't have a name. Then writer **Sylvia Wright** confessed in *Harper's Magazine* that for years she had felt sorry for the bonny Earl of Moray's wife, whenever she heard the song that told how:

> *They hae slain the Early of Moray, and Lady Mondegreen.*

A kind friend eventually explained that the entire misfortune was solely the Earl's—they *laid him on the green.*

Ms Wright's article on the subject released a tide of recognition in a public who had experienced precisely the same confusion with other songs. Some had been convinced that Rudolph was teased by a female fellow-worker: "Olive, the other reindeer, used to laugh and call him names." Others that Bob Dylan was singing "The ants are my friends, they're blowing in the wind," or that the Beatles were saying "She's got a chicken to ride." And that well-known bridge was not over "troubled Walter" after all, but "troubled water."

And so the word mondegreen settled firmly into the language (in academic terms, a mondegreen is closely related to a homonym, where two different words are spoken with much the same sound).

Money makes the world go around

This feels as if it should date back to early historical proverbs and the first urban mercantile societies. Indeed, a saying that was current in 1754, "Money governs the world," comes close. But the more flowing version with which we are familiar arose only in 1972. Christopher Isherwood's stories in *Goodbye to Berlin* had become the basis of John Van Druten's play *I Am a Camera*, which then metamorphosed into the New York musical *Cabaret* in 1966.

The show, starring Jill Haworth, Joel Grey, and Lotte Lenya, was extremely successful and a movie version was planned. For movie purposes, writers **John Kander** and **Fred Ebb** deleted some songs from the stage version, and created some new ones, especially designed for a movie-style delivery.

The song "Money Makes the World Go Around" was a dazzling duet between Liza Minnelli and Joel Grey. It made a considerable impact in the movie, and also put a new phrase into common usage.

Money talks

The power of money to change, improve, or smooth a difficult situation has been known since time immemorial. A selection of sayings exist to reminds us, from Horace's "All things are obedient to money" (c. 30 BC) to Giovanni Torriano's "Man prates but gold speaks" (1666) and "Money speaks in a language all nations understand" (1682).

In 1903 the *Saturday Evening Post* joked that if money did speak, it was usually saying "Goodbye."

But the neat, abbreviated version now in use came first from **P.G. Wodehouse** in *Something New* (1915). An impoverished young woman named Joan is told by her rich friend Aline that Aline's father has lost an ancient Egyptian scarab and is distraught. To Joan a scarab seems an ugly little geegaw to get upset about, until Aline remarks that her dad would give $5000 to anyone who could find it for him.

> *The whole story took on a different complexion for Joan.*
> *Money talks. A man who shouts that he will give five*
> *thousand for a thing may very well mean he will give five*
> *hundred—and Joan's finances were perpetually in a condition*
> *which makes five hundred dollars a sum to be grasped at.*

(The) moral majority

Initially this was a formal organization that arose in America as a result of some controversy within an earlier organization called Christian Voice. In 1979 Evangelist pastor **Jerry Falwell** founded the Moral Majority, made up of united Christian political action committees. Through the 1980s the organization became a powerful political lobby group for Christians in the U.S.

Towards 1989 support for the Moral Majority began to diminish, partly because its adherents felt the nation was in better moral health than during the previous decade. Falwell announced, "Our goal has been achieved."

But the name remained in use as a vague reference to that sector of the population that believed morality was on their side, when disagreeing with another part of the population whose morality they felt to be in question.

More bang for your buck

Originally the "bang" was meant quite literally. In 1954 a defense policy of "massive retaliation" was presented to the U.S. Council on Foreign Relations, relying on nuclear deterrents. *Newsweek* quoted Secretary of Defense **Charles E. Wilson** referring to the "plutonium explosion" policy as: "A bigger bang for a buck." Later usage reduced the alliteration and substituted the word "more," besides gradually eliminating the nuclear connotation. In modern usage it means more value for your money.

Motel

The word dates back to 1925 when travel by private car was burgeoning in California. In the pleasant town of San Luis Obispo, halfway between San Francisco and Los Angeles, architect **Arthur Heineman** designed and had built a hostelry which was deliberately planned to attract motorists—it had garages adjoining the accommodation. Mr. Heineman named it the Milestone, and added the word Mo-Tel.

Since this word was Heineman's own invention, it generated some confusion among people anxious to report that the "hotel" had misspelled its sign. But the abbreviation of "motor hotel" caught on, eventually contracting to motel and becoming an internationally common word.

The building in San Luis Obispo carries a plaque advising (quite correctly) that it is the world's first motel.

Movers and shakers

Often used in reference to rebels, financial wizards, and leaders in business and politics to describe those who are highly influential in their field, the breakers of perceived and actual barriers. But the original seems to suggest that the phrase's creator meant quite the opposite.

William (Arthur Edgar) O'Shaughnessy was a British poet, born in London in 1844 to Irish parents. (A relative, surgeon Sir William Brooke O'Shaughnessy, introduced cannabis to Western medicine and the telegraph to India). Young William worked at the British Museum, eventually specializing in ichthyology (the study of fishes) though he was a devotee of literature and writing. Several volumes of his poetry were published and his volume *Music and Moonlight* (1874) contains the "Ode," several lines of which have become familiar—albeit slightly out of context.

> *We are the music-makers,*
> *We are the dreamers of dreams,*
> *Wandering by lone sea-breakers,*
> *And sitting by desolate streams;*
> *World-losers and world-forsakers,*
> *On whom the pale moon gleams:*
> *Yet we are the movers and shakers*
> *Of the world for ever, it seems.*

The Ode was set to music by Sir Edward Elgar in 1912 and its first two lines are spoken by Gene Wilder as Willy Wonka in the movie *Willy Wonka and the Chocolate Factory*.

Ms.

Miss, Mrs. and Ms. have a common ancestor: they are all versions of the word mistress (from Old French maistresse, the feminine of maistre). Mistress was used to address all women, but it evolved into two forms designating a woman's marital status: Mrs. for a married woman; Miss for an unmarried one.

A further variation in parts of America was Miz for women, married and unmarried, both in fiction (Miz Scarlett in *Gone With the Wind*) and in fact (during the 1970s President Jimmy Carter's mother was universally known as Miz Lillian). Meanwhile, mistress had acquired the meaning of a woman who has an ongoing extramarital sexual relationship with a man.

By the late 1940s some women were beginning to agitate for a prefix that didn't identify their marital status. As early as 1949 there had been occasional low-profile mention of Ms. as a possible non-discriminatory courtesy prefix for all women, but it did not have a smooth passage into everyday language. The American Business Writing Association and also the National Office Management Association had viewed the term with favor, but the general public ignored it.

A turning point came in 1961. **Sheila Michaels** was a member of CORE (Congress of Racial Equality), and like other feminists was seeking an honorific that didn't disclose her private status. One day a newspaper dropped into her mailbox and she noticed what seemed to be a misprint in the address: Ms. She had never seen it before, but decided that this was what she sought.

There was still difficulty promoting the idea, but in a later radio interview discussing feminism, Michaels suggested that Ms. be adopted, and pronounced as she had heard Miz in her home state of Missouri. A friend of Gloria Steinem's heard the interview, and in 1971 suggested it to Ms. Steinem as the name for a new magazine about to be launched. The first issue of Ms. Magazine sold 300,000 copies in one week, and the "new" honorific started to take hold.

But there were still some roadblocks: the *New York Times* initially held out and would not publish the new word, in 1984 dismissing Ms. as "business-letter coinage too contrived for news writing." But in 1986 it succumbed.

Muck-raking

Long before the age of tabloid sensationalism or election campaign dirty tricks, **John Bunyan**'s *Pilgrim's Progress* was published in 1678. In it we are shown:

> ... *a Man that could look no way but downwards, with a*
> *Muck-rake in his hand.*

And we are told that he never looked up, but continued to rake the filth on the floor " ... and his Muck-rake doth shew his carnal mind."

Mumbo jumbo

British writer **Francis Moore** introduced the term to the English language in 1738. In his book *Inland Parts of Africa*, Moore reported on a custom in villages where men had several wives. If dissension arose between wife and husband, or among the wives, the weird and mysterious figure of Mumbo Jumbo would appear out of the jungle at night, shriek, curse, and dance outside the wives' sleeping quarters, and having announced a decision on their behaviour, would even administer a whipping to the offender.

Mumbo Jumbo was twice as tall as a man, dressed outlandishly in a costume of bark and wisps of bushes. It was clear to Francis Moore that the African village women were in awe and terror of a visit from Mumbo Jumbo. The fact that the man inside the costume was one of their own neighbors (or even their own husband) seemed to escape them—and made the story seem rather unlikely.

But Moore's report was completely backed up by the later Scottish travel writer, called (appropriately perhaps) Mungo Park, whose 1795 *Travels in the Interior of Africa* reported the same phenomenon—women in African villages were kept in subjection by the fear of Mumbo Jumbo.

English readers began to associate the term mumbo jumbo with arcane rituals and the puzzling language associated with them. Eventually this led to the term being used to describe any language causing bewilderment, confusion, or boredom.

My better half

In the *Odes* of the Roman poet Horace (23 BC), his reference to a "better half" meant—in the idiom of the time—a good friend of either gender ("animae dimidium meae," 1 *Odes* iii. 8.), in this case his friend Virgil. When the term went into English, the passage of time effected a change in reference so that the "other half" gradually came to mean a spouse, of either gender.

It first surfaces with this meaning during the Elizabethan age, when **Sir Philip Sidney**'s *The Countess of Pembroke's Arcadia* was published in 1590. The fair Parthenia reports of her dying husband, the knight Argalus:

> . . . *it seemed a little cheerful blood came up to his cheeks, like a burning coal, almost dead, if some breath a little revive it: and forcing up, the best he could, his feeble voice, "My dear, my dear, my better half," said he, "I find that I must now leave thee . . . "*

My heart was in my mouth

The ancient Roman work *Satyricon* (c. AD 66) is also known as *A Recital of Lecherous Happenings*, and in P.G. Walsh's translation the character of Niceros tells of watching a man in a graveyard take all his clothes off and urinate around them before turning into a wolf. Niceros's reaction was: "Mihi animam in naso esse" (The life spirit rose into my nose), rendered in English as, "My heart was in my mouth."

The more familiar version first appeared in English in a different context. In 1548 **Nicholas Udall** (known as "the flogging headmaster") completed the section he was in charge of translating from Ersamus's *Paraphrase of the New Testament*. Udall's translation included:

> *Hauyng their herte at their verai mouth for feare, they did not belieue that it was Iesus.*

(Udall was light-footed enough to compose songs for the coronation of Queen Anne Boleyn, be engaged by Queen Catherine Parr to do translations, and yet avoid being burned by Queen Mary Tudor, even though he was a Protestant and she burned several hundred of them.)

My husband and I

In 1953 **Queen Elizabeth II** made her second Christmas broadcast, this time from New Zealand. She explained to listeners: "My husband and I left London a month ago," a perfectly harmless remark, even abiding by normal protocols in placing herself after the other person mentioned. But for some unknown reason the phrase "my husband and I" became regarded as faintly comic, though Her Majesty continued to use it for the next fourteen years before making a subtle change to "Prince Philip and I."

She returned to the phrase with gentle irony in 1972, at a banquet in the London Guildhall for the couple's twenty-fifth wedding anniversary. Her speech began:

> I think that everybody really will concede that on this, of all days, I should begin my speech with the words "my husband and I."

My lips are sealed

The expression first saw the light in 1909 in *Mike and Psmith* by **P.G. Wodehouse** when Psmith promises not to reveal that Mike is about to play a cricket match.

Wodehouse used the term several times over the next three decades, most memorably in *Spring Fever* where Lord Shortlands confides to Mike Cardinal that he wants to marry his cook. His lordship's daughter Lady Teresa is horrified and begs Mike Cardinal not to spread it about. Mike Cardinal assures her:

My lips are sealed. Clams take my correspondence course.

(In December 1935, British Prime Minister Stanley Baldwin—who was perhaps a fan of Wodehouse—reversed the term in a speech to Parliament. Unwilling to comment on a crisis concerning Abyssinia, he said: "I have seldom spoken with greater regret, for my lips are not yet unsealed." But in general usage the Wodehouse version is preferred.)

N

Naff off

There is no decisive origin of the term, but between 1973 and 1977 it became familiar to British viewers in the television series *Porridge,* the word "naff" being deliberately scripted (by **Dick Clement** and **Ian La Frenais**) in place of the more obvious swear words which would have been the norm in the prison context.

In April 1982 the context shifted to the opposite end of the social scale when **Princess Anne** (not a woman to mince words) fell off a horse. She became the target of snapping paparazzi, to whom she snapped back in no uncertain tones: "Naff off!"

This elevation from the lower reaches of society to the pinnacle caused headlines and made the term available for use in general circumstances.

Namby pamby

During the eighteenth century, Ambrose Philips was a don of St Johns College, Cambridge, and in addition gained some recognition as a poet. But his poetic style and political affiliations incurred the wrath of the musician and poet **Henry Carey** (who wrote "Sally in our Alley" and was possibly the first person to sing "God Save the King").

Carey thought Philips' poetic style was half-witted. So he set out in 1725 to create a poem that would satirize it with an ingenious series of rhyming couplets—a stinging series of childish epigrams. Carey came up with namby-pamby as a word-play on the name Ambrose Philips, and entitled his poem "Namby Pamby—A Panegyric on the New Versification."

The poem was so successful that Philips was henceforth known as Namby Pamby, and Alexander Pope used the term in his satiric epic *The Dunciad*.

Since then the term has been used to label anything perceived as childish, ineffectual or insipid.

(A) nation of shopkeepers

Napoleon is believed to have said it (in French) as a put-down of the English, and his doing so made the description famous. But long before Napoleon, the term "nation of shopkeepers" had already been used in English, though not as a put-down. **Josiah Tucker**, the Dean of Gloucester Cathedral, first floated the idea of a shopkeeping nation in 1763 when he wrote:

> *A shopkeeper will never get more custom by beating his customers, and what is true of a shopkeeper is true of a shopkeeping nation.*

Just over a decade later Adam Smith, in *The Wealth of Nations* (1776), encapsulated the concept more concisely and put the words in neater order:

> *To found a great empire for the sole purpose of raising up a people of customers may at first sight appear a project fit only for a nation of shopkeepers. It is, however, a project altogether unfit for a nation of shopkeepers; but extremely fit for a nation whose government is influenced by shopkeepers.*

Navel gazing

The expression has its origin in real life—the members of some religious sects do actually go into a kind of trance by staring at their navels. There is even a formal word for it: omphaloskepsis. During the nineteenth century that was translated as "navel contemplators"—the direct ancestor of the contemporary form.

The term first appears in a book by **Robert Alfred Vaughan** in 1857: *Hours with the Mystics—A Contribution to the History of Religious Opinion*. In one fairly lengthy sentence, he reports on a visit to the holy monasteries of Mount Athos in Greece:

> *It seems that some of the monks (called, if I mistake not, Hesychasts) held that if a man shut himself up in a corner of his cell, with his chin upon his breast, turning his thoughts inward, gazing towards his navel, and centering all the strength of his mind on the region of the heart; and, not discouraged by at first perceiving only darkness, held out at this strange in-looking for several days and nights, he would at length behold a divine glory, and see himself luminous with the very light which was manifested on Mount Tabor.*
>
> *They call these devotees Navel-contemplators.*

The activity itself may not have caught on in any major way beyond Mouth Athos, but the term "navel contemplators" did. Over several decades of use, contemplating became gazing, and the image moved from the literal to the metaphoric—indicating excessive introspection, self-absorption, and an inability to take action.

Nerd

In contemporary times, a nerd is generally perceived as a person with an obsessively narrow focus on certain intellectual or technological matters to the exclusion of ordinary activities and social graces. Nerds are not necessarily admired, whereas a geek is a person who also has advanced knowledge but a more relaxed attitude to other aspects of life (most people who own a computer are happy to have a geek as a friend).

The first known appearance of the word nerd in print—which launched its growth into international use—was in the story *If I Ran The Zoo* (1950), by children's author **Dr. Seuss**, in which a character proclaims:

> *I'll sail to Ka-Troo And Bring Back an It-Kutch, a Preep and a Proo, A Nerkle, a Nerd, and a Seersucker, too!*

The story was illustrated with a grumpy-looking android not particular about personal grooming.

Never look a gift horse in the mouth

"Never inspect the teeth of a gift horse" (Noli equi dentes inspicere donati) is credited to Eusebius Sophronius Hieronymus (later known as St. Jerome), around AD 400.

The writings of Magdalen College School's headmaster **John Stanbridge** brought the term into English in 1509. In his book *Vulgaria*, among somewhat gloomy sentences for schoolboys to study ("I fear the master," "I am weary of study," "I shall be beaten") there is also:

> *A gyven hors may not be loked in the tethe.*

Never–never land

The term "never-never" had at least two uses before it became internationally known. Early British migrants to Australia during the 1800s referred to the remote, stark and sparsely populated outback areas of Australia as "The Never Never," and the term still survives there. Then in 1900 American writer Israel Zangwill used the phrase in the title of a play: *The Moment of Death; or, The Never, Never Land*.

It is not known whether **J.M. Barrie** picked up the term from these two sources, but its widespread use came after his play *Peter Pan* introduced the concept to British audiences in 1904.

In the play, Peter Pan describes the place as "the Never Land" without doubling "never," but in general usage the island's single never quietly developed into never-never. In that form it was often used to describe hire-purchase, where goods could be obtained and their full price paid in instalments over a long period.

Only the late Michael Jackson got it right. His fantasy farm recreating the whimsy of Barrie's mythical island was entitled Neverland without the repeat, exactly as Peter Pan (and J.M. Barrie) intended.

Never say never

Although it became world famous as the title of a James Bond movie, the expression had musical beginnings. Songwriter **Harry McGregor Woods** composed "When the Red, Red Robin Comes Bobbin' Along" (1926), "I'm Looking Over a Four Leaf Clover" (1927), and "Side by Side" (1927).

His 1935 song "I'll Never Say Never Again" was recorded that same year by the Boswell Sisters and by Ozzie Nelson. Over forty years later, actor Sean Connery reportedly told his wife that having played Bond in six movies, he would never do another—and she replied, "Never say never."

Soon after, Connery was signed for his last Bond outing, an adaptation of the Ian Fleming novel *Thunderball*, filmed in 1983 as *Never Say Never*.

(The) new black

The very versatile expression arose as a variation on a remark from the former editor of *Vogue* **Diana Vreeland**. In 1962, when commenting on fashions in India, her actual words were "Pink is the navy blue of India." At the time variations on pink predominated in Indian fabrics, whereas navy blue was the safely respectable color in New York.

The expression caught on and as black became the basic color for a certain level of fashion, Vreeland's original statement morphed into whatever color was fashionable that season becoming described as "the new black."

Nice work if you can get it

The 1937 movie *Damsel in Distress*, based on a P.G. Wodehouse story, doesn't have a high profile in film history. But one Gershwin song from that movie, sung by Fred Astaire, put a new phrase into the language.

In their study of *America's Songs*, Philip Furia and Michael L. Lasser tell how American lyricist Ira Gershwin found the genesis of that song in the caption to a British cartoon, which had put an amusing slant on a phrase known around Britain at the time.

Two London charwomen were shown discussing the daughter of a mutual friend. One woman confided to the other that the girl had become a whore. The second woman replied, "Nice work if you can get it." The cartoonist was later identified as **George Belcher**.

George Gershwin provided the tune, Ira added lines about "holding hands at midnight, 'neath a starry sky . . . ," the resultant song became a classic, and the charwoman's observation travelled far and wide.

No brainer

In 1942 Americans first saw a comic cartoon strip about a pleasant middle-class family of five called "The Berrys." The strip ran until 1974, drawn by **Carl Grubert**.

During the 1950s the term "no brainer" arose informally among Americans, meaning that a decision or solution was easy and obvious. The term first saw light in Grubert's cartoon in 1959, showing that during a game of Scrabble the father Peter chooses a word that to mother Pat seems so easy she dismisses his choice as a "no brainer." Before long the expression was in wide international use.

No great shakes

The reason for referring to "shakes" is obscure and may have arisen from the image of a dice being shaken but only an insignificant number thrown. "No great shakes" must have been a recognizable expression in early nineteenth-century Britain, but unlike some English words and expressions that have come into the language from an ancient Latin origin, this one is first registered in actual Latin.

In 1865, **Lord John Cam Broughton**, a British statesman, prolific author and friend of Byron, published his *Recollections of a Long Life*. There he recounted a memory of visiting an art gallery with a group of friends in 1816. Broughton found one piece of displayed sculpture somewhat lacking, and—presumably to avoid offending anyone connected with the piece—remarked to his friends:

Nullae magnae quassationes.

His group greeted the remark with laughter, having understood immediately that he was saying, "No great shakes."

No more Mr. Nice Guy

This developed from a stern dictum uttered by Leo Durocher, manager of the Brooklyn Dodgers baseball team from 1939 to 1946, and misquoted later as: "Nice guys finish last." In his autobiography Durocher pointed out that his original statement was actually four separate statements:

They're all nice guys. They'll finish last. Nice guys. Finish last.

Subsequent reporters and headline writers condensed his words into a neater epigram. (Although he denounced the restructuring of his original line, that did not stop Durocher from entitling his autobiography *Nice Guys Finish Last*.)

From this there developed an image of nice guys seeming to lack some fibre or strength. Three decades after Durocher, during the presidential election campaign of 1972, a slight development of Durocher's decree surfaced twice. A contender for the vice-presidency was Senator Edmund Muskie, whose polite manner and gentlemanly personality seemed to some to be ill-suited to a vigorous political arena. Journalist David Broderin referred to him as "cautious cool Mr. Nice Guy." The team strategy to realign his image into something more edgy and independent was identified as: "No more Mr. Nice Guy."

During the same campaign, journalist **Robert Novak** was denied a seat on presidential candidate Senator McGovern's campaign plane, and instead was despatched to the secondary craft carrying camera crews and technicians. Not pleased, Novak told McGovern's press aide Dick Dougherty:

From now on, no more Mr. Nice Guy.

Seizing the moment, Alice Cooper's "shock rock" song "No More Mr. Nice Guy" was released a few months later.

No news is good news

At one point in the lead-up to the problematic trial of the Earl of Somerset in 1616, **King James I** wrote to Sir George Moore, Lieutenant of the Tower of London, saying:

> *No newis is bettir then evill newis.*

No pain, no gain

Crisp and contemporary though it sounds, the term dates back to at least the sixteenth century. The ancestor of the expression is:

> *They must take pain that look for any gayn.*

It is found in *Workes of a Young Wit* from the prolific British poet **Nicholas Breton** in 1577. Over the centuries successive versions transpired, with compression and adjustments in spelling, until the concise "No pain, no gain" took hold.

Nose out of joint

The sour grimace of someone whose pride has been dented. The image has been around since 1581. Soldier and romantic writer **Barnabe Riche** in *Apolonius and Silla* wrote of the duke that:

> *It could bee no other then his owne manne, that has thrust his nose so farre out of ioynte.*

Over the years, thrust has been replaced by the slightly less aggressive put.

No such thing as a free lunch

As far back as the nineteenth century some bars would offer a "free" lunch providing that a drink had been bought. This was a thin disguise for gaining more revenue from drinkers who stayed on.

The reality—that getting something for nothing is unlikely—was referred to by a Washington journalist Paul Mallon who in 1942 pointed out that:

> . . . such a thing as a 'free' lunch never existed. Until man acquires the power of creation, someone will always have to pay for a free lunch.

In June 1949 journalist **Walter Morrow** in the San Francisco News came out with the more concise "no such thing as a free lunch," which the *New York Times* in January 1994 credited as the first use of that exact phrase.

The term was later popularized by science fiction writer Robert Heinlein, and economist Milton Friedman.

Not a penny more, not a penny less

There had been earlier expressions concerning pennies, but not with the neat plus-minus balance put together by **George Bernard Shaw** in *Pygmalion* (1914).

Eliza Doolittle has come to Professor Higgins' house so she may learn to speak like a lady in a flower shop. Her father Alfred misinterprets the (strictly business) relationship between Higgins and Eliza, and he insists that he must be paid for her presence in the Professor's house.

After both shock and argument, Higgins (who is unwilling to give up Eliza's language training) finally agrees, and Doolittle asks for five pounds. Uncharacteristically amiable, Higgins raises the offer to ten pounds. Alfred is horrified:

Ten pounds is a lot of money: it makes a man feel prudent like; and then goodbye to happiness. You give me what I ask you, Governor: not a penny more, and not a penny less.

The phrase made a good title for Jeffrey Archer's 1976 novel about financial see-saws.

Nothing comes from nothing

That nothing can be created when there is nothing with which to create, is a familiar philosophical concept throughout recorded history. It can be found in the fifth century BC in a poem by the Greek **Parmenides of Elea**, and later in Latin translation as "Ex nihilo nihil fit" (Nothing can be created from nothing).

Over 2,000 years later in English, there is prominent use of the line more than once by Shakespeare in *King Lear* (c.1608)—Lear to Cordelia: "Nothing can come of nothing."

An endearing version occurs in the movie *The Sound of Music* in a song sung by Julie Andrews and Bill Lee (dubbing for Christopher Plummer):

Nothing comes from nothing,
Nothing ever could . . .

No time like the present

A fairly obvious precept, but it didn't see the light of day in English until 1562 in a now obscure work: *Accidence of Armoury*, by G. Legh:

To be sure sir no time better than euen now.

A century later it appeared in its more recognizable form in a Drury Lane theater comedy *The Lost Lover* (1696), by a gently radical feminist writer **Mrs. Delariviere Manley**:

There is no time like the present.

Not in my back yard

The expression originated in America, mainly to describe those who opposed nuclear development, and was quickly shortened to the acronym NIMBY. While known in Britain, it only received major publicity when British MP and Environment Secretary **Nicholas Ridley** in 1988 publicly dismissed the attitude of rural dwellers who opposed housing in nearby developments as "pure Nimbyism." The terms (now usually lower case) nimby and nimbyism rapidly went into wider use.

Not turn a hair

After vigorous activity such as racing, the coat of a horse is likely to be ruffled and sweaty. It has "turned a hair," a familiar stable term as far back as the eighteenth century. If the horse has *not* turned a hair, it can be regarded as cool and calm.

Jane Austen took the term out of the stables and into wide readership in *Northanger Abbey* (1797). Catherine Morland meets her brother and John Thorpe after arriving in Bath, and Catherine remarks that their horse looked hot. John Thorpe remonstrates that the horse

> *. . . had not turned a hair till we came to Walcot church!*

Not what it's cracked up to be

During the fourteenth century, crack up meant to speak confidently and boldly (which survives in "cracking a joke") and also meant "to praise." So its negative—not cracked up—signified that the praise had been misplaced.

This negative version must have been in American usage prior to 1834, for it occurs in **Davy Crockett**'s *Narrative of the Life of David Crockett of the State of Tennessee*. Davy wrote the expression in a casual style that he seemed to expect readers would understand:

We worked on for some years renting ground and paying high rent, until I found it wasn't the thing it was cracked up to be; and that I couldn't make a fortune of it just at all.

A decade later the term turns up in *Martin Chuzzlewit* (1844), where Dickens uses it in a positive way in the sense of giving praise. Chollop tells Mark:

We are the intellect and virtue of the airth . . . our backs is easy ris. We must be cracked up or they rises and we snarls.

The positive use seems to have faded, but the negative—"not cracked up"—remains.

No woman can be too rich or too thin

Encapsulating as it does the aspirations of so many during the current and previous century, this line is too good to ignore. But the problem of clarifying who originally said it has bothered researchers for fifty years. It has been attributed to Dorothy Parker, Coco Chanel, Joan Rivers, the Duchess of Windsor, Rose Kennedy, Diana Vreeland, Barbara Paley, Gloria Vanderbilt, and Mrs. J. Gordon Douglas Snr.

There is also a strong possibility that the line was created by a man—Truman Capote. He is reported to have said it on TV, on the David Susskind Show around 1959, but the videotape has never been available for verification.

In 1970 the *Los Angeles Times* put its faith in the Duchess of Windsor as the originator of the line, but offered no provenance. One thing is a known fact: in June 1971 journalist **Marian Christy** from the Ohio newspaper *Elyria Chronicle* visited the Duchess of Windsor, and reported that the Duchess had the line embroidered on a cushion (on which one of her dogs customarily sat). But whether to remind herself of the ruling, or to advertise to visitors that she was the first to use it, nobody knows.

Nudge-nudge, wink-wink, say no more

Already extant as a music-hall innuendo, the nudge-nudge expression went into popular parlance after a *Monty Python* show broadcast in 1969. One sketch written by **Eric Idle** showed a bar-room encounter in which a dignified British gentleman is harassed about his wife's sex life by a brash bystander (played by Idle himself). Central to the discussion is the brash one's clumsy avoidance of direct questioning, saying instead, "Nudge nudge, grin grin, wink wink, say no more." The phrase, shortened to "nudge-nudge, wink-wink, say no more," rapidly went into English vernacular as a comic substitute for direct discussion of sexual matters.

Old Glory

The American flag acquired this nickname in 1831 when **William Driver**, as skipper of the brig *Charles Doggett*, was about to sail to the South Pacific—a trip which would include returning the descendants of the *Bounty* mutiny survivors from Tahiti back home to Pitcairn. The *New York Times* (September 15, 1918) reported that just before the brig left Salem, Massachusetts, a group of friends appeared and presented Driver with a "large and beautifully made American flag."

Driver named the flag Old Glory, and after retiring from the sea flew it from his Tennessee house every day—until the Civil War. It was later reported that he hid the flag by stitching it inside his bedcover until the Union army arrived, when he presented Old Glory to their general, to be hoisted on the Capitol.

Old soldiers never die

In 1855 a singing evangelist nun, Sister Abby Hutchinson, composed a tune to some anonymously written words:

> *Kind words can never die; cherished and blest,*
> *God knows how deep they lie, stored in the breast;*
> *Like childhood's simple rhymes, said o'er a thousand times,*
> *Go through all years and climes, the heart to cheer.*

Before long a mock version had arisen, first printed in London but also known in America to the cadets of West Point, satirically referring to the official rations provided to the military:

> *There is an old cookhouse, far far away*
> *Where we get pork and beans, three times a day.*
> *Beefsteak we never see, damn-all sugar for our tea*
> *And we are gradually fading away.*
> *Old soldiers never die,*
> *Never die, never die,*
> *Old soldiers never die*
> *They just fade away.*

In 1951 a former West Point cadet who had become **General Douglas MacArthur** made a speech to Congress, closing his fifty-two years of military service. Perhaps without realizing it was a mocking version of a Christian hymn, MacArthur recalled his student days and mentioned:

> *. . . the refrain of one of the most popular barrack ballads of that day which proclaimed most proudly that "old soldiers never die; they just fade away." And like the old soldier of that ballad, I now close my military career and just fade away.*

The "just" varies from time to time—becoming "simply" or "always" or "only"—and although nobody knows who said it first, General MacArthur's speech during those early days of American television riveted the nation and put the expression into common parlance.

On a razor's edge

Straight from the *Iliad* of **Homer** (800 BC). Robert Fitzgerald translates Nestor (from the section of the Greek population known as the Achaeans) saying to Diomedes:

Terrible pressure is upon us. The issue teeters on a razor's edge for all Achaeans—whether we live or perish.

The expression—as *The Razor's Edge*—became the title of a W. Somerset Maugham novel in 1944, which was made into a movie in 1946 (earning Ann Baxter an Academy Award).

One good turn deserves another

There is speculation that a version of this expression existed during the reign of Nero, but evidence is thin. Later, various convolutions can be found telling that one good turn "asks," "requires" or "deserves" another.

But in 1620, the **Rev. Joseph Hall**, Bishop of Norwich, introduced the form which settled into English and has been used ever since. A prolific writer on theological matters, his *Contemplations on the Historical Passages in the Old and New Testaments* discusses the relationship between Nabal's flocks and David's followers and comments:

One good turn deserves another.

(That's) one small step for (a) man, one giant leap for mankind

After four days in space, the crew of Apollo 11 started their descent towards the moon, landing on (Earth time) July 20, 1969. Astronaut **Neil Armstrong** was seen and heard live on telecast to Earth, saying:

That's one small step for (a) man, one giant leap for mankind.

NASA later explained that the word "a" before "man" had been obscured by static and was inaudible on earth. There has been much debate about whether Armstrong did or did not actually speak the "a."

There is unsubstantiated belief that before the Apollo left earth, the line had been supplied to Armstrong, perhaps by his wife or by a professional writer. Whether or not that is the case, Armstrong certainly had it ready before he landed—in his book *Chariots for Apollo* he refers to having "rehearsed" the line before speaking it.

One-upmanship

Besides his study of D.H. Lawrence, and the edited Coleridge letters, British writer, academic, radio producer, drama critic and wit **Stephen Potter** wrote a series of tongue-in-cheek guides to living.

Gamesmanship, published in 1947, dwelt on possible ways of achieving psychological advantages over fellow players. This was followed in 1950 by *Lifemanship*, advising (somewhat light-heartedly) how to find success in both social and business activities.

His later output included *Supermanship* and *Golfmanship*. But his standout work, an exposé of how to gain status by making other people feel inferior to oneself, was his 1952 book *One-upmanship*. The title not only put a new word into the language, but spawned other uses of the suffix "-manship," such as Adlai Stevenson speaking of the "brinkmanship" of John Foster Dulles.

(The) only thing we have to fear is fear itself

Even if inaccurately remembered and slightly misquoted, everyone knows **Franklin D. Roosevelt** said it. But there is some doubt that it was an original thought on his part. Sir Francis Bacon had written, "Nothing is to be feared except fear itself" (*Fortitudo*, 1623). Arthur Wellesley, Duke of Wellington wrote, "The only thing I am afraid of is fear" (1831), and philosopher Henry David Thoreau wrote in his diary, "Nothing is so much to be feared as fear" (1851).

Eleanor Roosevelt reputedly said that Franklin D. was very familiar with Thoreau's writings, and Roosevelt's speechwriter denied that he had put the "fear" phrase into the speech script.

It is certain, however, that in March 1933 when Roosevelt made his inaugural speech, he introduced the expression to a wider public than that familiar with Francis Bacon, The Duke of Wellington or Thoreau.

Roosevelt's "The only thing we have to fear is fear itself" is sometimes misquoted as "We have nothing to fear but fear itself."

Only . . . shopping days until Christmas

The idea of reminding people how much shopping time is left before Christmas is not new. On December 19, 1900, the *Los Angeles Times* displayed a reminder: "There are only (counting today) five more shopping days till Christmas." Four days later the *Washington Post* took up the cry: "Only one more shopping day until Christmas."

At the time **Gordon Selfridge** was working with Marshall Field and Company in Chicago. He may have picked up the idea from the newspapers mentioned, but certainly he soon instructed his staff to drive the same slogan, which put a real sense of urgency into the shopping lead-up to Christmas. Before long it was used worldwide.

On one's last legs

The image is believed to come from the practice (still current) of referring to sections of a journey as "legs"—of which the last would be the most tiring, and could end in collapse.

In this physical sense it was first seen in **Thomas Middleton**'s play *The Old Law* (1619). Commenting on the imminent demise of Eugenia's husband, a courtier says:

On his last legs I'm sure.

By 1672 the expression had become more metaphorical. John Ray applied it to insolvency and bankruptcy: "He goes on his last legs." From there the term has moved to apply to any object or idea— washing machines, shoes, computers, Government policy—seen to be getting close to its use-by date.

On the grapevine

Gaining information through informal sources, usually conversational. Before that meaning developed, American abolitionists helping escaped slaves sometimes used a system of hanging garments on a clothesline in a prearranged sequence of colors that gave out information to those observing. The "clothesline" became a synonym for "discreet and clandestine delivery of information."

The concept took a further step in 1859. Although he didn't say it, the association of information with grapes came to pass through the efforts of **Colonel Bee**, who set up a rudimentary telegraph system between Placerville in California and Virginia City in Nevada. The swaying of the trees stretched the wires until at times some lengths were lying on the ground and the general convolutions of the "telegraph" resembled the trailing of a Californian grapevine.

The efficiency of telegraph information was severely compromised and newspapers of the area began to refer to information of doubtful validity as "grapevine telegraph." This became abbreviated and developed into the concept of hearing rumor and gossip usually at some distance from its source.

(The) opera's not over until the fat lady sings

In 1976 Fabia Rue Smith and Charles Rayford Smith published *Southern Words and Sayings*, a collection of old sayings from the South. It included the (apparently familiar) expression:

> *Church ain't out 'til the fat lady sings.*

Sports instructor Ralph Carpenter of the Texas Technical University may have known the saying prior to that publication. In the same year, during a tense tie in a basketball match playoff, Carpenter made what was presumed to be his own variation on the existing expression, saying:

The opera ain't over until the fat lady sings.

Carpenter's remark was heard by comparatively few people at the time but was later published in the *Dallas Morning News* (March 1976). The remark reached the knowledge of San Antonio sports writer **Dan Cook**, who in May 1978 spoke the line during a televised sports match. This in turn was seen by celebrated sports broadcaster Dick Motta, who took a liking to the expression.

One thing led to another and the term went into use worldwide. None of the men involved claimed to have invented the line, but it is clear that Dan Cook's use of it on television in 1978 created the opening that put it into general circulation.

Other fish to fry

Renowned for her writings about provincial society, Scottish author **Margaret Oliphant** was certainly not above using an informal expression when a character's lifestyle required it. In *At His Gates* (vol 2, 1872) she wrote:

> *'But you may compose yourself about Ned,' added the father with irony. 'That little thing has other fish to fry.'*

Out of kilter

Kilter is a form of an old British dialect word, kelter, referring to something being in good condition or good health. Being out of kelter was to be somehow at odds with a desired state. Although the expression sounds fairly casual, it must once have been quite acceptable in a formal context. Its first known outing in print came from the high-ranking divine **Dr. Isaac Barrow**, whose lengthy sermon on *The Duty of Prayer* (c.1662) says:

> *If the organs of prayer be out of kelter or out of tune, how can we pray?*

Some time after this, the spelling and pronunciation of kelter, for no known reason, became kilter.

Out of sight, out of mind

British poet **Arthur Hugh Clough** translated Plutarch, was an examiner in the Education Office, and part of a British commission to study foreign military education. He also devoted a lot of time to being an unpaid secretary to his wife's cousin, Florence Nightingale. In 1853 Clough published *Songs in Absence*, one of which told its readers:

> *That out of sight is out of mind*
> *Is true of most we leave behind;*
> *It is not, sure, nor can be true,*
> *My own and dearest love, of you.*
>
> *They were my friends, 'twas sad to part;*
> *Almost a tear began to start;*
> *But yet as things run on they find*
> *That out of sight is out of mind.*

Almost immediately, Clough's line went into common usage. See also **Absence makes the heart grow fonder**

Out of the frying pan into the fire

Various configurations go back several centuries BC and involve falling from a hot pan (or cauldron) into coals, or from smoke into flames.

In 1532 the expression came into English when King Henry VIII's Lord Chancellor **Sir Thomas More** expressed unrest about the direction in which Christian observance might be moving. In criticising Bible translator William Tyndale, More described such heretics as:

Lepe they lyke a flounder out of a fryeng-panne into the fyre.

(Thomas More was a brave man—his religious disapproval extended to disagreeing with Henry's marriage to Anne Boleyn and His Majesty's separation from the Catholic church, for which impudence he was beheaded.)

(The) oxygen of publicity

There is some belief that the term was originated by London's Chief Rabbi, Lord Jakobovits, but it became internationally prominent when British Prime Minister **Margaret Thatcher** addressed the American Bar Association in July 1985, and her speech included the line:

Democratic nations must try to find ways to starve the terrorist and the hijacker of the oxygen of publicity on which they depend.

Later that month she repeated the expression to the *Sunday Times* during a press conference in Washington. It has been widely used ever since.

(Do not eat) oysters in a month with no "r"

The concept was first formulated by **William Butler** in 1599. His
Dyet's Dry Dinner proclaims:

> *It is unseasonable and unwholesome in all months that have
> not an R in their name to eat an oyster.*

This may have less to do with safety than with flavor and
conservation.

Northern oysters spawn during the warm months (May, June,
July, August), and their texture and flavor is not as satisfying during
this period. Apart from that, leaving them alone during warm
months helps sustain the future oyster population.

Sophisticated techniques of farming and refrigeration have
gone a long way to resolve these issues, so in general farmed oysters
are available and can be eaten in all months with or without an "r,"
though the persnickety prefer the supposedly superior qualities of
oysters from the wild.

However, Northern Hemisphere epicures who relish such
oysters may prefer to avoid them in months without an "r." But this
of course does not apply in the Southern Hemisphere, where wild
oysters spawn in the months that do have an "r," and are therefore
best eaten in the months without one.

Parking meter

This ubiquitous feature of urban life was patented in 1935 by inventor **Carlton Cole Magee** (U.S. patent #2,118,318). The first ones were installed in Oklahoma City and the company that manufactured them became known as the P.O.M. company, because Magee had called the device a Park-O-Meter. Over time, public usage morphed the name into parking meter.

(The) patter of little feet

Subject to several later variations (e.g., "pitter-patter," and "tiny" feet) the folksy original phrase emerged in 1859 in **Henry Wadsworth Longfellow**'s poem "The Children's Hour":

> *I hear in the chamber above me*
> *The patter of little feet,*
> *The sound of a door that is opened,*
> *And voices soft and sweet.*

Peace for our time

From 1662 onwards, the Nunc Dimittis section of the *Book of Common Prayer* has the line, "Give peace in our time, Oh Lord."

British Prime Minister **Neville Chamberlain** may have been influenced by that when on September 30, 1938 he returned from a meeting with Hitler, and spoke from No. 10 Downing Street. His words were:

> *My good friends, for the second time in our history, a British Prime Minister has returned from Germany bringing peace with honor. I believe it is "peace for our time." Go home and get a nice quiet sleep.*

This has often been misquoted as "peace in our time."

(The) people's princess

The expression has been used to refer to three British princesses. Her Royal Highness Crown Princess Charlotte Augusta was the only legitimate heir to King George IV and the public delighted in her throughout her short life. Charlotte's death in childbirth in 1817 when she was twenty-one caused an enormous outpouring of grief. People of every class cried in the streets; even destitute laborers wore ragged black armbands. Shops closed, memorial services were crowded, and the entire population seemed united in sadness. *The Times* leader wrote: "We never recollect so strong and general an exhibition and indication of sorrow."

Another "people's princess" was Her Royal Highness Princess Mary, Duchess of Teck (great-grandmother of Queen Elizabeth II), who lived a profligate but cheerful life in London, was constantly in debt and was much loved by the masses, in spite of her enormous size (weighing in at nearly 250 pounds, she was sometimes jocularly called "Fat Mary"—see *The People's Princess*, by W.S. Jackman).

After the death of Diana, Princess of Wales in 1997, the tide of mourning matched that following the death of Charlotte 180 years earlier. The speechwriter for Prime Minister **Tony Blair** included Diana with Charlotte and Fat Mary as a "people's princess."

Perish the thought

Originally with "that" instead of "the," the line comes from English playwright–actor **Colly Cibber**. Undaunted by Shakespeare's having already written an impressive drama about Richard III, Cibber wrote an alternative version in 1700 and presented it at Drury Lane with himself playing King Richard. After being visited by ghosts, the king says:

> *Perish that thought. No never be it said*
> *That fate itself could awe the soul of Richard.*

Personal computer

Accepting that the abbreviation "pc" means "personal computer," the concept of everyone-and-their-own-laptop dates back to 1962. In December that year, the *Hillsboro Press-Gazette* in Ohio carried some information regarding predictions made by eminent American physicist **Dr. John William Mauchly**. It was reported that he:

> *. . . has designed computers and thinks well of them. He envisions a time when everyone will carry his own personal computer.*

Indeed Mauchly became codesigner of the first commercial computer made in the United States.

(By 1982 *Computerworld* was using the abbreviation "pc," and in 1983 the *Los Angeles Times* started advertising "laptops.")

Pie in the sky

In the early twentieth century, a somewhat anarchistic labor organization called Industrial Workers of the World was known jocularly as the Wobblies (because of its initials). One of its unifying factors was songs. Every member was given a little songbook that contained rousing parodies of popular songs, such as "Hallelujah I'm a Bum" and "Nearer My Job to Thee."

In 1911 **Joe Hill** created a song parody directly aimed at the Salvation Army hymn "In the Sweet Bye and Bye." The Industrial Workers had taken offence at the Salvation Army's implication that there would be joy in the afterlife so long as one remained meek and compliant in this life. Hill's parody was called "The Preacher and the Slave" and, instead of the sweet bye and bye, referred to "Work and pray, live on hay, you'll get pie in the sky when you die."

This may have been rather unfair to the Salvation Army, but nonetheless the phrase went into the language very quickly and has never disappeared. In time the phrase's origin was forgotten and the expression came to depict a dream scenario or an unrealistic hope.

Pigs might fly

A Scottish publication, written in Latin in 1586, acknowledged the impossibility of pigs flying. It failed to reach a large audience but, in 1865, Lewis Carroll did. In *Alice's Adventures in Wonderland* the Duchess makes (as usual) a cryptic remark on the subject of pigs and flying:

> *'Thinking again?' the Duchess asked, with another dig of her sharp little chin.*
> *'I've a right to think,' said Alice sharply, for she was beginning to feel a little worried.*
> *'Just about as much right,' said the Duchess, 'as pigs have to fly . . . '*

Lewis Carroll must have been intrigued about pigs flying—or not—since the notion cropped up again in *Through the Looking Glass* in 1872:

> 'The time has come,' the Walrus said,
> 'To talk of many things:
> Of shoes—and ships—and sealing-wax –
> Of cabbages—and kings –
> And why the sea is boiling hot –
> And whether pigs have wings.'

It seems that **Lewis Carroll** can take credit for putting speculation about the ability of pigs to fly into common usage.

Pillars of society

Norwegian playwright **Henrik Ibsen**'s play *Samfundets Støtter* (1877) was translated by Robert Farquarson as *Pillars of Society*. The term comes from a scene where Bernick claims that in every man's heart there will be at least one black spot that he has concealed. Lona replies:

> *And you call yourself pillars of society?*

(A) place for everything and everything in its place

The discipline was long familiar to all men of the sea and a version was mentioned in print as early as 1640. But it came to land in 1827 when the American, the **Rev. Charles Augustus Goodrich** of Connecticut, wrote uplifting books for the young. Writing in *Neatness*, he referred to an "old adage" when giving the advice:

> *Have a place for every thing, and keep every thing in its proper place.*

(Mrs. Beeton picked it up in *Household Management*, 1861.)

Plain as the nose on your face

A slight adjustment of "Plain as the nose on a man's face," from *Gargantua and Pantagruel* by **François Rabelais** (c.1532), introduced into English in 1693 by Sir Thomas Urquhart's translation.

Planned obsolescence

The expression dates back to 1932. During a lull in business, **Bernard London**, a successful New York real estate agent, wrote a twenty-page pamphlet on the depressed economic situation of that time. He observed that, during the Depression, people were retaining their old cars and wearing their old clothes longer than statisticians had expected. He coined a new term in his pamphlet's title:

Ending the Depression Through Planned Obsolescence.

Mr. London's expression "planned obsolescence" didn't cause much of a stir at the time, or for the following twenty years, but then caught the attention of Brooks Stevens. He was a successful home furnishing businessman and also had an impressive record designing cars and motorbikes. Stevens took up the term and in a landmark speech to an advertising conference in 1954 he reasoned that obsolescence could be planned, so that people would want something new sooner than they actually needed it.

The term became subjected to critical scrutiny when Vance Packard's book *The Waste Makers* was published in 1960.

Pleased as Punch

Based on an Italian original—Polichinello—the comic puppet show had reached England by the seventeenth century and enjoyed great popularity; Samuel Pepys reported enjoying the show in

1666. Polichinello gradually became known as Punch, and although his puppet activities involved mayhem—even violence and child murder—Punch was eternally satisfied and benign, saying cheerfully, "That's the way to do it!"

Irish poet and writer **Thomas Moore** is reputed to have used the term "pleased as Punch" in a private letter in 1813, and then put the expression into the public eye in 1818. This was in a collection of satiric poems from Paris supposedly written by the fictional Fudge family, who were quite unafraid of wide political generali-sations on the situation in Europe.

Moore's letter to Lord Castelreagh (from "Phil Fudge") tells us:

> That Poland, left for Russia's lunch
> Upon the sideboard snug reposes
> While Saxony's as pleased as Punch,
> And Norway 'on a bed of roses'
> That, as for some few million souls,
> Transferred by contract, bless the clods!
> If half were strangled—Spaniards, Poles,
> And Frenchmen—'twouldn't make much odds.

Poke fun at

Pointing the finger or guiding the conversation into ridicule. The expression first saw daylight in 1837 when Cardinal the **Rev. H. Barham** published his *Ingoldsbury Legends* series, including "The Monstre Balloon":

> Oh! fie! Mister Nokes,—for shame, Mister Nokes!
> To be poking your fun at us plain-dealing folks –
> Sir, this isn't a time to be cracking your jokes,
> And such jesting, your malice but scurvily cloaks . . .

(The) policemen are getting younger

Writings by the eminent British musician Sir Arnold Bax were published in autobiographical form in 1943 entitled *Farewell My Youth*. Sir Arnold wrote:

> *There are no compensations to weigh against advancing years—no, not one.*

This appeared to remind Sir Arnold of one of his many conversations with British novelist **Arnold Bennett**. During this particular talk, Bax recounted that Bennett had remarked:

> *. . . the recognition of his own middle age came at an appalling moment when he realised for the first time that the policeman at the corner was a mere youth.*

Pouring oil on troubled waters

Using actual oil on troubled waters had been a practice known as far back as the years BC. Pliny the Elder mentions it in AD 77. The expression reached English in AD 731, in *Historia Ecclesiastica* written by the Benedictine monk **The Venerable Bede**. He told of a priest being given a container of oil when he was sent as escort for a young woman from Ireland to marry King Oswin of Deira (Yorkshire). If a storm arose, he was instructed to pour oil on the water. This came to pass, and the water was calmed.

The original Latin was: "Assumpta ampulla, misit de oleo in pontum, et statim, ut praedictum erat, suo quievit a fervore." After being translated into English in 1565, the expression went into common usage in its metaphorical sense—pouring oil on troubled waters brings calm to an argument or volatile group situation.

Power is a great aphrodisiac

Christopher Hibbert's biography: *Napoleon: His Wives and Women* reports Bonaparte's belief (spoken in French) that women "belong to the highest bidder." British novelist **Grahame Greene** changed tack slightly and narrowed the concept when he commented in a *Radio Times* interview (1964) that:

> *Fame is a powerful aphrodisiac.*

Over time popular usage modified Greene's original statement, so that "fame" alternated with "power" as being a great aphrodisiac, and "great" sometimes became "the ultimate."

(Seven years after Grahame Greene's original remark, in January 1971, *New York Times* journalist Hedrick Smith wrote of statesman Henry Kissinger: "Power, he has observed, is the great aphrodisiac," but doesn't say when or where Kissinger "observed" it. This one hearsay report has often been referred to as the source of a widespread belief that Kissinger changed Grahame Greene's original remark. But evidence of Kissinger actually saying this has proved elusive.)

Pragmatism

The word is based on the Greek pragma, meaning deed, or act. In 1878 the philosopher and physicist **Charles Sanders Peirce** wrote a paper called "How to Make Your Ideas Clear" in the *Popular Science Monthly*. Peirce invented the word "pragmatism" to describe a guiding principle for scientists considering a concept in the mind in relation to the practical effect it would have in action.

His philosophies were subject to much academic discussion, and although the word pragmatic had existed since the 1500s, Peirce is credited with expanding it into pragmatism. The word duly went into common usage, though gradually with a rather less arcane application.

In contemporary times the word has taken on a meaning similar to "practicality"—the judgement of a situation according to a strict assessment of facts rather than theory.

(The) price of everything and the value of nothing

The line first occurs in the novel *The Picture of Dorian Grey* (1891) by **Oscar Wilde**, as:

> *Nowadays people know the price of everything and the value of nothing.*

Later, Wilde adapted the line himself by defining a cynic as, "A man who knows the price . . . " etc.

(The) Proms

The word promenade basically means a stately parade or a walk in a public place for pleasure and/or display. In the United States a prom usually refers to a school dance. But an entirely new reference developed with the evolution of promenade concerts in Britain.

In 1894 a meeting took place between British musician Henry Wood and entrepreneur **Robert Newman**. Newman was aware that symphonic concerts attracted audiences already accustomed to classical music. He discussed with Henry Wood the possibility of concerts with a more popular repertoire, presented in an informal atmosphere. The result in August 1895 was the start of a concert series for which Newman coined the name: Mr. Robert Newman's Promenade Concerts.

The presentation proved very popular indeed; besides normal seating, a large area of the Queens Hall (the original venue) was reserved for holders of very inexpensive tickets, who were permitted to eat, drink, stroll around, and smoke (though asked not to light matches when a singer was performing).

Henry Wood gradually evolved a program of popular and familiar items, mixed with unfamiliar and new material, talented young performers, and the works of foreign composers whose music had not before reached an English audience.

The Proms are now a firm part of the British musical landscape. However, although a large floor area is retained without any seating for informal attendees, there is no more eating, drinking, or smoking during a performance, and the "Prommers" tend to stand still, rather than stroll about.

Pull all the stops out

Each pipe in a pipe organ makes a different sound, and each is fitted with a stop. Pulling out a stop releases the air flow through that pipe, creating its unique sound, and the organist can create sound pictures by skilfully pulling out the desired combination of stops and allowing various pipes to have their say. The more stops pulled out, the more pipes are giving forth sound, hence the greater the volume.

This image of using the organ's full resources became a metaphor for an extravagant effort or a situation using every resource available. The metaphor first appears in **Matthew Arnold**'s *Essays in Criticism* (1865):

> *Knowing how unpopular a task one is undertaking when one tries to pull out a few more stops in that powerful but at present somewhat narrow-toned organ . . . the modern Englishman.*

Pull my leg

The origins of the term are generally believed to have something literal to do with pulling (or tripping) someone's leg. But by the end of the nineteenth century the expression had moved into metaphor, meaning a trick, a fanciful tale, or an amusing joke.

Used in that manner it first appeared in print in **William Brown Churchward**'s book *Blackbirding in the South Pacific* (1888). A suspect deal involving oil is being discussed with a Frenchman who reported having been cheated earlier by a character named Mike:

> *You can send me word by some of the boats if you can't come yourself. I shall be very anxious until I know, and then I shall be able to pull the leg of that chap Mike. He's always about here trying to do me.*

Pull your finger out

A legendary explanation is that loaded cannon had gunpowder poured into a small ignition hole blocked with a wooden rod. During battle, because of the urgency of the situation, after being poured the powder was held in place with a stuck-in finger. At the moment of firing, the call would come to "pull the finger out."

(Another more modern explanation prefers the remark to refer to advice among the military regarding intimate foreplay.)

After World War II the expression moved into general—but subdued—use to indicate a need for more energetic activity, or to finish an allotted task more quickly.

Its most prominent outing came in October 1961, when London's *Daily Mail* reported that **Prince Philip,** while addressing a meeting of British industrialists, said:

> *I could use any one of the several stock phrases or platitudes about this. But I prefer one I picked up during the war. It is brief and to the point: Gentlemen, I think it is about time we pulled our fingers out.*

(Let the) punishment fit the crime

Sir William Gilbert's clever words to Sir Arthur Sullivan's perfectly suited tune (in *The Mikado*) could well be the foremost example in the public mind of this expression.

But in fact Gilbert and Sullivan were following many footsteps after the Roman politician **Marcus Tullius Cicero**, who in 70 BC when writing about law and crime opined:

> *Noxiae poena par esto—Let the punishment be proportionate to the offence.*

Purple prose

Long before Mills and Boon, there were those who viewed with disfavor any over-ornate writing with extravagant use of flowery language. One such was the Roman poet Quintus Horatius Flaccus, aka **Horace**, who in 18 BC wrote *Ars Poetica*, criticising "purpureus pannus." This was translated into English by **Queen Elizabeth I** as "purple prose," which ever since has been a descriptor for what in later times is sometimes called pulp fiction.

See also **It Was a Dark and Stormy Night**

(On the) qt

It means reliable information given confidentially. How this came to be qt is unclear unless it is simply the first and last letters of quiet. The term was in use late in the nineteenth century, and came to print in *A Mummer's Wife* (1884) by Irish novelist **George Moore**. In a conversation between Kate and Miss Mender, Kate says:

> *'Mr Lennox will be here on Monday. I've just got a letter from him.'*
>
> *'Oh, I'm so glad; for perhaps, this time, it will be possible to have one spree on the strict q.t.'*
>
> *Kate was thinking of exactly the same thing, but Miss Mender's crude expression took the desire out of her heart, and she remained silent.*

Why Kate (or George Moore) thought of "qt" as crude, we don't know. Soon after, it came to be regarded as discreet but entirely respectable.

R

Read my lips

The term attracted international comment at the 1988 Republican National Convention when George Bush accepted the nomination to run for President. Peggy Noonan was George Bush's speechwriter, and she included the expression in his outline of one predicted policy: "Read my lips—no new taxes," and the sound bite went around the world.

But the line predates that occasion by at least thirty years. In 1958 songwriter **Joe Greene** composed "Read My Lips," which was recorded for Liberty Records with the Russ Garcia orchestra (LRP-3062). Greene was a respected songwriter whose output was recorded by an A-list: Ella Fitzgerald, Carmen McRae, Julie London, Fats Waller, the Mills Brothers, Stan Kenton, Ray Charles, Dinah Washington, even the Muppets. Greene's line "Read my lips" moved into rock vernacular and other songs arose that appropriated the title. It was also borrowed by a movie, a racehorse, a sports coach, *Coronation Street* dialogue, and—eventually—an American President-to-be.

(In Britain, seven years after George Bush's use of the term, Education and Employment Secretary David Blunkett caused a stir at the 1995 Labour Party conference by declaring: "Watch my lips: no selection, either by examination or interview, under a Labour government." It was later explained that in attempting to parody

Bush he had forgotten to include the word "further" before "selection.")

Reality television

Strictly speaking, reality television is any telecast that shows something happening in real life: Olympic Games, the coronation of Queen Elizabeth II, any sports match or political debate. But since the 1950s, the term reality television began to apply to contrived situations intended to entertain and fiercely pretending to be reality but in fact carefully arranged to occur within forty-four minutes, pause for commercial breaks, and occasionally have an invisible band or orchestra lurking somewhere in the wings.

The use of "real" people began innocently enough with entertainment programs. In 1950 American TV producer **Ralph Edwards** initiated both *Truth or Consequences* and *This is Your Life*.

By 1954 **Art Linkletter** was hosting *People Are Funny*. All three programs showed—apart from the host—only ordinary people, unscripted and spontaneous. Linkletter told the *Milwaukee Journal*:

> *Ralph Edwards and I invented reality television.*

Later the term came to be regarded as pejorative, as the so-called reality shows became structured, with considerable modification and editing being involved. Linkletter said of this that he and Ralph Edwards never demeaned people: "We never dreamed they'd have people eating bugs on TV."

Rearrange the deck chairs on the Titanic

The first known mention of the *Titanic*'s deck chairs came from Elizabeth Carpenter, who was press aide to Mrs. Lyndon Johnson in the White House. When interviewed by the *New York Times* in January 1969, Ms Carpenter commented:

All the new people want an office close to the President's. You should see them scramble. It's like fighting for a deck chair on the Titanic.

Her comment didn't directly link the chairs with any suggestion of disaster. But musician and conductor **Joseph Eger** did. Writing to the *New York Times* in May 1972, referring to the Lincoln Center's plans for young people's performing arts, Joseph Eger said:

Administrators are running around straightening out deck chairs while the Titanic *goes down.*

Eger's deck chair image caught people's imagination, and one of its better-known utterances came from Rogers Morton, public relations manager for Gerald Ford's election campaign in 1976. After Ford had lost five out of six primaries, Morton produced this variation on Joseph Eger's remark:

I'm not going to rearrange the furniture on the deck of the Titanic.

In later general usage, deck chairs were favored over furniture.

(Incidentally, the term's leap into popularity was seen as a marketing ploy by at least one enterprising entrepreneur: the Titanic Deck Chair Company of Nantucket produced accurate replicas of *Titanic* deck chairs as trendy items of garden furniture.)

Red sky at night . . . shepherd's delight

The best-known (and possibly the earliest) purveyor of this piece of weather wisdom was **Jesus of Nazareth**, who may have been quoting a known Israeli proverb. He spoke in Aramaic, and his words have gone through at least four different translations since then. The Revised Standard Version of the Bible reads:

When it is evening, you say, "It will be fair weather; for the sky is red." And in the morning, "It will be stormy today, for the sky is red and threatening." (Matthew 16: 2-3)

Over the centuries this piece of wisdom became contracted into a more pithy form, and has sometimes mistakenly been attributed to sailors and shepherds. They were probably already aware of these weather factors, since the situations mentioned had a great effect on their lives, but there can be little doubt that being launched by Jesus helped make the expression famous.

Red tape

It has a contemporary ring but is based on historical fact. The records of Henry VIII's negotiations with the Pope in 1527 concerning his desire to annul his marriage to Catherine of Aragon still exist. The ancient documents are tied together with red tape.

The use of such tapes remained a common practice over 300 years later; bundles of legal and Government documents were tied with red tape (in fact, a reddish pink).

The first known comment associating red tape with official obfuscation came from **Oliver Cromwell** in 1652. Thomas Carlyle's edition of Cromwell's speeches and letters contains this comment:

> *In fact red tape has, to a lamentable extent, tied up the souls of men in this Parliament and the Commonwealth of England. They are becoming hacks of office.*

In 1840 Carlyle himself referred to "red tape clerks" in a speech, but Charles Dickens' character David Copperfield (1869) probably drew more attention to the term than any prior use. After Copperfield has become a Parliamentary reporter, he writes of his daily exposure to tangled bureaucracy:

Britannia, that unfortunate female, is always before me, like
a trussed fowl: skewered through and through with office pens
and bound hand and foot with red tape.

Robot

It is believed that when **Karel Capek** first had an idea for a drama featuring mechanical men, it was his brother Josef Capek who suggested they be described by the Czechoslovakian word "robata," meaning "drudge worker."

Capek's 1921 play *R.U.R.* (*Rossums Universal Robot Corporation*) launched the word. It immediately came into common use to describe not only actual mechanical operators, but also human behavior of a repetitive and thoughtless nature. In 1942 Isaac Asimov further developed Capek's word into "robotic."

Rock and roll

Member of a high school band called Sultans of Swing, **Alan Freed** became a radio sports announcer in Ohio in 1942. Later moving to Cleveland and broadcasting music sessions, he specialized in playing jazz and pop. By 1951 he had become a rhythm and blues fan, calling himself Moondog and thumping his fist on a telephone book in time to the recordings he played.

The two words "rocking" and "rolling" had been teamed in various songs, but not representing what we now identify as rock 'n roll. In the 1934 movie *Transatlantic Merry Go Round* the Boswell sisters sang "Rock and Roll," referring to the motion of a ship ("rolling rocking rhythm of the sea . . . ").There was also minimal and somewhat clandestine use of the expression as a synonym for sexual activity.

But whether he knew that or not, Alan Freed heard the new style developing among bands and recordings, and announced that *this* sound was "rock 'n roll" because of the "rolling surging beat." The term quickly became universal, eventually contracted to just "rock."

(A) rolling stone gathers no moss

The term is identified with a world-famous rock group and an almost world-famous magazine. But in fact the basis of the line dates back to a slave from Iraq who was taken in servitude to Italy during the first century BC.

Publilius Syrus won freedom because of his wit and wisdom, one piece of which said:

> *People always moving, with no roots in one place, avoid*
> *responsibilities and cares.*

The thought was developed into Latin sayings such as "Planta quae saepius transfertur non coalescit" and "Saepius plantata arbor fructum profert exiguum," to the effect that trees that are uprooted and replanted too often are unlikely to be fruitful.

Erasmus added the concept of "rolling stones," and in 1362 the term came into English through **William Langland** (attributed author of *Piers Plowman*), who introduced the moss:

> *Selden moseth the marbelston that men ofte treden.*
> *(No moss grows on stone frequently trodden on.)*

Room at the top

Born into a poor family in rural America, **Daniel Webster** displayed acumen at an early age and nurtured an ambition to become a lawyer. When he mentioned this ambition to others he was dissuaded, because the legal profession was said to be overcrowded. He replied (c.1805):

> *There is room enough at the top.*

His determination and his intellect did not let him down. Webster not only became a lawyer admired for his oratory but also a Senator and eventually Secretary of State.

His expression went into the vernacular and in 1957 became the title of a novel, *Room at the Top* by John Braine, which caused a considerable stir, followed by the 1958 movie of the same name which caused a similar stir (six Oscar nominations and two wins).

Rose-colored glasses

The rose has been seen as an emblem of natural beauty for millennia. And traditional wisdom in the theater profession held that a rose-pink gel over the lighting made the stage, and anyone on it, look more attractive. Adding a similar tint to glasses would seem then to make everything take on a pleasing glow (though in actuality anything green might become a muddy grey).

The image first appears in **Thomas Hughes'** *Tom Brown at Oxford* (1861). The character Hardy when visiting Oxford finds it "a sort of Utopia" and:

> . . . *continued steadily to behold towers and quadrangles and chapels, and the inhabitants of the colleges, through rose-coloured spectacles.*

(Sometimes referred to as "rose-tinted spectacles" or "rose-colored glasses.")

(A) rough diamond

Fairly obviously, it means a diamond before it has been cut into facets and polished. But in metaphorical use it usually refers to a person whose qualities though sterling may not be immediately ascertained because of external shortcomings.

This use was introduced by **John Dryden** in his *Preface to Fables Ancient and Modern* (1770) in which he referred to the writing style of Chaucer as:

> . . . *a rough diamond who must be polished first ere he shines.*

Royal walkabout

For many years Queen Elizabeth II when in public kept strictly to designated places, made a stately progress along cleared paths, and spoke only to carefully positioned people.

But in March 1970 when visiting New Zealand, the Queen alighted from her car and suddenly walked straight toward the waiting crowd, talking at random to whoever came into her space and moving among the crowd with dignified goodwill. The public was delighted. *Daily Mail* writer **Vincent Mulchrone** described the incident as a "walkabout."

Initial reports of this caused mild confusion in Australia. In that country walkabout is a term used to describe the aboriginal cultural practice of disappearing into the bush or desert for an unspecified time, living on ancient survival skills.

This meaning seemed at odds with the notion of a Royal personage stepping from a gilded frame to chat to people in the street. But adding the word "royal" solved it. However because the Queen continued to do it frequently, people got used to the idea and just "walkabout" now suffices.

Rudolph the Red-nosed Reindeer

The image of Santa Claus as we know him was virtually invented in 1822 by the poet Clement C. Moore in his famous poem "A Visit from St. Nicholas." Moore provided Santa with eight named reindeer and that image remained stable for 117 years—until the advent of Rudolph.

In 1939 the American chain store Montgomery Ward was considering some Christmas advertising material written by a freelancer called **Robert May** in Chicago. One of his offerings was a feel-good poem, about an unglamorous reindeer with a red nose who yearned to be on Santa's team and eventually triumphed.

The store executives liked the poem but didn't like the reindeer's name: Rollo.

Changing it to Reginald didn't help. Robert May had a young daughter, and for no known reason she suggested Rudolph. Montgomery Ward executives said yes.

The story of Rudolph was printed as a Christmas-purchase giveaway, and several million of them were given away. An animated movie cartoon followed and then Johnny Marks set the poem to a tune that was recorded by major star Gene Autry. The result was a sensation, and Rudolph entered international Christmas mythology.

(A) rum go

A puzzling, unexpected, and slightly uncomfortable situation. The term had been in use in the early 1800s, and was launched into print in 1836 by **Charles Dickens** in *The Pickwick Papers*. Sam tells Mr. Pickwick of his suspicions that a certain coach's proprietor is not to be trusted and they are being given

> *rayther a rum go.*

Sacred cow

The term is a simple statement of fact in areas where the Hindu religion is paramount, since Hindus regard cows as indeed sacred. In America during the late 1800s, "sacred cow" became a metaphor referring to something held in unreasonably high regard by some people, and referred to cynically by others as beyond criticism.

The metaphorical use had crept into newspapers by 1890, but without a name attached. Apparently the first attributable use was in the formidable publication *The Armies Of Labor—A Chronicle of the Organized Wage Earners* (Yale University Press, 1919) by political scientist and lawyer, **Professor Samuel P. Orth**.

> *Emma Goldman, who prides herself on having received her knowledge of syndicalism "from actual contact" and not from books, says that "syndicalism repudiates and condemns the present industrial arrangement as unjust and criminal." Edward Hamond calls the labor contract "the sacred cow" of industrial idolatry.*

In similar vein, the metaphorical use of sacred cow spread throughout the English-speaking world.

Sally Lunn

In the streets of Bath during the late 1700s one could buy a particular brioche-like cake with a creamy, spicy flavor. It may have been called by the French name *soleil et lune*, or may have been sold by a young woman called Solange Luyon/Sally Lunn (the Sally Lunn Museum prefers the latter version). Either way, **William Dalmer**, a local baker, secured the recipe and started making the cakes himself around 1780, promoting them by composing a song that nowadays would be called a singing commercial:

> *Buy my nice Sally Lunn,*
> *The very best of Bunn,*
> *I think her the sweetest of any . . .*

The song spread far beyond Bath; the style of cakes with Sally Lunn's name were sung about in Gilbert and Sullivan's *The Sorcerer*:

> *The eggs and the ham*
> *And the strawberry jam,*
> *The rollicking bun*
> *And the gay Sally Lunn!*

Cakes called Sally Lunns are still sold in Britain and elsewhere. However, at this distance in time there is some confusion about the exact nature of the original Sally Lunn cakes, and the name has become attached to several versions.

Salome

She is widely perceived as the siren in the Bible who shed seven veils—but her name and veils have no biblical basis whatever. Matthew 14:6 and Mark 6:22 tell the story, describing the young woman only as Herodias's daughter and never mentioning her style of dancing.

In AD 94 the Roman-Jewish historian **Flavius Josephus** appears to have invented a name for her—Salome—and the misconception grew that her name was mentioned in the Bible.

Eighteen hundred years later came **Oscar Wilde**'s play *Salome* (1891). Wilde apparently knew the centuries-old Babylonian legend of the goddess Ishtar venturing into the underworld, surrendering a veil-like garment (or a piece of jewelry—the versions vary) at each of the seven gates to Hades, finally arriving naked at her destination. In Wilde's play, when Salome announces she is ready to dance, the stage directions read: "Salome dances the dance of the seven veils." In 1905 Richard Strauss's opera *Salome* followed suit, featuring evocative music for that same sequence of Salome's "seven veils" dance. The seven veils fantasy was here to stay.

(Being) savaged by a dead sheep

In 1978, British Labour politician and Chancellor of the Exchequer **Denis Healey** was criticized in parliamentary session by a Conservative minister, Sir Geoffrey Howe. Denis Healey's response was to refer to the encounter as like "being savaged by a dead sheep."

Say it with flowers

In the early 1920s the Society of American Florists was seeking to update their marketing. The publicity committee chairman **Henry Penn** approached the O'Keefe Advertising Agency. The agency's president **Major Patrick O'Keefe** found a line written by Bishop Arthur Cleveland Coxe:

Flowers are words even a babe can understand.

Mr. Penn felt the line was too long, Major O'Keefe agreed, and between them they abbreviated the line to: "Say it with flowers."

Scientist

One of the commonest words in the language didn't exist until 1833. We read, write, and speak about early pioneers of science, but in their own era those people were not known as scientists. The more usual appellation was "men of science," or even "natural philosophers" (in the sense of being examiners of nature).

One of the most eminent of these in nineteenth-century Britain was **William Whewell**, who was an authority on architecture, theology, politics, astronomy, geology, mechanics and mineralogy. Whewell was a fellow of the Royal Society and President of the British Association for the Advancement of Science. As well as science matters, he loved to play with language, and invented terms such as "ion" and "cathode".

When asked by the poet Coleridge in 1833 if there could be a word to describe people devoted to the study of science, William Whewell came up with the simple solution: scientist. The word went into universal use. So Whewell kept going and invented the word "physicist" as well.

Screw loose

Although the mid-nineteenth century was hardly as equipped with mechanical contrivances as the twentieth century, there were enough about to make the image of a screw being loose quite a valid image of dysfunction (streetcars, sewing machines, brick-makers, lawn mowers, yale locks . . .)

Charles Dickens turned the literal loose screw into the metaphorical in *Martin Chuzzlewit* (1844) when Mark Tapley tells Mr. Martin:

> *I've had my eye on you any time this fortnight. I see well enough there's a screw loose in your affairs. I know'd well enough the first time I see you down at the Dragon that it must be so, sooner or later.*

Self-help

A simple enough term (whether concerning personal growth, or a shop where you select you own purchases), but someone had to think of it. That someone appears to have been **Thomas Carlyle** in his philosophical satire *Sartor Resartus* (1833):

> *Thus from poverty does the strong educe nobler wealth; thus in the destitution of the wild desert does our young Ishmael acquire for himself the highest of all possessions, that of Self-help.*

Twenty-six years later (1859, the same year as Darwin's *Origin of Species*), Scottish author Samuel Smiles' book *Self Help*, outlining help for those who sought personal development, became a classic bestseller. Its opening sentence was: "Heaven helps those who help themselves."

Sex, drugs, and rock'n'roll

The form of hedonism later referred to as a rock'n'roll lifestyle had been burgeoning since the 1960s. The ethos was encapsulated by the title of the 1977 song "Sex, & Drugs & Rock'n'Roll" recording by the Blockheads, written by their star **Ian Drury** with **Chaz Jankel**.

The term quickly went into the vernacular.

She who must be obeyed

During his childhood, novelist **H. Rider Haggard** had a nanny who used to threaten him with an ugly doll which was referred to as "She who must be obeyed." In his later novel *She—A History of Adventure* (1887) the "She" who must be obeyed was Ayesha, an African sorceress who is immune to death (her name is a variation on an Arabic word meaning "she who lives").

Further use occurred when screen writer John Mortimer created the television character of Horace Rumpole, who frequently said it about his wife Hilda.

Shop till you drop

The expression is derived from a crucial moment in **Noel Coward**'s play *Still Life* (1936). The play tells of a couple, both married to other people, who have been having a passionate affair and are meeting to say goodbye because he has been posted to Africa.

Their heartbreaking farewell is interrupted by a noisy gossiping acquaintance laden with parcels (originally played by actress Everley Gregg) who stumbles to their café table and flops down beside them, announcing:

I've been shopping till I'm dropping.

Coward was a master of internal rhyme, but even shorn of its present participles, the abbreviated form retained its pleasing alliteration and quickly went into popular parlance.

Shut your face

Obviously a way of asking (telling) someone to be quiet. There are some who believe the concept dates back to knights of old whose armor had moveable face-plates, which when shut effectively prevented speech. Even if that were correct, in the later absence of armor from normal life the term assumed a distinct air of impoliteness.

A few centuries post-jousting, the expression appeared in print in **Upton Sinclair**'s *King Coal* (1917):

And suddenly the boss whirled upon him. "Get the hell out of here!" he shouted. "If you don't like it, get your time and quit. Shut your face or I'll shut it for you."

Significant other

By formal definition, a "significant other" is a person of importance in someone's life—as regards their emotions, behavior, and indeed how they spend their time. It may be a sibling, fiancé, parent, spouse, other family relation or business colleague.

During the 1980s and 90s, the field of reference narrowed slightly—there was an unspoken assumption that a significant other was a person's lover, life partner, or in some way shared a sexual and emotional connection (without gender restriction).

The original term dates back several decades, to 1953, when it was coined by American psychiatrist **Dr. Harry Stack Sullivan** in his book: *The Interpersonal Theory of Psychiatry*.

The work deals with the relationships between individuals and the network of others surrounding them. An individual may be:

> . . . *vulnerable to being arrested or impeded in direct chronological and otherwise specific relationship to the emotional disturbance of the significant other.*

Armistead Maupin's book *Significant Others* (1987) brought wide (and more accessible) American coverage to the term. And in 1989 the expression received amused attention in Britain when the TV series *Only Fools and Horses* featured Del-Boy referring grandiloquently to his girlfriend as his significant other.

Six degrees of separation

In 1929 Hungarian writer Frigyes Karinthy's short story "Chain Links" investigated the concept that technology was making the world smaller. Because of increased travel and communication, any two people could be connected through acquaintance with five intermediary people.

This story came to be seen by social commentators as a possible first step toward a study of "degrees of separation." Five intermediaries became six when playwright **John Guare** explained in an interview with David Finkle that Marconi had connected the world with wire, and it had been calculated that to connect with anyone anywhere on the planet could require 5.82 relay stations. Comparing this with social connections, Guare decided that six would be a better round number.

His play *Six Degrees of Separation* opened in New York in 1990, ran for over a year and was subsequently made into a movie. The expression has remained in the language to describe a fascinating possibility.

Six of one and half a dozen of the other

The saying was in use early in the nineteenth century, meaning that when an alternative is available, the choice between the two may be straightforward—or tricky.

It was captured by Captain **Frederick Marryat** in *The Pirate* (1836). Jack and Bill are discussing the advantages of having "wives" wherever the sea takes them. Jack agrees that a wife in every port is fine, but he misses seeing the children that might result:

> *I knows the women, but I never knows the children. It's just six of one and half-a-dozen of the other; ain't it, Bill?*

Skating on thin ice

It refers to either speaking carefully on a potentially dangerous topic, or more straightforwardly taking a risk and challenging danger. The image was captured by American poet, philosopher, orator and essayist **Ralph Waldo Emerson** in an essay on "Prudence" (1841):

> *Our Yankee trade is reputed to be very much on the extreme of this prudence. It takes bank-notes, good, bad, clean, ragged, and saves itself by the speed with which it passes them off.*

Iron cannot rust, nor beer sour, nor timber rot, nor calicoes
go out of fashion, nor money stocks depreciate, in the few
swift moments in which the Yankee suffers any one of
them to remain in his possession. In skating over thin ice,
our safety is in our speed.

Skeleton in the cupboard

When popular literature was in its Gothic period, there was a
fascination with bodies in priest holes, bricked walls revealing
hidden bones, and corpses being snatched for medical
experiments. Then the notion of hiding a skeleton in a cupboard
(or closet) began to acquire a metaphorical edge, referring to an
unsavoury secret that a person or family was keen to keep hidden.

Figurative use of a skeleton in a closet was made by
W.H. Stowell in a magazine called *Eclectic Review* in 1816. But the
image took off when the more famous writer **William
Makepeace Thackeray** put it into print.

His first reference to a skeleton as an embarrassing secret was
about his own figure. In 1845, writing for *Punch,* he explained that
eating too much was making his garments tight, so his name and
address were written inside his coat breast-flap in case he were
found speechless in the street:

> *A smiling face often hides an aching heart; I promise you*
> *mine did in that coat, and not my heart only, but other*
> *regions. There is a skeleton in every house.*

Thackeray went back to the skeleton image several times, and
moved it into the closet when he wrote *The Newcomes: memoirs of
a most respectable family* (1855):

> *. . . persons with whom our friends have had already, or will*
> *be found presently to have, some connexion. And it is from*

these that we shall arrive at some particulars regarding the Newcome family, which will show us that they have a skeleton or two in their closets.

Sledging

Verbal abuse, particularly by sportsmen to their opposition, during a match. The term is used in cricket to describe loud annoying comments delivered by fielders close to a batsman.

This practice goes back to the 1800s, but the name for it arose from the actions of Australian fast bowler **Grahame Corling**. He didn't create the term, but his tendency to make outspoken comments led to its creation. During the 1960s Corling made a particularly pungent faux pas in front of an embarrassed waitress at a cricket party, prompting a team member to say, "You're as subtle as a sledgehammer."

At the time, soul singer Percy Sledge had a hit song in Australia, and his name amalgamated with Corling's gaffe. The image of a sledgehammer became associated with rude remarks so that when players ridiculed a batsman they were sledge hammering, eventually abbreviated to sledging.

Slept her way to the middle

Rachel Abramowitz's book about female power in Hollywood *Is That a Gun in Your Pocket?* (2000) reports that Sherry Lansing's first step upwards from aspiring actress to studio executive in 1975 caused a male producer to remark that Lansing had "slept her way to the middle."

But since Abramowitz refrained from naming the man who said it, or when, we can't honor him as the originator. The term's more public launch and with acknowledged authorship was in actor/writer **Dirk Bogarde**'s novel *Voices in the Garden* (1981), albeit in a rather more blunt version. The short-time boyfriend of a nondescript actress (who plays "someone's mother on television and does voice-overs for custard commercials") says of her:

> *Decca York is the only woman I know who has screwed her way to the middle.*

Repeats of the line have tended to bowdlerise it back to the Hollywood version. *Voices in the Garden* became a television drama in 1993 with an all-star cast led by Joss Ackland, Samuel West, and Anouk Aimee.

Small but perfectly formed

Diplomat, author, British Member of Parliament and Britain's ambassador to France **Sir Alfred Duff Cooper** married the famous beauty Lady Diana Manners, daughter of the Duke of Rutland. In 1914 Duff Cooper wrote a letter to Lady Diana about a party at Belvoir, her father's castle, joking about his own slight build:

> *I really did enjoy Belvoir you know . . . You must I think have enjoyed it too, with your two stout lovers frowning at one another across the hearth rug, while your small, but perfectly formed one kept the party in a roar.*

The letter was published by their daughter (Artemis Cooper) in 1983.

Small fry

The young of some kinds of fish have been referred to as fry for several centuries and there are examples of it crossing over sometimes to refer to children. But it was **Harriet Beecher Stowe**'s widely read *Uncle Tom's Cabin* which put the term into the public domain:

Roars of laughter attended the narration, and were taken up
and prolonged by all the small fry who were lying, in any
quantity, about on the floor, or perched in every corner.

Smoking gun

The expression's ancestor is a line from **Arthur Conan Doyle**'s story "Gloria Scott" (1893) involving dirty doings on a ship of that name. The original line reads:

> *We rushed into the captain's cabin . . . there he lay . . . while*
> *the chaplain stood with a smoking pistol in his hand . . .*

Over the following years, pistol slowly changed to gun.

Smooth-shaven

Smoothness was hardly an unknown condition, but in times past men without beards were generally referred to as "smooth-skinned" or "smooth-faced." English poet **John Milton** introduced the term "smooth-shaven" c.1635 in *Il Pensoroso*. Milton was actually referring to a lawn-like patch of grass when he wrote:

> *And missing thee I walk unseen,*
> *Upon the dry smooth-shaven green . . .*

In vernacular usage the term moved from the lawn to refer to a man's smooth-shaven face.

Snug as a bug in a rug

The line occurs in a comedy by the prolific Irish playwright **Francis Gentleman** in 1769. A character says of a widow that if the rumor of her having money is true, he will "have her as snug as a bug in a rug."

Benjamin Franklin may have seen the play; he certainly knew the line. For in 1772 he wrote a charming letter to Miss Georgiana Shipley whose pet squirrel Skugg had died. His suggested epitaph for the buried creature was:

> *Here Skugg*
> *Lies snug*
> *As a bug*
> *In a rug.*

Sober as a judge

British judges apparently had a fine reputation when **Henry Fielding** wrote this line in *Don Quixote in England* (1733):

> *Oons sir—do you say that I am drunk?*
> *I say, sir, I am as sober as a judge.*

Spam

In 1937 the Hormel Food Co. launched a competition to find a name for a canned meat product. Apparently the company didn't want to call it "pork loaf" (though that's what it was) and was not permitted to call it ham because the meat was shoulder, rather than hindquarter. A prize of $100 was to be made available to a name the firm approved.

Kenneth Daigneau from New York came up with the name Spam—a condensed version of spiced ham—but without claiming it to be actual ham.

Thirty-three years later the British comedy group Monty Python's Flying Circus performed a bizarre television sketch in which a run-down café served only ludicrous variations of Spam. The customers' indignation climaxed in a ridiculous song whose lyrics consisted simply of the word Spam repeated.

The sketch was first broadcast on December 15, 1970. Its

popularity, and the association of spam with something unwanted but in oversupply, is credited with the word coming to mean junk email.

(There is no truth in the rumor that the title of the original Hormel tinned Spam was an acronym for "Something Posing as Meat.")

Speak softly and carry a big stick

Although sometimes referred to as being of West African origin, the expression is most indelibly associated with **Theodore Roosevelt**.

The American Treasures of the Library of Congress traces its first use in a letter from Roosevelt (dated January 26, 1900, before he was President) to Henry L. Sprague, in reference to support being withdrawn for a state insurance commissioner whose honesty had been found wanting.

In later years, as President, Roosevelt said "Speak softly and carry a big stick" publicly several times, once referring to it as "an old adage." No connection with Africa has been found.

(It's sometimes misquoted as "Walk softly and carry a big stick.")

Spill the beans

By itself, spill indicates something has been allowed out of where it should have remained (as in "blood was spilled") or, metaphorically, that information has been released—inadvertently or unwisely.

There are different stories explaining how beans got into the picture: ancient Greek voting was done with beans; or Turkish fortune-tellers poured beans from a cup and "read" the resulting configuration. There is no solid evidence behind these.

But spilling beans certainly crept into informal American usage in the early 1900s. The first author to use it was **Thomas K. Holmes** in *The Man from Tall Timber* (1919). We learn that, in front of acquaintances she had hoped to impress, Mrs. Lemoyne is claimed joyously by a frowsy old woman who knew her years before when they had worked together in Shattuck's eating house.

> *"And mother certainly has spilled the beans!" thought Stafford in vast amusement. For Mrs. Lemoyne, once having been caught by Aunt Tabby, saw the futility of clinging to any of her city airs and graces.*

(The) squeaky wheel gets the grease

With various wordings, the image has been around for several hundred years. But in 1870 American poet Henry Wheeler Shaw—who wrote as **Josh Billings**—in his poem "The Kicker" neatly nailed the image in the form we now know it:

> *I hate to be a kicker,*
> *I always long for peace,*
> *But the wheel that does the squeaking,*
> *Is the one that gets the grease.*

(The) stately homes of England

While most of the output of British poet **Felicia Hemans** is neglected, at least two of her lines are famous:

> *The boy stood on the burning deck, when all but he*
> *had fled . . .*

This is from "Casabianca" (1826). And in "The Homes of England" (1827) she wrote:

> *The stately homes of England,*
> *How beautiful they stand,*
> *Amidst their tall ancestral trees,*
> *O'er all the pleasant land!*

A century later, Hemans' poem was satirized by Noël Coward:

The stately homes of England,
How beautiful they stand
To prove the upper classes
Have still the upper hand . . .

British eccentric and writer Quentin Crisp, in his 1968 autobiography *The Naked Civil Servant*, referred to himself as "a stately homo of England."

State of the art

The term originally used the word state in its meaning of status, and referred to engineering, which historically is regarded as an art because it creates things that never existed before.

The earliest known use of the term in print was in 1910, when it appeared in a manual written by **H.H. Suplee**:

In the present state of the art this is all that can be done.

The art being referred to is the engineering of gas turbines. In a modern context the term retains a connection with its engineering background, since "state of the art" now often refers to new and improved versions of some form of technology.

Steal my thunder

In 1709 the Drury Lane theater staged a new play, *Appius and Virginia*. Its author was aware that if during a part of the action the audience could hear something resembling thunder, the play's dramatic atmosphere would be greatly enhanced. He invented the effect of stage thunder by hanging a wobbly metal sheet on wires, and then shaking it and beating it. The thunder effect was very successful but the play wasn't, and had only a short run.

Shortly after, the play's author **John Dennis** returned to the theater to see its production of *Macbeth*. During the performance he immediately recognized that his own invention was being used by the theater company. He called out:

They will not let my play run, but they steal my thunder!

Within a short time his cry had come to mean any situation where credit is being seized at the expense of where it is actually due.

(A) stiff upper lip

Somehow perceived as exemplifying British stoicism, the term's ancestry appears to be from elsewhere. London *Telegraph* writer Mark Steyn (October 19, 2004) cites evidence that stiff upper lip was actually of American origin, being referred to in the *Massachusetts Spy* newspaper in June 1815, and must have traveled to England and Bertie Wooster much later.

Its first appearance with acknowledged authorship was in 1833, in *The Down Easters* by American poet, critic and novelist **John Neal**:

What's the use o' boo-hooin, I tell ye! Keep a stiff upper lip; no bones broke don't I know?

Storm in a teacup

There were various changes before we settled on a storm and a teacup. Around 70 BC Cicero wrote about a lot of fuss over something relatively unimportant as "billows in a ladle."

Many centuries later Americans spoke of a tempest in a teapot. *The United States Democratic Review* in 1838 chided the Supreme Court over a minor matter concerning a University with these words: "This collegiate tempest in a teapot might serve for the lads of the University to moot." And tempest in a teapot has remained in common usage in America.

The British version was first brought into public prominence by American-born playwright **William Bayle Bernard**, who had lived in Britain since he was thirteen. He wrote over 100 plays, and the London farce *Storm in a Teacup* (1845) nailed the expression down into its now familiar form.

Straight from the horse's mouth

A horse's age can be assessed by examining its teeth. So whatever the age a horse trader tells a prospective customer, a look at the teeth will quickly show if the trader is telling the truth—the horse's mouth is the highest authority.

From this simple fact there developed a sense that information said to be from the horse's mouth was liable to be accurate, rather than skewed.

The expression had been known to stable hands and racing aficionados for decades. But it took **P.G. Wodehouse** to put the term into print as a metaphor for the first time, in August 1928 ("The Reverent Wooing of Archibald," *Strand Magazine*).

Archibald Mulliner is in love with the imperious Aurelia Cammarleigh, and he finds himself outside her curtained window just as she is about to tell her friend what she really thinks of him:

> *The prospect of getting the true facts—straight, as it were, from the horse's mouth—held him fascinated.*

Wodehouse was followed closely by Aldous Huxley in *Brave New World* (1932):

> *Straight from the horse's mouth into the note-book, the boys scribbled like mad.*

(Wodehouse must have liked the term; he used it again later in *Right Ho, Jeeves*:

I bunged my foot sedulously on the accelerator in order to get to Aunt Dahlia with the greatest possible speed and learn the inside history straight from the horse's mouth.)

Strictly for the birds

This expression of disbelief or dismissal must have been known—at least in Illinois—by the early 1940s, but was not perhaps in universal use. Then came its first known public expression in October 1944 when the "Sports Roundup" column in a Massachusetts newspaper, the *Lowell Sun*, interviewed a sergeant in the military about sports at the Camp Ellis Internment Camp in Illinois. **Sergeant Buck Erickson** said:

> *Don't take too seriously this belief that we have football at Camp Ellis solely for the entertainment of the personnel—that's strictly for the birds. The army is a winner . . . the army likes to win—that's the most fortunate thing in the world for America.*

(Sergeant Erickson may have been being polite for the occasion: Christine Ammer's *The American Heritage Dictionary of Idioms* tells that the more vulgar version of the term is "shit for the birds," alluding to birds' habit of picking seeds out of horse droppings. Hence the notion that something "for the birds" is worthless.)

Strike while the iron is hot

This is not the iron you use on shirts, but the old-fashioned blacksmith sort. When the blacksmith wishes to shape a horseshoe from a strip of iron, he must first heat it, and then bend it while it is hot.

But **Geoffrey Chaucer** was the first to use it in the meta-phorical sense: when circumstances seem propitious for a particular outcome, then action should be taken. In *The Tale of Melibee* (c.1386), the young people scorn the wisdom of their elders and clamour for war, crying out:

Whil that iren is hoot, men sholden smyte.

Superman

The concept—if not the realization—of a human more than normally powerful dates to 1883, when German philosopher Friedrich Nietzsche introduced the notion of the Übermensch in *Also Sprach Zarathustra*.

Twenty-two years later the same idea surfaced in English. **George Bernard Shaw** knew of Nietzsche's work, but was cautious about translating the word über. He settled on super, and "superman" appeared for the first time in 1905 as the title of Shaw's play *Man and Superman*.

Shaw's superman was one who could both direct and follow the will of the universe while suppressing his own. Both Shaw and Nietzsche envisaged the "super" part of their super-being as mental and moral, rather than physical, strength.

Using the name borrowed from Shaw, but combining it with an image somewhat more accessible to the general public, Jerry Siegel and Joe Shuster created the athletic figure of Superman. He was first launched in 1933, and started appearing in Action Comics in 1938. He grew into an American icon, the central figure of countless cartoons, radio shows, films and a musical.

The adventures of Superman were easier on the audience's patience than the play from which his name came—Shaw's *Man and Superman* lasts on stage over four hours.

Supermarket

Derived from Latin, the original meaning of "super" is "above," which survives in words like superintendent. But since George

Bernard Shaw's creation of the term superman, in English the prefix "super" has acquired the meaning of great size, outstanding qualities, and exceeding the norm.

Large shops that differed by supplying a wide range of foodstuffs rather than a single speciality began to appear spasmodically in the United States as early as 1916. By 1930 there were many chain groceries, complete with parking lots, and not dissimilar to their modern counterparts. But in general they were referred to as "groceterias," although the Big Bear stores sometimes used the expression "Super Market."

In November 1933 **William H. Albers** opened a shop in Cincinnati with a sign over it saying Supermarket, the first known public display of the word. Historians William H. Young and Nancy K. Young in their survey *The 1930s* assign Albers' shop as the first formal corporate use of the term with the registration Albers Super Mkts. Inc.

Supermodel

George Bernard Shaw attached the word "super" to a man in 1905. Prominent actors and sportsmen were being described as "superstars" from 1936. Soon after, in 1942, the *Chicago Daily Tribune* announced that "Super" models would be appearing in a fashion parade.

Then in 1953 a book appeared written by New York model agent and writer **Clyde Matthews Dressner** called *So You Want To Be A Model!* Predicting success for those who had the requisites, his advice included:

> She will be a super-model, but the girl in her will be like the girl in you—quite ordinary, but ambitious.

It was a rather extraordinary misunderstanding: that a super-model would be quite ordinary.

But Dressner's use of the hyphenated term super-model was the earliest known step toward usage, which gradually abandoned the hyphen and sometimes adopted an upper-case S—the Supermodel.

And a new form of aristocracy was born.

(A similar case of dropping the hyphen occurred in 1969 when Andrew Lloyd Webber saw a photo caption describing Tom Jones as an (un-hyphenated) "superstar." Webber attached the same label to Jesus and the hyphen disappeared.)

Suppose they gave a war and nobody came

In 1936, arising from the Great Depression, American poet **Carl Sandburg** wrote the poem "The People, Yes," in which a little girl is depicted seeing her first military parade. She speaks the line:

Sometime they'll give a war and nobody will come.

In 1961 a letter published in the *Washington Post* misquoted Sandburg's line as: "Suppose they gave a war and nobody came." Journalist Charlotte E. Keyes came across the letter, and not realising that the Sandburg quote was inaccurate, cut it out and kept it. In 1966 when she wrote an article for *McCall's* about an anti-war protestor, she used the (mis)quote as the article's title. This put the inadvertently adjusted line into wide circulation, and despite its inaccuracy, it surpassed the original in familiarity and soon went into common use.

Survival of the fittest

Darwin's *Origin of Species* (1859) clarified his theory that every species develops or evolves from a previous one by a process of natural selection. The book was studied by British philosopher **Herbert Spencer**, an esteemed commentator on ethics, religion, economics, politics, philosophy, biology, sociology, and psychology.

He too was interested in evolution, and in 1864 published his *Principles of Biology* that included his new term "survival of the fittest," which he compared with Darwin's natural selection.

Eventually Darwin decided that survival of the fittest was an acceptable interpretation of his own theories, and he included it in the fifth edition of his own work.

Suspension of disbelief

When a narrative has an element of fantasy that requires the observer to set practical judgement aside and become involved in the story in spite of its implausibility.

The term was created by **Samuel Taylor Coleridge** in *Biographia Literaria* (1817). His wish was that a reader of poetry would cooperate with:

> . . . *a willing suspension of disbelief for the moment, which constitutes poetic faith.*

Svengali

Svengali was a charismatic fictional figure with a controlling personality focused on organising the behavior of someone less resilient. The name is still widely used when referring to certain sporting coaches, parents with show-business ambitions for their children, and policy advisers in politics.

The name arose after British artist **George du Maurier** made a suggestion to his friend Henry James about a plot involving a manipulative personality who exerts a hypnotic power over someone weaker. But James didn't like the idea. When Du Maurier began to have trouble drawing because of failing eyesight, James suggested that he try writing his own prose fiction, rather than illustrating other people's works.

Du Maurier took up the suggestion and his 1894 novel *Trilby* was the result.

Trilby was a sensation—the story of a young woman with an indifferent singing voice who was transformed into a vocal star by the power of Svengali, her Hungarian mentor.

Professor Stephen Connor, Academic Director at Birbeck College, London, comments that:

> *The name Svengali is one of Du Maurier's happiest inspirations; suggesting some Nordic-Oriental cross-breeding, it also has wisps of the words 'English,' 'angel', 'sanguinary' and 'vengeance' in it. Crossword addicts will spot straight away that it can almost be unzipped into the word 'enslaving,' as well as, disconcertingly, forming a perfect anagram of the modern phrase 'sang live.'*

Echoes of the Trilby-Svengali relationship recur in Gaston Leroux's novel *Phantom of the Opera* (1911) and George Bernard Shaw's *Pygmalion* (1912).

Tabloid journalism

The word tabloid was invented in 1884 by Henry Solomon Wellcome of Burroughs Wellcome pharmaceutical company to describe a new kind of concentrated medicinal tablet.

In 1896 Irish-born **Alfred Harmsworth** (later Lord Northcliffe) launched a London newspaper called *Daily Mail*, self-described as "The Busy Man's Daily Newspaper." Its innovations included banner headlines, a more economical and easy to read prose style, considerable coverage of sports, and the inclusion of news specifically for women.

Because the new newspaper style was compressed, compact, economical in size, with contents concentrated into easily assimilated form, Harmsworth referred to it as "tabloid," like the new pill.

The word's association with compressed medicines rapidly faded and instead became firmly affixed to newspaper style. Initially referring only to size and accessibility of content, the term slowly became associated with a particular style of sensational journalism and took on its pejorative connotation.

Take care of number one

Referring to oneself as number one sprang into print in 1829 with the publication of **Frederick Marryat**'s *Adventures in the Life of Frank Mildmay*. Young seaman Mildmay came to be in charge of catering on a ship sparsely supplied with food, resulting in quarrelsome mealtimes:

> *Aware of the dangers and difficulties of my position,*
> *I was prepared accordingly. On the first day that I shared*
> *provisions, I took very good care of number one . . .*

Take down a peg

There are murky interpretations of what "peg" may have referred to in the early centuries of the expression's use. It might have been the pegs used to display a ship's flags (the higher the pegged flag, the greater the prestige), or a marker peg in a wine barrel. But whatever peg it was, by the late nineteenth century the term had settled into meaning that the bubble of someone's arrogance was about to be punctured.

In this context, it appeared in the novel *Marcella* by Australian-born Mary Augusta Arnold, a prolific novelist writing as **Mrs. Humphry Ward**. In 1894 she wrote:

> *I knew perfectly well that she had said to herself, 'Now*
> *then I must take that proud girl down a peg, or she will be*
> *no use to anybody;'—and I had somehow to put up with it.*

Take the cake

Cake has always been perceived as a treat, but it is not clear whether "taking the cake" derives from American high-strut dancing competitions, resulting in the winning of a cake.

Around 420 BC, Aristophanes refers to a cake as a symbol of winning, and several centuries later Shakespeare referred to "cakes and ale" as a part of good living.

So cake had a long history of signifying an honor or marking a special occasion. In 1836 prolific writer William T. Porter published "A Quarter Race in Kentucky" in the New York magazine *Spirit of the Times* and wrote:

> *They got up a horse and fifty dollars in money a side, each one to start and ride his own horse, the winning horse take the cakes.*

Early use of the term in America sometimes made the cakes plural, but the version currently in use, with just one cake, came from **Theodore Dreiser** in *Sister Carrie* (1900) after Carrie tells Drouet she can no longer live with him:

> *"Well that's a fine finish," said Drouet. "Pack up and pull out, eh? You take the cake. I bet you were knocking about with Hurstwood or you wouldn't act like that."*

(By extension, the cake is sometimes replaced by "the biscuit.")

Taking an early bath (or shower)

During a sports match a participant might leave the field because of injury, or be sent off after committing a misdemeanor.

During the 1960s prolific British sports commentator **Eddie Waring** popularized the thinly disguised euphemism "He's goin' for an early bath" as if the player was merely heading for the changing rooms ahead of the full team.

The term moved into wider use and is applied to anyone leaving a situation earlier than originally intended—and against their inclination to remain.

Teach your grandmother to suck eggs

There have been several versions down the centuries: Don't teach your grandmother to spin (from 1542, when all grandmothers knew how to spin), or to grope ducks (!), or to steal sheep, or to sup sour milk.

Sucking eggs settled in 1738 with **Jonathan Swift**'s *A Complete Collection of Genteel and Ingenious Conversation*:

> Go teach your Grannam to suck Eggs.

Teddy bears

In 1902 President Theodore Roosevelt (aka "Teddy") inspected the boundary between Mississippi and Louisiana, and combined the official trip with some bear hunting. By the fifth and final day of the hunt, the President had still failed to bag a bear. So when another man in the hunting party had the opportunity to capture a bear cub, he did so and tied it to a tree before offering Roosevelt the opportunity to shoot it. The President declared this was unsporting, and firmly declined to shoot the cub.

The incident aroused considerable publicity, very favorable toward the president. Confectionery shop owner **Morris Michtom** suggested to his wife that she make a toy bear to decorate their shop window. So she made a cuddly little bear out of velvet with shoe-button eyes. They called it "Teddy's Bear." The single toy in the window was a huge success, and orders were placed for dozens more.

The Michtoms sent their first bear to President Roosevelt and acquired permission to use his name. They closed the sweet shop and in 1903 set up a toy company which made literally millions of teddy bears. All over the world, children began a love affair with the charming toy named by Morris and Rose Michtom. One of their original 1903 bears is in the Smithsonian Museum.

(In 1921 A.A. Milne bought a teddy bear at Harrods for his son Christopher Robin, who called it Edward instead of Teddy. Five years later, Milne began his stories about his son's collection of stuffed toys, centred around Edward Bear, whose nickname Winnie the Pooh came from the black bear Winnie in London zoo, and a swan the family had named Pooh. Christopher Robin Milne's original teddy bear Edward is on display in the New York Public Library.)

(The) Teflon President (or Prime Minister, CEO, MP, Senator . . .)

Democratic representative in the House of Representatives **Patricia Schroeder** addressed the floor of the House in 1983, saying:

> *Ronald Reagan is attempting a great breakthrough in political technology—he has been perfecting the Teflon-coated presidency. He sees to it that nothing sticks to him.*

The description was so accessible it became appropriated and widely used; Reagan was soon being described as "Teflon-coated" or "the Teflon President," or said to be wearing a "Teflon suit." The term was also quickly applied to any major public figures who seemed to weather political storms unscathed.

There but for the grace of God go I

A modified version of the remark passed by sixteenth-century preacher **John Bradford**, whose Protestant beliefs fell foul of the impassioned Catholic monarch Queen Mary Tudor. Imprisoned in the Tower of London in 1553, Bradford witnessed first-hand Mary's persecution of those who wavered from her Catholic doctrines. While imprisoned in his cell Bradford watched as

Protestant prisoners were taken to the executioner, whereupon he is reputed to have remarked:

> *There but for the grace of God goes John Bradford.*

In time, Queen Mary with reference only to her personal interpretation of the grace of God, decreed his fate and John Bradford was led to his own death (by burning) in 1555.

There's no accounting for taste

Although the familiar English version has a contemporary ring, it dates back to 1794 (and indeed much further; classical Latin tells us De gustibus non est disputandum—there is no disputing about tastes).

Mrs. Ann Radcliffe's novel *The Mysteries of Udolpho* introduced the term into English, though in the plural:

> *I have often thought the people he disapproved were much more agreeable than those he admired—but there is no accounting for tastes.*

Udolpho is often called the first or quintessential Gothic novel. It abounds with crumbling castles, Italian brigands, an heiress in financial decline, an evil Marchioness, and apparently supernatural happenings. Jane Austen had a fine old time sending it up in her *Northanger Abbey*.

There's no place like home

The idea can be found eight centuries BC in the ancient Greek farmer-poet Hesiodos whose 800-verse *Works and Days* collection contains (in Greek) the line: "There's no place like home." By 1546 this had traveled into English as "Home is homely though it be poore in sight."

But the most familiar outing came in 1823 in Sir Henry Rowley Bishop's opera *Clari*. Bishop composed seventeen operas and over 100 operettas, ballets, and symphonic works. But after all that, only one of his compositions remains in people's memory—the leading lady's solo from *Clari:* "Home Sweet Home."

It owes its success and longevity to the plaintive melody, and the words provided by American writer **John Howard Payne**. Payne had arrived in London penniless and eventually created, adapted or translated sixty theater works. The public loved "Home Sweet Home" and over a hundred thousand copies of the sheet music were sold in the first year. But Payne's payment was small, and he returned to America. The song opens with:

> *'Mid pleasures and palaces though we may roam*
> *Be it ever so humble, there's no place like home . . .*

In East Hampton, NY, a picturesque old house believed to have belonged to John Howard Payne's grandfather is preserved as a memorial to Payne. The house is known as the "Home Sweet Home Cottage."

Thick as thieves

An old French expression encapsulates the concept that thieves are inclined to form a certain discreet brotherhood of collusion. Versions can be found in Pierre de Bourdelle Bratome's *Lives of Fair and Gallant Ladies* (1666) as "like thieves at a fair" and Balzac's *Domestic Peace* (1832) has it as "military fellows work together like thieves at a fair."

In English, the slightly adjusted French phrase first surfaced in 1866 as "thick as thieves" when used by author **Thomas Hook** in *The Parson's Daughter*.

Things aren't what they used to be

A common enough opinion, but the first time the now familiar wording is known to have appeared was in America in 1941.

Because of a union strike, jazz music star Duke Ellington was unable to do some night-time broadcasts and his son Mercer Ellington stood in for him. The younger Ellington used the opportunity to broadcast some of his own compositions, including a blues number—"Things Aren't What They used To Be"—whose name and lyrics came from **Ted Persons**.

This predated by nineteen years Lionel Bart's use of the same title for his quintessentially Cockney musical *Fings Ain't What They Used To Be*, which opened in London in 1960.

Things that go bump in the night

The expression is part of an anguished—and very old—prayer or litany from Cornwall. Nobody knows how old, or who might have composed it. But in 1926 the Cornish Arts Association made a collection of traditional adages originating from, or based around, the fishing village of Polperro, and illustrated with poker-work line drawings on wood.

So to that association, and to **Frederick Thomas Nettling-hame** who put it all together, we give credit for being first to print—and rescue—a fondly regarded expression in general English.

> *From ghoulies and ghosties*
> *And long leggety beasties*
> *And things that go bump in the night –*
> *Good Lord deliver us.*

The Cornish Litany is found in the Cornish Studies Library in Polperro.

Third World

The first known use of the term Third World was in 1952 by French anthropologist and historian **Alfred Sauvy**. He described what he called the Third World as being comparable to the Third Estate of the French Revolution:

> . . . at the end this ignored, exploited, scorned Third World like the Third Estate, wants to become something too.

Three years later the Bandung Conference in Indonesia brought together 1,000 representatives of fifty states. French diplomat Georges Balandier then referred to twenty-nine African and Asian nations as "third world." The term stuck, and quickly came to refer to nations perceived as underdeveloped, especially those with significant poverty issues.

Over time the "undeveloped" aspect of the description has been softened—the Third World nations are now usually defined as "developing."

Thirty days has September

Prior to England adopting the Gregorian calendar (1752), each fourth year had a "leap" day. However, that day was accepted simply as part of the preceding day's date, so is not mentioned in the first known rhyme cataloguing the months—**Richard Grafton**'s 1562 *Chronicles of England:*

> *Thirty dayes hath Nouember,*
> *Aprill, Iune, and September,*
> *February hath twenty-eight alone,*
> *And all the rest have thirty-one.*

In 1696, *Return from Parnassus* carried a new version of Grafton's original, which is the basis of the form now familiarly used:

Thirty days hath September,
April, June, and November;
February eight-and-twenty all alone,
And all the rest have thirty-one:
Unless that leap-year doth combine,
And give to February twenty-nine.

Throw the baby out with the bathwater

The origin is German—Das Kind mit dem Bade ausschütten (1512)—and it didn't appear in English until 1849. **Thomas Carlyle** wrote an essay for *Frazer's Magazine* concerning the slave trade (also published separately in 1853). Carlyle was knowledgeable about all things German and while opining about the necessity of being kind to slaves, he included an English version of the old German proverb:

> *The Germans say 'You must empty-out the bathing-tub,*
> *but not the baby along with it.' Fling-out your dirty water*
> *with all zeal, and set it careering down the kennels; but*
> *try if you can keep the little child! How to abolish the*
> *abuses of slavery, and save the precious thing in it alas,*
> *I do not pretend that this is easy . . .*

Throw the book

The term was in circulation among the American criminal underworld as a warning of what might happen if a planned crime should go wrong. The book would be thrown—meaning the maximum punishment the law allowed could be incurred.

In 1933 *Collier's* magazine published "Three Wise Guys," a **Damon Runyon** story about Blondy Swanson, Miss Clarabelle Cobb and a speakeasy. During the story, this line occurred:

> *The judge throws the book at him when he finally goes to bat.*

And the expression then moved into the public arena.

(In the same year *Collier's* published another Damon Runyon story, "The Idyll of Miss Sarah Brown," which later became *Guys and Dolls*.)

Throw your hat in the ring

The expression was once a literal statement. At nineteenth-century boxing evenings, a punter would demonstrate his willingness to fight by simply throwing his hat into the ring. The practice was known in Britain as well as America, and was first referred to in print when English poet **John Hamilton Reynolds** (aka **Peter Corcoran**) wrote "The Fancy" in 1820:

> *And dauntless man step full of hopes*
> *Up to the P.C. stakes and ropes*
> *Throw in his hat, and with a spring*
> *Get gallantly within the ring*

(P.C. means "Pugilist Club.")

The term became metaphorical, usually referring to entering some kind of contest. There is no doubt that **Theodore Roosevelt** made this figurative use famous when in 1912 he was asked if he planned to run for President, and replied:

> *My hat's in the ring—the fight is on and I'm stripped to the buff.*

Till the cows come home

Cows occupy their time fairly languidly all day, then head for home when milking is due—taking their time about getting there. So to say something will last until the cows come home implies that will be of a reliably long duration.

The saying originated from a line in a **Beaumont and Fletcher** play *Scornful Lady* (1616), now slightly adjusted from the original, which was:

Kiss till the cow comes home.

Time is money

It sounds like twenty-first century business mantra, but in fact recognition of the concept dates back to several centuries BC in ancient Greece.

In English, Sir Thomas Wilson hinted at it in *A discourse upon Usuary* (1572): "They saye tyme is precious." Francis Bacon came closer in his *Essays*, writing "Of Dispatch" (1625): "Time is the measure of business as money is of wares; and business is bought at a dear hand."

But the tidiest phrasing came from American journalist and diplomat **Benjamin Franklin** in *Advice to a Young Tradesman—Written by an Old One* (1748):

> *Remember that TIME is Money. He that can earn Ten Shillings a Day by his Labor, and goes abroad, or sits idle one half of that Day, tho' he spends but Sixpence during his Diversion or Idleness, ought not to reckon That the only Expence; he has really spent or rather thrown away Five Shillings besides.*

Tin pan alley

During the early part of the twentieth century, the premises of New York music publishers, writers and lyricists were mainly to be found on West 28th Street, between Broadway and Sixth Avenue.

Monroe Rosenfeld was a lyric writer who turned journalist for a series of articles he wrote in the *New York Herald* about the burgeoning music business. As Mr. Rosenfeld moved along the street among music publishing offices, the sound of pianos and singers demonstrating songs to publishers was inescapable—and disconcertingly discordant. The comparison Mr. Rosenfeld made was to the noise of many tin pans being clanged together. He described the area as: Tin Pan Alley.

To a T

It means eminently suitable, or "exactly." The expression may have arisen from an old term—to a tittle—meaning a miniscule amount, and some see it as referring to the exact neatness achieved by the draughtsman's T-square.

Neither explanation has a firm provenance, but what we do know is that the term first appeared in print during the 1600s, which makes the T-square connection unlikely.

James Wright was the author of a satire called *The Humours and conversations of the town, Expos'd in Two Dialogues. The First of the men. The Second of the Women.* (1693). In this book we find:

> *All the under Villages and Towns-men come to him for Redress; which he does to a T.*

Today is the first day of the rest of your life

The line originated in the Haight-Ashbury district of San Francisco during the peak activity of a community activist theater group called The Diggers. They were named after a seventeenth-century group of British radicals who initiated an early form of belief in the communal ownership of land.

Starting in 1966, the San Francisco group sought to enhance freedom through anarchic street theater, handing out food to those who needed it, giving free concerts, organising street parades with radical themes (e.g., "The Death of Money"), and the publication of papers reminiscent of early English pamphlets and broadsheets. These pamphlets launched various slogans that became catch-phrases, including "Do Your Own Thing."

In 1967 a **Diggers** pamphlet published this advice:

Today is the first day of the rest of your life.

An occasional alternative version developed—that tomorrow is the first day of the rest of your life.

Toe rag

Known to both tramps and prison inhabitants during the 19th century, the term reached print in 1864.

J.F. Mortlock was twice sentenced for offences in England, twice transported to Australia as a convict, and twice returned to England. His book *Experiences of a Convict* explained that since socks were generally unavailable to prisoners, they would wrap their feet in strips from an old shirt, called "in language more expressive than elegant—a toe rag."

After long service, the condition of these strips of cloth may well explain why the expression toe rag had become a term of contempt within a decade of Mortlock's book being published.

To err is human, to forgive divine

The idea was in circulation both in Latin and in English during the 1500s and 1600s. But **Alexander Pope**'s *Essay on Criticism* in 1711 captured the meaning in the epigrammatic form in which it is best remembered.

Tom and Jerry

It seems an unlikely leap from the streets of early nineteenth-century London to the cartoon drawing boards of Hanna Barbera. Nevertheless the urban sketches of English sportswriter **Pierce Egan**, collected and published in 1821 as *Life in London, or Days and Nights of Jerry Hawthorne and His Elegant Friend Corinthian Tom*, are the first known teaming of the names Tom and Jerry.

Pierce Egan's Tom and Jerry were roistering bucks, constantly encountering trouble on "rambles" and "sprees," and the book was a great success, engendering a stage adaptation and a drink devised to represent the pair of rakes. The Tom and Jerry drink—a kind of eggnog with both brandy and rum—survived long after the book had faded. Damon Runyon mentions it in "Dancing Dan's Christmas" over 100 years later, and the drink's name is believed to have inspired the names of the Oscar-winning cartoon cat and mouse.

(There would seem even less connection between Egan's London dandies and Simon and Garfunkel, but that duo's original name in 1957 was Tom and Jerry.)

See also **Bunch of fives**

Tomorrow is another day

An ordinary enough remark, but it didn't really enter the vernacular until 1936 when **Margaret Mitchell** wrote it as the last line of *Gone With The Wind*—Scarlett O'Hara resolving that on the following day she would start planning her campaign to get Rhett Butler back, and saying determinedly:

> *After all—tomorrow is another day.*

The 1939 blockbuster movie ended with Vivien Leigh announcing the same line, making the phrase even more familiar to thousands who hadn't already read the book.

Tongue in cheek

It is difficult to know why "tongue in cheek" signifies irony and that something being said is not to be taken seriously. Actually doing it—putting the tongue in the cheek—is virtually unknown, besides being rather awkward to achieve (especially when speaking).

Nevertheless the term is freely used to indicate doubtful integrity, having been launched by **Sir Walter Scott** in *The Fair Maid of Perth* (1828). A pompous and ridiculous looking little man is perched atop a very large horse when:

> . . . *some wag of the lower class had gravity enough to cry out, without laughing outright "There goes the pride of Perth"* . . . *It is true, the fellow who gave this all-hail thrust his tongue in his cheek* . . .

Too clever by half

Sheridan gives the first hint in *School for Scandal* (1771) when Charles Surface tells Sir Peter that Joseph is "too moral by half." But the true ancestor of the contemporary expression came from British poet, author and soldier **George Whyte-Melville**, a former cavalry officer in the Crimean war, who used the term "too clever by half" when writing of Crimea and the siege of Sebastopol in his novel *The Interpreter* (1858).

(A jocular version—"too clever by three quarters"—has occasionally been used to describe Stephen Fry, Clive James, Jonathan Miller, Tom Stoppard, and others of similarly impressive breadth of mind.)

Took to my heels

The ancient Roman comedy playwright **Publius Terentius Afer** wrote about taking to his heels in the second century BC.

The move into English came with a few variations. Shakespeare in *Henry IV*, Part 1 offers: " . . . play the coward with thy indenture, and show it a fair pair of heels . . ."

By the 1800s *taking* to one's heels can be found in R.L. Stevenson, John Buchan, Conan Doyle, Daniel Defoe, Captain Frederick Marryat, and many others, having settled into popular usage.

To the victor the spoils

Bearing in mind that in this context "spoils" means trophies, prizes, and profits, rather than spoiled things, the phrase is often used in reportage of sports events or election results.

It is a condensed version of a statement put into circulation in 1832 by the Governor of New York **William Learned Marcy** when he addressed the Senate concerning the attitudes of the Jackson administration. Marcy said:

> *They see nothing wrong in the rule that to the victor belong the spoils of the enemy.*

(Ninety years later F. Scott Fitzgerald deliberately reordered the term in *The Beautiful and the Damned* (1922): "The victor belongs to the spoils.")

Touch and go

The origin of the touching and going referred to has several claimants. Land lubbers say it refers to the horse and carriage era, when if two carriages brushed against each other even momentarily there could be danger. But Admiral Smyth's *Sailor's Word Book* (1867) places the image firmly at sea, as in "rounding a ship very narrowly to escape rocks, or when under sail she rubs against the ground with her keel." In any case (including later frequent use by airplane pilots) the element of accidental danger can be present.

But the first prominent use of the term in public does not imply any sense of danger; its use is strictly metaphorical, in this case meaning to speak briefly on a topic and then quickly moving on. The term occurs in a sermon delivered by Protestant church-man and martyr **Hugh Latimer** preaching to King Edward VI in 1549:

> *As the text doth rise, I will touch and go a little in every place
> . . . I will touch all the foresaid things, but not—too much.*

Trophy wife

The concept of a strong successful man with an impressively decorative wife has been around for several thousand years, and described in the same way. Victorious warriors of ancient Greece and Rome aimed to capture, and make wives of, the most beautiful women among their enemies. The custom is mentioned in Ariosto's *Orlando Furioso* (1516):

> *Those arms that Marganor were wont to wield*
> *Were here dispos'd, his cuirass, helm and shield*
> *In trophy wife—and near they bade to place*
> *Their new decree to bind the future race.*

Over 400 years after *Orlando Furioso* the American editor **Julie Connelly** may have picked up a vibe that there was a rekindling of interest in the ancient term. She certainly gave it a new front-rank exposure. William Safire, writing in the *New York Times* (May 1994) said of her:

> *The term trophy wife, now firmly ensconced in the language,*
> *was coined by Julie Connelly, a senior editor of* Fortune

*magazine. In a cover story in the issue of Aug. 28, 1989,
she wrote: "Powerful men are beginning to demand trophy
wives. . . . The more money men make, the argument goes,
the more self-assured they become, and the easier it is for
them to think: I deserve a queen."*

Truth is stranger than fiction

The original lines are:

> *'Tis strange,—but true; for truth is always strange;
> Stranger than fiction: if it could be told . . .*

Lord Byron wrote this in *Don Juan* (1823). General usage in
the vernacular eventually resulted in an abbreviated version.

TTFN (Ta-ta for now)

During the lead-up to WW II, the phrase TTFN arose as a reaction
to, and a slight send-up of, military abbreviations, which were
being heard quite frequently.

TTFN may have arisen in the Air Force, but an enormously
popular radio show made it famous in Britain.

It's That Man Again started in 1939 starring Tommy Handley
and ran for ten years. A year into its run, actress **Dorothy
Summers** took over the role of Mrs. Mopp, charlady to Mayor
Handley, and the scriptwriters began and ended her scenes with
two memorable lines. Mrs. Mopp always arrived with a clatter,
calling out "Can I do you now sir?" and when she left she bellowed
"TTFN."

Somewhat later, 1968 in Los Angeles, when the soundtrack of
Disney's movie *Winnie Pooh and the Blustery Day* was being laid
down, the actor playing the voice of Tigger was Paul Winchell,
whose English wife was very familiar with the term TTFN.
Although Disney himself was unsure about it, Paul Winchell

inserted TTFN into Tigger's dialogue, giving the impression to some moviegoers that it comes from A.A. Milne, which it doesn't.

Whether or not Dorothy Summers' writers picked it up from military jargon, there is little question that she launched the phrase onto the wider English-speaking world.

Tweedledum and Tweedledee

In London during the 1700s, a hot topic of conversation concerned the varying quality of new offerings from classical musicians. One disputed point was whether Handel's music was the equal of, or superior to, that of the Italian musician Bononcini.

John Byrom, who invented shorthand, also invented comic names for those two composers when he wrote a satirical poem (c.1725) comparing them. It ended with the lines:

> *Strange that such high dispute should be,*
> *Twixt Tweedledum and Tweedledee.*

Over 140 years later, Lewis Carroll took up the names and allocated them to two fat brothers Alice met through the looking glass.

Two countries separated by the same language

The basic observation was first expressed by **Oscar Wilde** in *The Canterville Ghost* (1888), a story about an American family in England coming to terms with a ghost in an English castle. He writes of the American Mrs. Otis:

> *In many respects she was quite English, and was an excellent example of how we really have everything in common with America nowadays except, of course, language.*

Later developments modified Wilde's original observation into England and America being two countries (or nations) separated (or divided) by one (or a common, or the same) language. One or other of these is often attributed to George Bernard Shaw, but no evidence exists that Shaw ever commented on the matter, either orally or in writing. Wilde takes the honor.

Ugly as sin

What some regard as sins seem attractive to others. But there is no escaping the dark connotations of the word sin. English poet Alexander Pope referred to sin as being unpleasant to behold:

> *Sin is a creature of such hideous mien*
> *That to be hated needs but to be seen.*

But **Sir Walter Scott** in *Kenilworth* (1821) first put "ugly" and "sin" together. The young lad known as Hobgoblin tells Tressilian:

> *Though I am as ugly as sin, I would not have you*
> *think me an ass, especially as I may have a boon to*
> *ask of you one day.*

Ugly duckling

There is a hint of Cinderella—even of Pygmalion—but Hans Christian Andersen's duckling story (1843) is entirely original, and not based on any earlier myth or folklore. In 1846, **Mary Howell** provided the first translation of Andersen's story from Danish into English—the first of many that appeared in other languages.

The story is seen as a metaphor for personal transformation, although the title is commonly heard to refer to someone or something which appears ill-favored. *The Ugly Duckling* has formed the basis for animated movies, symphonic story-telling, a pop song, and the Olivier Award-winning musical *Honk*.

Uncle Sam

He was a real person—**Samuel Wilson**, born in the United States in 1766. An experienced meat inspector, he was engaged by the U.S. Army during the Anglo-American war in 1812 to inspect meat. He declared meat to be acceptable by initialling the barrels, not with "S.W." (his initials), but with "U.S." because his fellow workers referred to him and addressed him as Uncle Sam.

Uncle Sam Wilson was known to be a man of great fairness, reliability and honesty. The coincidence of the initials echoing United States, and the affectionate respect in which Uncle Sam Wilson was held, gradually led to the name being equated with the nation as a whole.

By 1852 there were cartoons depicting a benign old man (his red, white, and blue striped suit came later), and his acquaintances and colleagues had no complaint about his being associated with all things American.

He died in 1854 in Troy, New York, and a statue in that town commemorates him as the original Uncle Sam. In 1961 the Congress formalized the matter by passing a resolution affirming that Samuel Wilson was the inspiration for the symbolism of Uncle Sam.

Uncle Tom Cobleigh and all

Commonly invoked when attempting to describe briefly a comprehensive guest list, or any situation where simply everyone with the slightest connection to the event, whatever it is, turns up!

The line comes from a charming old song called "Widdicombe Fair" and although its exact writer is unknown, **Uncle Tom**

Cobleigh is believed to have been a real person, from the village of Spreydon in Devon. Legend has it that he fathered every red-haired child within a thirty-mile radius—without ever marrying. The local tavern features an inscription commemorating the ride to Widdicombe Fair in 1802:

> *Tom Pearse, Tom Pearse, lend me your grey mare*
> *All along, down along, out along lee*
> *For I want for to go to Widdicombe Fair*
> *With Bill Brewer, Jan Stewer, Peter Gurney,*
> *Peter Day, Daniel Whiddon, Harry Hawk,*
> *Old Uncle Tom Cobleigh and all*
> *Old Uncle Tom Cobleigh and all.*

Underdog and Top dog

The concept of a "top dog" arose originally from the observation that any group of dogs—a wild pack, or even just two in a domestic setting—produces an alpha male which dominates.

Then the term shifted to the once-popular sport of dogfighting, with two references—one actual, and one predictive. During a fight the superior dog could be seen on top. If a particular dog had a track record for often achieving supremacy, those taking bets on a forthcoming fight would refer to it as a top dog, while a newcomer, or fighter with an unimpressive track record, would be the underdog.

The latter term moved away from dogfighting and into wider metaphorical use following the publication of a poem by **David Barker,** a lawyer in Maine, and also an active writer and poet. "The Under-Dog in the Fight" was first published in 1859, and when Barker died, the *New York Times* commented (September 16, 1874) that his poem had been "extensively copied." It was in fact copied and re-published so many times that corruption crept into the original words, but the vernacular use of the term underdog became commonplace.

The Under-Dog in the Fight

I know that the world, the great big world,
From the peasant up to the king,
Has a different tale from the tale I tell,
And a different song to sing.
But for me, and I care not a single fig
If they say I am wrong or right,
I shall always go for the weaker dog,
For the under-dog in the fight.

I know that the world, that the great big world,
Will never a moment stop
To see which dog may be in the fault,
But will shout for the dog on top.
But for me I shall never pause to ask
Which dog may be in the right.
For my heart will beat, while it beats at all,
For the under-dog in the fight.

As a vernacular expression, top dog appears to have crept into common usage later than underdog.

Under the weather

Clearly a reference to seasickness: etymologists of maritime expressions, Bill Beavis and Richard G. McCloskey (in *Salty Dog Talk*), explain that originally the expression was "under the weather bow"—the weather bow being the side of the ship receiving the full blast of rotten weather—and quite the most unpleasant place to be if feeling queasy.

The first known recording of the term ashore is its mention by American author **Donald Grant Mitchell** (aka Ik Marvel) in *Fudge Doings* (1855).

Young Mr. Fudge is travelling for the first time on a steamer and starts to need to lie down a great deal, calls a steward frequently, loses his appetite, develops a parched yellow expression, and finds that wine tastes different and cigars have lost their appeal. He writes to a friend:

> *The engines keep up an infernal chatter: prefer sailing*
> *myself. Besides—one has no appetite: the truth is, I've*
> *been a little under the weather.*

In later decades the expression lost its direct relationship to seasickness, and began to describe a hangover, a failed romance, financial strain—or any other discomfort.

United Nations

At the end of World War II high-level discussions between President Roosevelt and Prime Minister Winston Churchill, who was staying at the White House, sought an agreement between allies. On January 1, 1942, Roosevelt in his wheelchair, and Churchill straight from a bath, met in Churchill's bedroom to discuss and if necessary revise the Department of State's proposal, which was provisionally called Declaration of Associated Powers.

President Roosevelt showed preference for a name change to Declaration of United Nations. Churchill firmly agreed, and quoted some lines from Byron's "Childe Harold's Pilgrimage":

> *Here, where the sword united nations drew*
> *Our countrymen were warring on that day!*
> *And this is much, and all which will not pass away.*

The following day the Soviet ambassador and the Chinese Foreign Minister signed the Declaration of United Nations.

(The) usual suspects

A notable line from the 1942 movie *Casablanca*. Claude Raines as the French police chief Renault gives the order:

> *Round up the usual suspects.*

Written by twins **Julius E. Epstein** and **Philip G. Epstein.**

Vamp

A vamp is a woman who cruelly uses sexual fascination to enslave a man. By a curious set of circumstances, she owes her name to **Rudyard Kipling**—after he was inspired by Sir Philip Burne-Jones.

In 1896, the year that *Dracula* was first published, a striking painting by Burne-Jones was exhibited at the New Gallery in London. It showed a woman in melodramatic pose and flowing attire, bending back from the body of a man who seemed to be dead, and whose open shirt showed teeth marks on his exposed chest. The painting was called *The Vampire*.

Fully clothed though the subjects were, the painting was seen as both erotic and dangerous, and caused much comment. Inspired by the Burne-Jones painting, Rudyard Kipling was intrigued enough to write a poem with the same name, "The Vampire," published in 1896.

The poem concerned the sadness of a man's loss of pride in the face of the manipulations of beautiful women. Its most memorable line reduces womankind to: "a rag, a bone, a hank of hair."

The poem caught the attention of Robert Hilliard, who was inspired to write a play on the theme of man destroyed by a rapacious woman. As its title, he chose the Kipling poem's opening line: *A Fool There Was*. The play appeared on Broadway in 1909 with Hilliard taking the lead as a diplomat whose life and career are ruined by a scheming charismatic woman. His opposite number, the leading female character, was known throughout simply as The Vampire.

Film producer William Fox bought the rights, and chose an obscure twenty-nine-year-old actress from Cincinnati named Theodosia Goodman to play The Vampire. Recreated by publicists **John Goldfrap** and **Al Selig** as Theda Bara (of Eastern royal blood, born under the pyramids and suckled by serpents), she made a sensation and the type she represented in her role as The Vampire quickly became known as the vamp.

There was no known comment from Kipling, but the word has retained that meaning ever since.

Variety is the spice of life

Euripides put it quite gently in 408 BC: "A change is always nice," and over 2,000 years later Aphra Behn produced a modified version (1681): "Variety is the soul of pleasure."

But British poet **William Cowper** in "The Task" (1785) put it in the way it's been said ever since:

> *Who waits to dress us arbitrates their date*
> *Surveys his keen reversion with keen eye*
> *Finds one ill-made another obsolete*
> *This fits not nicely, this is ill-conceived*
> *And making prize of all that he condemns*
> *With our expenditure defrays his own ...*
>
> *Variety's the very spice of life,*
> *That gives it all its flavor.*

Viewer

Before television actually began in Britain, there was no satisfactory word to describe the people who would be watching it. The rather clumsy term "looker-in" was gradually replaced by "televiewer," which was equally awkward.

In 1936 the BBC opened its studio and transmitter at Alexandra Palace in London. The event was marked with a telecast ceremony, during which the Chairman of the BBC, **R.C. Norman,** greeted the "viewers."

This is believed to be the first time the word viewer was used publicly to describe television-watchers.

Virtual reality

Somehow evoking the computer age, the term virtual reality actually dates back to 1938 when computers were still beyond the horizon. It occurs in *The Theatre and its Double* by French poet and director **Antonin Artaud**, who wrote about virtual reality in theater, where for many centuries images, objects, and characters strove to create a reality that everyone present knew was illusion.

Three decades later the expression began to move way from theater and to imply computer imagery. Myron Krueger wrote of artificial reality, which is also mentioned by Damien Broderick in *Judas Mandala* (1982).

Fifty years after Artaud created the term, it was revisited by eminent computer scientist Jaron Lanier, who developed populated virtual worlds, created the first avatars and founded a firm which sold VR product.

The popularity of things virtual led to the ancillary expression virtual community.

See also **Cyberspace**

W

(A) walk on the wild side

In 1951 Jimmy Heap recorded a song called "The Wild Side of Life." Neither the recording nor the song attracted much attention until country music star Hank Thompson re-recorded it in 1952 and had a major hit. Written by Arlie Carter and William Warren, the song depicted the sad breakup of an affair because of a woman's drift toward "places where the wine and liquor flow, where you wait to be anybody's baby."

In the early 1950s American author **Nelson Algren** heard the song often and its title and setting influenced his 1956 novel *A Walk on the Wild Side*, which became a 1962 movie with Laurence Harvey, Jane Fonda, Anne Baxter, and Barbara Stanwyck. The movie's title song "Walk on the Wild Side" (Mack David and Elmer Bernstein) was quite different from the Hank Thompson offering that had originally caught Algren's attention. But a third song was yet to come—the best known of the three.

Lou Reed had discussed the possibility of making a theater musical of Algren's novel. Although he didn't continue with the theater project, Reed did compose his own 1972 version of "A Walk on the Wild Side," which bore no relation to the earlier two songs. Reed's version became one of his longest-lasting hits, and took the expression into wider international recognition than ever before.

Warts and all

It was, and is, not uncommon for portraitists of celebrities to present their subject as attractively as possible. Long before airbrushing or photoshopping—or even photography—a royal personage would despatch a portrait of himself (or herself) to distant potential marriage partners, and expect the compliment to be returned. Sometimes the portraits proved more seductive than the reality.

But when **Oliver Cromwell** took power in England as Lord Protector in 1653, a less obsequious atmosphere reigned. Cromwell sat for a portrait by Sir Peter Lely. It was reported some time afterward that Cromwell had told Lely:

> *I desire you would use all your skill to paint my picture truly like me, and not flatter me at all; but remark all the roughness, pimples, warts and everything, otherwise I will never pay a farthing for it.*

And indeed the Lely portrait shows Cromwell's slight imperfections and at least one sizeable wart (verified by his death mask). Although his reported remark was "warts and everything" the shortened version has been attributed to Oliver Cromwell ever since.

We are not amused

She didn't say it, though it's often confidently attributed to Queen Victoria as evidence of her dour and restrictive attitude toward anyone else's fun. But there is absolutely no evidence that she ever made that remark.

In her 1999 biography of Queen Victoria, eminent historian Elizabeth, Countess Longford (who was given access to all Victoria's letters and papers), says the legendary "We are not amused" is pure invention. On the contrary, Lady Longford points out that the Queen's writings often contained the line "I was much amused."

Weasel words

Substitute words to deprive a statement of its force, or avoid a direct commitment. The term first appeared in print in 1900, written by **Stewart Chaplin** in *Century Magazine*, in an article called "The Stained Glass Political Platform." Chaplin was reporting on preparations being made by two young politicians, and explained:

> *Weasel words are words which suck all the life out of the words next to them, just as a weasel sucks an egg and leaves the shell. If you heft the egg afterwards it's as light as a feather and not very filling when you're hungry— but a basket full of them would make quite a show and bamboozle the unwary.*

Sixteen years later Theodore Roosevelt used it in a speech which made it famous, and it went into common use.

Examples perceived as weasel words or phrases are: "restructuring" and "streamlining operations in response to market forces" (meaning people are going to be fired); "take out" (bomb or otherwise destroy); and "ethnic cleansing" (genocide).

(A) week is a long time in politics

The line is attributed to British Prime Minister **Sir Harold Wilson** and there is little doubt that he actually created it, although there is no certainty about *when* he said it. Even Sir Harold himself wasn't sure.

The *Oxford Dictionary of Quotations*, while firmly allocating the expression as a Wilson original, skips the time factor with the notation that he "used it a number of times."

We have ways of making you talk

Bringing an immediate image of ruthless German military questioning of prisoners of war, or James Bond when he's really up against it, the line owes its origin to a 1930 novel by Major Francis Yeats-Brown: *The Lives of a Bengal Lancer.*

Five years later the novel was used as the basis for a highly successful movie (seven Oscar nominations). The screenplay took liberties with the original book, and a string of screenwriters were credited with doing so: **Grover Jones**, **William Slavens McNutt**, **Waldemar Young**, **John L. Balderston**, **Achmed Abdullah**, and **Yeats-Brown** himself.

Between them they conjured the line:

We have ways of making men talk

spoken by the character Mohammed Khan planning an Indian uprising against the British.

Over time the line suffered a minor corruption through being inaccurately remembered and quoted as: "We have ways of making you talk."

Well he would, wouldn't he?

In 1963, during the trial of a man charged with "living off immoral earnings," London-based model/dancer **Mandy Rice-Davies** gave evidence of having an affair with Lord Astor.

When told by the prosecuting counsel that Lord Astor denied this, Rice-Davies replied: "Well he would, wouldn't he," a simple remark that then and since has been widely quoted (and sometimes adapted as, "Well he would (*say that*), wouldn't he?"

Wendy

In the nineteenth century the girl's name Wendy occurred only rarely in English, usually as a form of Guinevere, or as a shortened version of the Welsh name Gwendolyn. But famous author **Sir James Barrie** had a friendship with a little girl called Margaret Henley who had trouble pronouncing "r." Legend has it that she referred to Barrie as her "fwendy" and sometimes her "fwendy wendy." Margaret died when she was only six.

It is believed that Barrie found her death greatly affecting, and also that her inability to say "r" helped engender the name of a character he was about to immortalize. The world was introduced to *Peter Pan, the Boy Who Wouldn't Grow Up* in 1904, in which Peter met Wendy, the daughter of the Darling family, and took her to Never Land.

From being uncommon, the name Wendy quickly became popular—a popularity that has always been attributed to the delightful character in Barrie's play. (And little Margaret Henley's father was the inspiration for R.L. Stevenson's character Long John Silver.)

Went phut

We can thank **Rudyard Kipling** for introducing this useful word into English. Kipling's *Story of the Gadsbys* (1888) says:

> *I came out here, and the whole thing went phut. She wrote to say that there had been a mistake, and then she married.*

Nobody is entirely sure where Kipling found the word; a similar word appears in Hebrew and in Thai. But Kipling's familiarity with things Indian makes it seem likely that it is a version of the Hindi word phatna, which means "burst."

(Kipling's Gadsbys are not to be confused with F. Scott Fitzgerald's Gatsbys.)

Wham bam, thank you ma'am

Familiar during World War II among men in the armed forces referring to brief and random sexual encounters, the term first went into the public arena when the song "Wham Bang Thank You Ma'am" composed by **Hank Penny** was recorded in 1950 by an upcoming young singer called Dean Martin (Capitol 6469-4).

What you see is what you get

Dreamed up by the Central Camera Co. in Chicago, the line first surfaced in May 1936 when the company ran an advertisement in the *Chicago Tribune* for a new Keystone 8 mm "natural color" movie camera:

> *All you do is sight your subject through the telescopic finder and press the automatic button. That's all there is to it. What you see is what you get.*

The catchphrase has since been used in dozens of contexts other than color photography, but without its wording being changed.

(Many years after 1936, the abbreviation WYSIWYG has come to mean a system which allows the user of a computer to view something very similar to the end result while the document is still being created.)

When in Rome, do as the Romans do

Christianity remained fluid during the first 400 years of its existence, many of its customs and observances not having settled into an international pattern.

St. Augustine was from Africa, and after having had a mistress for fifteen years (and a son), he moved to Rome in AD 383 to study philosophy. He became accustomed to the Christians in Rome fasting on a Saturday.

Augustine was offered a job in Milan as a professor of philosophy and on arriving there he found that Christians did not fast on Saturdays. He was curious, and Aurelius Ambrosius— **Bishop Ambrose of Milan**—advised him:

> *Cum fueris Romae, Romano vivito more, cum fueris alibi, vivito sicut ibi.*
>
> *(When you're in Rome, then live in Roman fashion; when you're elsewhere, then live as there they live.)*

(Augustine gradually espoused Christianity and in AD 387 was baptized, together with his illegitimate son. He was canonized in 1298 and is the patron saint of theologians and brewers.)

When the going gets tough the tough get going

The *Charleston Daily Mail* in May 1954 quoted this line as being the favorite expression of football coach **Frank Leahy** (Francis William Leahy), who had resigned that year as coach for Notre Dame. His original wording is said to be:

> *When the going gets tough, let the tough get going.*

Later, a slightly modified version was given much wider exposure when Joseph P. Kennedy (father of President John Kennedy) frequently used it.

When you get what you want you don't want it

A link between **Oscar Wilde** and Marilyn Monroe at first seems unlikely, but a line from Wilde's *Lady Windermere's Fan* (1892) was:

In this world there are only two tragedies—one is not getting what one wants, and the other is getting it.

Irving Berlin may or may not have known Wilde's works, but in 1920 he came up with a song version with the same observation:

After you get what you want you don't want it.

Its first recording by Van and Shenck in 1920 was an American hit, surpassed in 1946 by Nat King Cole. But Marilyn Monroe's 1954 rendition in the movie *There's No Business Like Show Business* put the song, and the concept of being beware of getting what you want, in front of a worldwide audience. Custom and usage resulted in the slight change from Berlin's (and Wilde's) words into "When you get what you want …"

(The ancient Chinese maxim, "May you get what you wish for," is regarded as a curse.)

When you've got it—flaunt it!

Written by **Mel Brooks** for the 1968 movie *The Producers*. Zero Mostel, playing the role of financially strapped Broadway producer Max Bialystock, sees from his office window someone arrive in the street below in a white Rolls Royce.

In ironic desperation at his own plight, Bialystock shrieks at the unfortunate stranger:

That's it baby—when you've got it, flaunt it, flaunt it!

While there's life, there's hope

The expression appeared in a play with the unattractive title *The Self Tormentor* in Rome, c.163 BC. It was picked up over a millennium later by the Dutch scholar Desyderius Herasmus Roterodamus (Erasmus for short).

The translation into English by **Richard Taverner** (1539) started out as:

The sycke person whyle he hath lyfe, hath hope.

A century later the saying had been whittled down to "While there's life, there's hope."

(The) whole shebang

This expression can be used to describe the sum total of anything, without a thought to what a shebang actually is. Whatever its origin (possibly the Irish word shebeen), **Walt Whitman** made it clear what the word meant in nineteenth-century America in his *Specimen Days* (1862):

> *Besides the hospitals, I also go occasionally on long tours through the camps, talking with the men, &c. Sometimes at night among the groups around the fires, in their shebang enclosures of bushes.*

Hence, a type of rustic dwelling. But its meaning had clearly widened ten years later. **Mark Twain** in *Roughing It* (1872) was using the word to mean a vehicle:

> *You're welcome to ride here as long as you please, but this shebang's chartered, and we can't let you pay a cent.*

By the end of the century shebang meant "anything and everything"—the whole lot.

Who wants to be a millionaire?

The title of a duet composed by **Cole Porter** and sung by Frank Sinatra and Celeste Holm in the 1956 movie *High Society*. The two characters are attending a wealthy socialite's wedding, and they sing the duet surrounded by a display of extraordinarily lavish wedding presents brought to the young bride (played by Grace Kelly).

The song's lyrics emphasise that the couple singing is not impressed by the leisured lifestyle and luxury goods set out before them, since they are happy with each other.

Curiously, when the song title was used as the name of an internationally successful television game show, it rapidly became clear that almost everyone else in the world *does* want to be a millionaire.

Why should the devil have all the good tunes?

Often mistakenly attributed to other prominent Christians, the statement was originated by a preacher in London. In 1782, the first stone was laid for an independent Methodist and Congregational church in Southwark. The building was designed to be round, in the belief that this prevented the devil from being able to hide in any corner.

In 1783 the building opened as The Surrey Chapel (sometimes spelt Surry). The pastor of the chapel was the **Rev. Rowland Hill**, who took a close interest in the quality of church music. In his biography of Hill, E.W. Broome reports that the pastor saw no reason why "the devil should have all the good tunes," and thus allowed some of them to be sung in his chapel.

(The) wild blue yonder

In 1937 a song competition was held in the U.S. to find a song that reflected the unique identity of their airmen. The magazine *Liberty* cooperated by offering $1,000 as a prize for the winning song. During a survey period of two years, over 700 entries came in, but were somewhat disappointing. At the last minute, a song arrived entitled "Army Air Corps Song," with the opening lines:

Off we go into the wild blue yonder,
Climbing high into the sun.

Composer-lyricist **Captain Robert MacArthur Crawford** was declared the winner.

A slight change in the title came in 1947 when the U.S. Air Force was founded and the use of the term Army Air Corps ceased to exist as an entity. Accordingly, the name of the song became "U.S. Air Force Song." The song became popularly referred to as "The Wild Blue Yonder," and early printings of the sheet music advised that the line "Off with one hell of a roar" could be replaced with "Off with a terrible roar" to suit the broadcasting ethos of the time.

In 1979 General Lew Allen Jr., Chief of Staff of the American Air Force, announced that the song was now the official service song.

Window-shopping

The first known public use of the term was in 1922, in **Charlotte Rankin Aiken**'s how-to-make book *Millinery*. Aiken was a director of the Lasalle and Koch Dry Goods department store in Toledo, Ohio and author of books on shop management.

Her use of quote marks suggests that the term was already in use, though not yet regularly in print:

The first step in making a hat at home, if one does not know exactly how one wishes to make it, is to leave home and go "window shopping" and also to look through the millinery departments in the stores.

(A) woman needs a man like a fish needs a bicycle

More than a decade prior to the feminist movement of the 1970s, American philosopher Charles S. Harris at Swarthmore College observed in a college publication that "A man without faith is like a fish without a bicycle" (1958).

Some years later, and across the Pacific Ocean, Australian author, editor, and documentary film maker **Irina Dunn** was studying for an Honors degree in Language and Literature and happened to read Harris's line. Being, as she later admitted to *Time*, "a bit of a smart-arse," she paraphrased the line as "A woman needs a man like a fish needs a bicycle."

In 1970 Irina Dunn boldly wrote the line inside two toilet doors—one at Sydney University, and the other in a Woolloomooloo wine bar. The expression spread widely and became a familiar part of the women's liberation movement.

(It was often attributed to Gloria Steinem, but the latter wrote to *Time* in 2000 to clarify that Irina Dunn was the true progenitor.)

Word for word

The noble art of understanding exactly what is meant. In his collection *The Legend of Good Women* (c.1385) **Geoffrey Chaucer** told his readers in the chapter on Dido, Queen of Carthage that he could understand Virgil precisely:

> *I coude folwe, word for word, Virgile,*
> *But it wolde laste al to longe while.*
> *This noble queen, that cleped was Dido,*
> *That whilom was the wif of Sytheo,*
> *That fayrer was than is the bryghte sonne,*
> *This noble toun of Cartage hath bigonne …*

Would you buy a used car from this man?

During the lead-up to the American presidential election in 1960 when rivalry between John Kennedy and Richard Nixon was a hot topic, Mort Saltzman was editor of the *UCLA Daily Bruin* newspaper, and tells:

> *I published an editorial cartoon drawn by a free-lance*
> *cartoonist, **Dennis Renault**, an on-again, off-again student.*
> *It depicted Nixon with his famous 5 o'clock shadow and*
> *the caption said, "Would you buy a used car from this man?"*
> *The shit hit the fan.*

The original cartoon was made into a poster and displayed far and wide. Its caption quickly went into the language landscape, and was later adapted in many situations where doubt was being suggested about someone's abilities—and trustworthiness.

Yadda Yadda

There has been quite a long line of verbal replacements for "etc., etc.," such as yackkety yak, blah–blah–blah and yap yap yap.

The development of Yadda Yadda came through a complex series of "filler" words thought to imitate many people talking (yatata yatata), plus an influence from Yiddish (yatta yatta; yaddega yaddega).

The Yadda Yadda version was established in American vaudeville routines as early as the 1940s. It was introduced to a wider number of show business audiences twenty years later by comic **Lenny Bruce** in a monologue featuring the character of a prison riot leader, who answers "Yadda yadda" to every question put to him. Indeed, Lenny Bruce is regarded as the "father" of Yadda yadda.

But to be fair, the launch into international recognition came in April 1997 when scriptwriters **Peter Mehlman** and **Jill Franklyn** included Lenny Bruce's "Yadda yadda" expression in an episode of the *Seinfeld* show, in which the term became a comic fixture for some time afterward.

Yahoo

Scholars have agonized over the derivation of this word. Is it from Sanskrit? Australian aboriginal? Chinese? Hebrew? Burmese? Russian? But there is no strong evidence for any of them.

Jonathan Swift simply made up a new word himself when he wrote *Gulliver's Travels* (1726). The yahoos were a brutish race—loutish, violent and ugly—who had a bad smell and slept in mud.

In 1994 two electrical engineering students at Stanford University, David Filo and Jerry Yang, created a list of favorite Internet links, which as it grew had to be divided into many categories. It became *Jerry and David's Guide to the World Wide Web*. Seeking a new name, they created the slightly comic *Yet Another Hierarchical Officious Oracle*, then wisely checked if it happened to be a real word.

Their dictionary told them that yahoo—the initials of their new name—was a widely used slang term referring to a rude unsophisticated youth. Filo and Yang were sufficiently intrigued to abandon their complex title and settle for just YAHOO.

Within a year they had a million-hit day, and then a torrent. By 1996 they had forty-nine employees. In 2005 Yahoo services were in use by over 345 million individuals per month. Which makes the two enterprising men quite the opposite of Jonathan Swift's initial concept of a yahoo!

Yes man

He who unfailingly agrees with whomever he wishes to please, was first noticed in print at the hand of **Thomas Aloysius Dorgan** (known as "TAD"), American sports writer, prolific cartoonist, and purveyor of colorful and sometimes new language.

In 1913 a published drawing of his showed a number of newspaper employees, each one labeled "Yes man," all eagerly agreeing with their editor. After this the term went into wide usage.

You ain't heard nothing yet

The expression was often used by entertainer **Al Jolson** in his stage appearances—once notably when he was scheduled to sing in a concert straight after Enrico Caruso. The audience gave the opera star's item a huge ovation, then Jolson came onstage and boldly announced, "You ain't heard nothing yet." Classical music fans were not pleased about this, but Caruso was reportedly quite amused.

In 1926 when Vitaphone started experimenting with sound dics playing in sync. with a movie screen, Al Jolson was "filmed with sound" singing three songs that same year.

But the turning point for sound movies—and Jolson's favorite expression—came in 1927. By then, movies with sound had played music or effects such as trains rumbling or swords clashing. Spoken words were still being treated ultra-cautiously, and only a very few had been heard coming from a movie screen. As was normal at the time, *The Jazz Singer*, the first full-length movie-with-sound-and-songs, would have dialogue only as printout title-sequences telling the story.

When the studio set-up was ready for the movie's big musical number and the microphones already switched on, Jolson—the diehard vaudeville performer—completely against the movie-maker's plans, suddenly burst into a spoken introduction to his song:

> *Wait a minute, wait a minute I tell yer, you ain't heard nothin' yet!*

The spoken lines had been accidentally recorded on the film's "soundtrack," and the director made a bold decision and added another scene where the characters talked.

The result changed the movie-making industry overnight. *The Jazz Singer* launched a new word into the language—talkies—and Al Jolson's line became a catchphrase for the rapid output of movies in which people actually spoke dialogue.

You are what you eat

The phrase owes a lot to French gastronomist **Anthelme Brillat-Savarin** (of sufficient status that a French cheese is named after him), who in his 1825 book *The Physiology of Taste* wrote:

> *Dis-moi ce que tu manges, je te dirai ce que tu es.*
>
> *(Tell me what you eat and I will tell you what you are.)*

The expression made a somewhat unconventional entrance into English through an American newspaper, the *Bridgeport Telegraph*, in an advertisement in 1923 (with unattributed translation, and a strange misspelling) for the United Meet (*sic*) Markets:

> *Ninety per cent of the diseases known to man are caused by cheap foodstuffs. You are what you eat.*

This policy is believed to have arisen through the enthusiasm of nutritionist Victor Lindlahr who at the time was paying great attention to health and diet, and in 1942 published his book *You Are What You Eat*.

You can't be serious . . . you cannot be serious

American professional tennis player **John McEnroe** won seven Grand Slam singles titles—three at Wimbledon, four in the U.S. Open, and was World No. 1. Not a shrinking violet, his behavior was often seen to be rebellious.

In 1981 during a match at Wimbledon he disagreed with an umpire's opinion and made this clear with the shouted remark, "You can't be serious," followed immediately by the slightly more formal, "You *cannot* be serious."

This much publicized mini-tirade became the title of his 2002 biography (co-written with James Kaplan), which went to the top of the *New York Times* bestseller list. McEnroe was inducted into the Tennis Hall of Fame in 1999.

You can't have your cake and eat it too

This came into print in 1546 as part of a collection by dramatist and balladeer to King Henry VII's court, John Heywood, of sayings that were already known to him:

> *Wolde ye both eate your cake and have your cake?*

A sixteenth-century reading audience would be small compared with a more literate nation over 200 years later when Keats wrote his poem "On Fame" (1816).

He placed the "cake" line simply as a heading to Verse 2. One has to acknowledge that his literary standing makes **John Keats** a stronger candidate for launching the expression into wider recognition:

> *On Fame*
>
> *"You cannot eat your cake and have it too"—Proverb*
>
> *How fevered is the man who cannot look*
> *Upon his mortal days with temperate blood,*
> *Who vexes all the leaves of his life's book,*
> *And robs his fair name of its maidenhood;*
> *It is as if the rose should pluck herself,*
> *Or the ripe plum finger its misty bloom ...*

You can't make an omelette without breaking eggs

This image exists in just about every language in Europe and probably beyond.

It was first introduced in English by **Major-General Thompson**, MP for Bradford in *Audi Alteram Partem (Hear the other side)—Letters of a Representative to his Constituents* (1859):

> *The conclusion is that we are walking upon eggs, and whether we tread East or tread West the omelette will not be made without the breaking of some.*

Nearly forty years later, Robert Louis Stevenson in *St. Ives, Being the Adventures of a French Prisoner in England* (1897) when the narrator shows his damaged hands to a young woman, the expression settles into the form it has retained:

> *My dear Miss Flora, you cannot make an omelette without breaking eggs—and it is no bagatelle to escape from Edinburgh Castle.*

You can't take it with you

The concept is noted in the Bible: "For we brought nothing into this world, and it is certain we can carry nothing out" (1 Timothy 6,7). It reappeared rather more colloquially when expressed in Captain Marryat's *Masterman Ready* (1841):

> *Masterman was a bachelor, of nearly sixty years, without any near relations. It is true, that he was very fond of money; but that, they said, was all the better, as he could not take it away with him when he died.*

But the clear and neat contemporary version came when American writers **George Kaufman** and **Moss Hart** (leaning more on the Book of Timothy than on Marryat as inspiration) opened their play *You Can't Take It With You* in New York. The play won a Pulitzer Prize the following year and its title became part of everyday speech.

You get what you pay for

Reputedly said in a firm tone of voice by actress Elizabeth Taylor when queried about her astronomical fees for movie appearances. But the expression was nearly 500 years old by then.

It is first seen in the *Exposito Canonis* (c.1495) of German philosopher **Gabriel Biel**:

> *Pro tali numismate tales merces.*
>
> *(You get what you pay for.)*

You'll never work in this town again

It sounds very Hollywood, but in fact first arose among nineteenth-century straight-talking English industrialists.

In 1882, the committee of the Guild of Preston was awaiting Queen Victoria's son, His Royal Highness Prince Leopold, Duke of Albany who was due to arrive for a visit. But a message arrived from the Royal Household saying that the Prince had "a slight indisposition" and was not able to attend.

The Committee chairman remarked:

> *Reet. He'll never work in this town again.*

(They were a bit tough—and might not have known that Prince Leopold was a haemophilia sufferer.)

You pay your money and you take your choice

Believed to be a slogan of London market stallholders, the saying came before the general public when the term was first seen in print in 1846. There had been a Prime Ministerial crisis in Britain when Robert Peel resigned, followed by a time of government indecision, and the new leadership was unclear but hovering over several possible starters.

On January 3, 1846, a *Punch* cartoonist drew a picture showing a young girl standing with her father, watching a group of important-looking men go by.

She asks: 'Which is the Prime Minister?'

His reply: 'Whichever you please my little dear. You pays your money and you takes your choice.'

Your country needs you

In July 1914 and aware of the approaching signs of war, Britain's Field Marshall Lord Kitchener initiated confidential preparations for a campaign to alert the public and recruit more soldiery. Advertising writer Eric Field quietly created an image of the Royal coat of arms, and the slogan "Your King and Country Need You," and put his work on standby.

It was ready to publish on August 5, 1914, the day after war was declared, as the Government's official recruitment poster.

Three months later artist **Alfred Leete** revised Field's design and created a slightly parodied version showing a fierce-looking Lord Kitchener glaring out. Leete also shortened Eric Field's original slogan to "Your Country Needs You." This simplified version was so much more effective than the original that Leete's version was accepted by the Government as the flagship of its recruitment campaign, which encouraged three million men to volunteer for service.

Leete's design and its crisp slogan became famous internationally, and was frequently copied, most notably by America with Uncle Sam announcing "I want YOU for the U.S. Army," which first appeared in 1916 two years after the British version, and was revised in America for World War II.

The last word

Shakespeare
by Bernard Levin

If you cannot understand my argument, and declare "It's Greek to me,"

>*you are quoting Shakespeare;*

if you claim to be more sinned against than sinning,

>*you are quoting Shakespeare;*

if you recall your salad days,

>*you are quoting Shakespeare;*

if you act more in sorrow than in anger, if your wish is father to the thought, if your lost property has vanished into thin air,

>*you are quoting Shakespeare;*

if you have ever refused to budge an inch or suffered from green-eyed jealousy, if you have played fast and loose, if you have been tongue-tied, a tower of strength, hoodwinked or in a pickle, if you have knitted your brows, made a virtue of necessity, insisted on fair play, slept not one wink, stood on ceremony, danced attendance (on your lord and master), laughed yourself into stitches, had short shrift, cold comfort or too much of a good thing, if you have seen better days or lived in a fool's paradise—why, be that as it may, the more fool you, for it is a foregone conclusion that

>*you are (as good luck would have it) quoting Shakespeare;*

if you think it is early days and clear out bag and baggage, if you think it is high time and that that is the long and short of it, if you believe that the game is up and that truth will out even if it involves your own flesh and blood, if you lie low till the crack of doom because you suspect foul play, if you have your teeth set on edge (at one fell swoop) without rhyme or reason, then—to give the devil his due—if the truth were known (for surely you have a tongue in your head) *you are quoting Shakespeare;*

even if you bid me good riddance and send me packing, if you wish I was dead as a door-nail, if you think I am an eyesore, a laughing stock, the devil incarnate, a stony-hearted villain, bloody-minded or a blinking idiot, then—by Jove! O Lord! Tut, tut! for goodness' sake! what the dickens! but me no buts—it is all one to me, for

you are quoting Shakespeare.

Sources

Wherever possible, the source and context of examined expressions have been included within the text of their entries. The following list is not comprehensive, but refers to the main sources which provided further information:

Ammer, Christine, *The American Heritage Dictionary of Idioms*, Houghton Mifflin, Boston, 1997

Apperson, G.L. ed., *The Wordsworth Dictionary of Proverbs*, Wordsworth Editions, Hertfordshire, 1993

Ayto and Green, *Don't Quote Me*, Hamlyn Paperbacks, Middlesex, 1981

Ayto and Simpson, *Stone the Crows*, Oxford University Press, 2008

Ayto, J., *Twentieth Century Words*, Oxford University Press, 1999

Benet, William Rose, *The Reader's Encyclopedia,* A & C Black, London, 1973

Brown, Lesley ed., *The New Shorter Oxford Dictionary*, Oxford University Press, 1993

Burnam, Tom, *Dictionary of Misinformation*, Ballantine Books, New York, 1980

Chambers, James, *Charlotte and Leopold—The True Story of the Original "People's Princess,"* Old Street Publishing, London, 2007

Chapman Robert L. and Kipfer, Barbara Ann, *American Slang*,
Harper Perennial, 1998

Coxe, William, *Memoirs of the Life and Administration of Sir Robert
Walpole, Earl of Orford*, Cadell & Davies, 1798

Fleming, Tom, *Voices Out Of The Air*, Heinemann, London, 1981

Fraser, Antonia ed., *The Lives of the Kings and Queens of England*,
Weidenfeld and Nicolson, London, 1975

Freedland, Michael, *Al Jolson,* W.H. Allen, 1972

Harper, Joseph ed., *The Ultimate Book of Notes and Queries,*
Atlantic Books, London, 2002

Hendrickson, Robert, *The Facts on File Encyclopaedia of Word and
Phrase Origins*, FOF Publications, New York, 1987

Hole, Georgia, *The Real McCoy*, Oxford University Press, 2005

Jack, Albert, *Red Herrings and White Elephants*, Metro Publishing,
London, 2004

Jackman, S.W., *The People's Princess*, Kensal, 1984

Longford, Elizabeth, *Queen Victoria*, Sutton Publishing, Phoenix
Mill, 1999

McCann, Liam, *The Sledger's Handbook: How to Deliver the Perfect
Cricketing Insult*, AAPPL Publishers, 2006

Mort, Simon ed., *Longman Guardian New Words*, Longman, Essex, 1986

Muir, Frank, *The Frank Muir Book*, William Heinemann, London, 1976

Partridge, Eric, *A Dictionary of Catch Phrases*, Routledge and Kegan Paul, 1977

Pickering, David, Isaacs, Alan and Martin, Elizabeth eds., *Brewer's Twentieth Century Phrase and Fable*, Cassell, London, 1991

Richards, Kel, *Wordwatching*, ABC Books, 2006

Room, Adrian, *Brewer's Modern Phrase & Fable*, Cassell, London, 2000

Shales, T.W. and Miller, J.A., *Live From New York*, Little, Brown and Co., New York, 2002

Titelman, Gregory, *The Random House Dictionary of Popular American Proverbs and Sayings*, Random House, New York, 2000

Walsh, William, *The Handy Book of Literary Curiosities*, Gibbings and Co., London, 1893